THE
COMPLETE
WILDERNESS
TRAINING BOOK

THE COMPLETE WILDERNESS TRAINING BOOK

HUGH McMANNERS

DK Publishing, Inc.
www.dk.com

A DORLING KINDERSLEY BOOK
www.dk.com

Project Editor LYNN PARR
Senior Art Editor LEE GRIFFITHS
Designer COLETTE HO
Managing Editor KRYSTYNA MAYER
Managing Art Editor DEREK COOMBES
DTP Designer DOUG MILLER
Production Controller ROSALIND PRIESTLEY
US Editor JILL HAMILTON
US Consultant PAUL G. MARCONI, EMT-P,
EXECUTIVE DIRECTOR, WILDERNESS MEDICAL ASSOCIATES

First paperback edition, 1998
4 6 8 10 9 7 5 3

Published in the United States by
DK Publishing, Inc.,
95 Madison Avenue,
New York, New York 10016

Copyright © 1994, 1998
Dorling Kindersley Limited, London
Text copyright © 1994, 1998 Hugh McManners

McManners, Hugh.
  The complete wilderness training book / by Hugh McManners. -- 1st
American ed.
    p.   cm
Includes index.
  ISBN 0–7894–3750–3
  1. Survival skills--Handbooks, manuals, etc. 2. Wilderness survival--
Handbooks, manuals, etc. I. Title.
GF86.M35 1993
613.6'9--dc20
                                                                  93–5686
                                                                  CIP

Color reproduced by GRB, Milan
Printed and bound in Singapore by Star Standard Industries (Pte.) Ltd.

IMPORTANT NOTICE

Some of the techniques described in this book
should be used only in dire emergencies, when the
survival of individuals depends upon them.
Consequently, the publishers cannot be held
responsible for any injuries, damage, loss, or
prosecutions resulting from the use or misuse of the
information in this book. Do not practice these
techniques on private land without the owner's
permission, and obey all laws relating to the
protection of land, property, plants, and animals.

CONTENTS

Introduction 6

CHAPTER 1 ARE YOU A SURVIVOR?

Physical Condition 12
Nutritional Needs 14
Adapting to the Environment 16
Fitness 18

CHAPTER 2 BASIC EQUIPMENT

The Right Clothing 22
Footwear 24
Personal Camp Kit 26
Basic Survival Kit 28
Sleeping Bags and Beds 30
Tools 32
Ropes and Knots 34
Using Ropes 36

CHAPTER 3 LIVING IN THE WILD

Choosing a Campsite 40
Choosing a Tent 42
Erecting a Tent 44
Dismantling a Tent 46
Building a Shelter 48
Snow Shelters 50
Tropical Shelters 52
Long-term Shelters 54
Running a Safe Camp 56

Campfires 58
Building a Fire 60
Lighting a Fire 62
Striking Camp 64

CHAPTER 4 FINDING WATER

The Importance of Water 68
Collecting Water 70
Natural Water Sources 72
Water Purification 74
Carrying and Storing Water 76

CHAPTER 5 FINDING AND PREPARING FOOD

Food for Traveling 80
Edible Plants 82
Poisonous Plants 84
Roots, Tubers, and Bulbs 86
Nuts and Fruit 88
Fungi and Lichen 90
Plants as Food 92
Invertebrates 94
Invertebrates as Food 96
Freshwater Fish 98
Saltwater Fish 100
Angling Equipment 102
Angling Techniques 104
Fishing Nets and Traps 106
Using Fishing Nets and Traps 108
Preparing Fish for Cooking 110
Cooking Utensils 112
Stoves and Ovens 114
Cooking Methods 116
Preserving Food 118

CHAPTER 6 ON THE MOVE

Travel Planning 122
Finding Direction 124
Using Maps 126
Finding Your Location 128
Navigation Basics 130
Assessing the Weather 132
Preparing to Move 134
Walking 136
Walking in Snow and Ice 138
Traveling Over Snow 140
Crossing Deserts 142
Traveling Through Jungles 144
Safe Climbing 146
Emergency Climbing Techniques 148
Crossing Water 150
Dangerous Water 152
Building a Raft 154
Using Rafts and Boats 156
Using Vehicles 158
Other Transportation 160

APPENDIX A
Abandoning Ship 162
Surviving at Sea 164
Dangerous Creatures 166
Natural Hazards 168
Extreme Weather 170
Signaling 172

APPENDIX B
First Aid 174

Glossary 184
Checklist for Survival 187
Index 188
Acknowledgments 192

INTRODUCTION

ONE OF THE GREAT PHILOSOPHERS is thought to have remarked, "Any fool can be uncomfortable" – probably after a washed-out camping holiday. Whether attempting to dry out your bedding on a rainsoaked campsite, or trying to stay alive after some unexpected disaster, it helps immeasurably to know the basic principles of outdoor life. These include how tents and shelters are erected, choosing or making sleeping bags and beds, building a fire, and preventing or treating blisters and other health complaints. Understanding more specialized principles of survival, such as safe navigation across different types of terrain, or water purification, is as interesting and useful to recreational users as it is vital and life saving to those unfortunate enough to become "survivors."

EXPECTING THE UNEXPECTED

In the Commandos, the day-to-day motto is, "Always expect the unexpected." Years of training in wet and potentially dangerous places paid off – we maintained equipment for operations worldwide and often found ourselves working in hostile environments. Special forces people are realistic about what they have to do, so having thought it all through in training, we had no problems when we had to do it for real. Nevertheless, we were certainly coping with "the unexpected."

By contrast, for civilians facing nothing more hazardous than the possibility of car breakdowns or bad weather, preparing for various disaster situations may appear ridiculous. However, even the mildest family walk, particularly in hill country, can suddenly turn dangerous if the participants are unaware of the basic principles of weather prediction, first aid, navigation, clothing, and footwear. It is only through understanding more about life in the wild, that many common disasters can be avoided – or at least identified before they become severely life threatening.

Preparing for the unexpected is a constant process of trying to understand how things work, then drawing parallels between what is part of our own experience and what we understand, and strange, different things of which we have no experience. Even though we may choose to visit wilderness areas and undeveloped countries, we usually remain spectators, kept apart from the reality of everyday life in those places by the nature of our urban lives, which are filled with modern technology. Yet we must shed our comfortable wrappings if we want to understand how life really works – if we were to be set down on a remote tropical island after a plane crash, for example, we would be unlikely to have bottled water, prepacked, precooked meals, or even sunglasses, and urban accoutrements such as credit cards would be useless.

It is to our benefit, therefore, to make a serious effort to step outside our cushioned, shielded lives. If we can understand where we fit into the wild world, honestly assessing our physical and mental strengths and limitations, we can make the next step, becoming players in the real world, regardless of where that might be.

LIFE-SAVING KNOWLEDGE

It is impossible to predict what disasters may occur, so you cannot learn specific survival skills to cover every option. Understanding basic principles is far more important than learning techniques by rote, particularly since most techniques require some modification every time they are used. Nothing is easy, no matter how well trained you might be, but if you learn the basics, you will be able to adapt to different situations. Modern technology often masks the basic principles by which all physical work is done. We create machines for every job, freeing ourselves from tasks that would otherwise take up most of our time. We forget the physics by which everything from weather to the tools we improvise actually functions.

We may have learned and understood a great deal in our lives so far, but much of this knowledge is locked away in our minds, and we are not always able to apply it to real-life situations. Urban life generally tends to make us inflexible in the practical application of our knowledge – simply because we almost never find ourselves in the kind of survival situations where there is no option but to improvise.

THE PRINCIPLES OF SURVIVAL

All manner of principles are important in the wild. Every half-forgotten school physics, chemistry, or biology lesson could save hours of experimentation. As children, we constantly make tools and other artifacts, learning how to apply basic principles – a process that stops as we grow up and begin buying ready-made items from shops. In the wild, we must return to our childhood in many ways, and relearn how to improvise and invent. We must work as adults, however, considering engineering principles such as stressing, strength, and tensioning, which have to be combined with a very clear idea of the purpose of what we are making. This process is governed by necessity – if we do not get it right, we get wet, stay hungry, or remain cold.

Combining step-by-step instructions with photographs and artworks, this book contains information on a wealth of practical skills, demonstrating an easy transition from urban living back to the wilds in which our primitive ancestors had to survive. The knowledge this book contains may one day save your life, if you suddenly find yourself having to survive – even temporarily – as our ancestors did, for example after an accident, disaster, or vehicle breakdown, or in extreme weather, when services have been cut off.

On the other hand, you might want to set off backpacking into the wilderness for a vacation away from the pressures and complications of urban life. Whatever your situation, this book will be invaluable to you, providing much of the data you need, with information dealing with a wide range of specialized subjects.

PHYSICAL AND MENTAL CONDITION

In Chapter One, the physical and mental condition of urban dwellers is discussed, with comparisons to other animals and to primitive peoples living in inhospitable terrain, where they have had to adapt to survive. In survival situations, harsh natural laws are suddenly imposed upon us, and reality breaks through the rose-colored glasses of modern life. Suddenly, physical fitness becomes important. By being as physically fit as possible, we not only increase our chances of survival after a disaster, but we also know exactly what our bodies are capable of doing. We can improve our physical fitness by doing simple but effective exercises and by following the dietary rules for all-around good health.

THE RIGHT EQUIPMENT

Chapter Two discusses the equipment you might need in the wilderness, ranging from the right clothing, sleeping bags, and tools, to a personalized survival kit that you make up yourself. In addition to comparisons between manufactured articles, this book shows you how to make items yourself if you do not have the proper equipment. When the right materials are not available, construction methods must be amended, designs altered, and compromises made – just about anything can be made from a few branches and pieces of string. Although improvised equipment is not particularly neat and must be used with care, this does not matter in the slightest, as long as it does the job. Throughout this chapter – and, indeed, throughout the book – conservation of natural resources is stressed. There is no need to damage the environment. Indeed, by fitting in with the natural environment, we stand a much better chance of surviving, both as individuals and as a species.

THE BASICS OF CAMP LIVING

If you do find yourself in a survival situation, the first thing you must do is find shelter, either by erecting a tent or by building a shelter from natural materials. Chapter Three considers the types of shelter needed for different terrain, such as tropical forests and polar regions. Fire is the next most important consideration in a survival situation – a fire can cook your food, keep you warm, purify your drinking water, and maintain your morale. Building and lighting different fires are also discussed. Chapter Four discusses the importance of water to the human body, and shows how to find it. Water in the wilderness is unlikely to be pure, and may transmit diseases that could threaten your life. Water purification methods are therefore emphasized in this chapter. After water, you will need to find food. Chapter Five considers the types of food you can buy to take on a backpacking trip, as well as how to recognize and gather various kinds of wild food, from plants and invertebrates to fish. You will learn how to prepare wild food for eating, as well as ways of preserving food for times when it is otherwise unavailable.

TRAVELING IN THE WILD

You may not have any experience of traveling in true wilderness areas, but as long as you know the basic principles of living in each place, your chances of surviving there will be greatly increased. Chapter Six explains the rigors of traveling in areas as diverse as the jungle and the desert, polar regions, and rocky mountains. Techniques such as packing your gear efficiently, crossing rivers, and walking correctly to minimize injury are discussed, together with basic navigational skills that you can use around the world, and basic rock-climbing techniques for emergencies. Travel may involve the use of motorized vehicles, rafts, canoes, and other watercraft, and dog sleds as well as walking, and methods of making, loading, and using such transportation are also included.

DON'T PANIC!

Survival depends on making the right decisions. Only by understanding what might happen in a survival situation is it possible to see far enough ahead to predict potential disaster, and to then take the correct action to prevent it. In survival situations, we are thrown suddenly into something we cannot avoid, where very few of the skills we use daily are relevant. Our first problem is accepting what has happened. Panic and depression are the great enemies of thought, preventing people from using their built-in will to survive. A logical and honest assessment of the situation, resources, and options will determine those first critical steps.

Appendix A discusses major disasters and dangerous situations, along with their causes, and how you can predict and prepare for them, as well as surviving in their aftermath. Then follow examples of perilous situations in which you might find yourself, such as being adrift on the open sea in a liferaft, or being confronted by a dangerous animal, natural disasters such as earthquakes and volcanic eruptions, and extreme weather such as hurricanes. Signalling to potential rescuers is also explored in some detail.

Appendix B discusses basic first-aid techniques, with special emphasis on coping in a survival situation, when you cannot just telephone for an ambulance. It also gives information on worldwide infectious diseases, and how to avoid them.

IT'S UP TO YOU

Above all, survival demands mental toughness and very clear thinking. The logical evaluation of everything you know and a hard-headed assessment of your own abilities and those of the members of your party may lead to unpalatable conclusions and difficult decisions. Unlike in normal life, however, in a survival situation you determine your own future, and your decisions can mean life or death.

Although this book shows you how things might be done, in a true survival situation, you must do them all yourself. If things do not work out as described on these pages, you will have to sort them out yourself. However, by following the specific details in this book and adapting the basic principles, you will greatly increase your chances of survival, even in the most adverse conditions.

CHAPTER ONE

ARE YOU A SURVIVOR?

BY NATURE, WE are all survivors, driven by the desire to live rather than die, fired up by fear whenever our lives are threatened. However, in purely physical terms, we are poorly equipped to stand up either to the environment or to our natural enemies. Way back down our evolutionary line, this weakness became an enormous advantage, forcing the ape-creatures from which we developed to use their brains to overcome adversaries stronger than themselves. The more these early humans used brain rather than brawn, the more advantage they achieved over their natural enemies, and the more their brain power and dexterity developed. We are descended from the ones that continued to think, experiment, and persevere, and who adapted to change, thus surviving while others perished. As nature's best survivors, all we require in order to translate our day-to-day survival techniques into unfamiliar environments is some additional knowledge and a few practical skills.

NATURAL SURVIVOR
Although urban dwellers are generally out of touch with the natural world, and find it more threatening than their ancestors did, they can easily adapt to surviving in the wild if they have to. The biggest threat to survival is fear, but this can be overcome with a little knowledge and imagination.

PHYSICAL CONDITION

Humans are physically inferior to many other animals. Their advantage, however, is lack of specialization. They have the intelligence and dexterity to create new skills and to adapt to new situations. In an urban environment, humans do not use their bodies as much as they would in the wild. Primitive people are thus much more the masters of their own destiny than their urban counterparts.

THE HUMAN BODY

Smell
Humans have a good sense of smell, although it is not as powerful as that of animals such as dogs. In the wild, smell is useful for identifying food, the presence of other creatures, and dangers such as forest fires.

Hearing
Wild animals are used to listening for danger. Urban dwellers, however, live in a noisy environment that can reduce the sensitivity of their ears, and their desire to listen carefully.

Taste
Taste buds on the tongue allow humans to perceive sour, sweet, salty, and bitter flavors. The brain interprets information from the taste buds and from the food's smell to give a particular taste.

Breathing Rate
The breathing rate of humans depends on how much oxygen the brain thinks the body needs. The rate increases during exertion or fright, and at high altitudes, where the air contains a lower amount of oxygen.

Spine
Humans are still designed to walk on four legs, and back trouble is often the price for standing upright on two.

Opposing Thumbs
Humans have thumbs and fingers that can work independently and grip objects. This dexterity allows for the production and use of complex tools, an ability that greatly contributes to their adaptability.

Joints
Certain joints, such as the knees, are weak and prone to injury. In urban life, humans do not get enough exercise. This exacerbates these design weaknesses.

Feet
With all the weight of the body resting on the feet, injuries and other foot problems are common, especially in rough terrain.

Brain
The large, complex brain more than makes up for the inadequacy of other human senses. Because of this, people can think logically, as well as having a sense of history, a conception of the future, and the ability to philosophize about their place in the universe.

Sight
Humans have a field of vision of about 210 degrees, around 120 degrees of which overlaps to create stereoscopic sight. This enables people to see in three dimensions and to judge distances. They can also see in full color in daylight.

Teeth
Humans have teeth both for cutting meat and for grinding and chewing plants. The teeth are thus adapted for an omnivorous diet.

Heart
By pumping oxygen-rich blood around the body, the heart keeps all the other organs working. Without regular exercise, however, the heart becomes unfit, stopping the rest of the body from functioning properly.

Skin
As well as protecting internal organs, skin controls body temperature through sweating. Having lost most of its protective hair over the centuries, human skin now has to be shielded from sun, rain, and cold.

The Human Animal
Humans are hardly a physical match for other predators. In the wild they can become prey, unable to defend themselves with claws, teeth, or beak, or to protect themselves with a carapace or hide. They lack the eyesight and sense of smell of other hunters, and the speed to outrun game. They cannot maintain body temperature in some environments without special clothes. Humans are, however, natural survivors, forced through physical weakness to develop their dexterity and intelligence – the ultimate survival skills.

HOW SOME ANIMALS HAVE ADAPTED

Dormouse
Small and nervous, with a correspondingly fast metabolism, the dormouse hibernates during winter when there is little or no food. During hibernation, its heart and breathing rates slow, and its body runs off the fat deposits it has built up before its long sleep.

Shrew
Because of its small size and quickness, the shrew has a high metabolic rate. However, it must eat almost continuously to stay alive.

Fennec
The fennec's huge ears can swivel to accurately locate the smallest of sounds, enabling the animal to hunt by night and day. Their large surface area allows dissipation of excess body heat in the fennec's desert environment.

Whale
Although the whale is a mammal, needing to breathe air, it is well adapted to its ocean environment, and can hold its breath for up to 20 minutes when diving very deep for food. However, through being so well adapted, it is also very limited, and is therefore unable to escape from that environment.

CLOSE TO HUMANS

Apart from apes, humans are physiologically very close to pigs. In common with humans, the pig is able to eat both meat and vegetation, and its organs and general physiology compare well with the human body, although it has more body fat and a thicker skin than a human. In the past, cannibals on Pacific Ocean islands spoke of eating "long pig" – a reference, perhaps, to the similarity between pork and human flesh.

Domestic Pig
The pig has a very similar physiology to a human's.

EFFECT OF ENVIRONMENT

The wilderness is not a garden of Eden. Even simple complaints that the urban dweller takes for granted, such as tooth decay, lack of hygiene, and ordinary infection, are potential killers. Urban life is not that much better, often creating as many health problems as it solves. These can range from headaches caused by excessive noise to cancer resulting from radiation poisoning.

- A low oxygen content in the air at high altitudes can make breathing difficult, and aggravate respiratory disorders such as emphysema.
- Tobacco smoke and other air pollution can lead to lung cancer and respiratory disorders such as asthma.
- Polluted water and water contaminated with disease-carrying organisms can be responsible for internal problems.
- In extreme cases, chemicals in food, as well as pesticides on crops, can sometimes cause allergies, cancer, damage to ovaries, liver, and testes, and hyperactivity.
- Ultraviolet rays from the sun cause skin cancer and skin aging.
- Dust and pollen in the air are often responsible for allergies such as hay fever, as well as respiratory disorders such as asthma, fibrosis, and pneumonia.
- Extreme levels of noise cause deafness and tinnitus, as well as headaches and stress through irritability.
- Skin contact with industrial solvents, or inhalation of their vapor, may cause allergic reactions or damage to liver and kidneys.
- Radiation, for example from machines or nuclear power plant leakage, often causes sperm-cell damage, resulting in children being at risk from leukemia and birth defects.
- Stress, usually a result of fast-paced urban living, can cause a variety of physical and mental problems, such as colitis and peptic ulcer.

MENTAL ATTITUDE

Whatever the severity of a situation and the individual's physical capability to cope, mental attitude is the real key to survival. Human beings are great survivors, using their brains to keep one step ahead of their animal competitors. Urban living uses only a small part of a human's physical and mental attributes. In a wilderness survival situation, humans have to relearn many manual skills. Common sense is one of the most basic and valuable of human characteristics, but much more important than even this is the will to survive.

NUTRITIONAL NEEDS

THE PHYSICAL CHARACTERISTICS of animals are determined by the food they eat. For example, herbivores have multiple stomachs to digest tough grasses, along with grinding teeth for grazing, while carnivores have teeth for tearing meat and bodies adapted for stealth or speed. Humans, however, are omnivores, which means they can live either on meat or without it, and have teeth both for shearing meat and for grinding vegetable matter. If existing on a vegetarian diet, they must ensure that it provides the full range of vitamins and minerals that eating another animal would give them instantly.

BUILDING BLOCKS OF LIFE

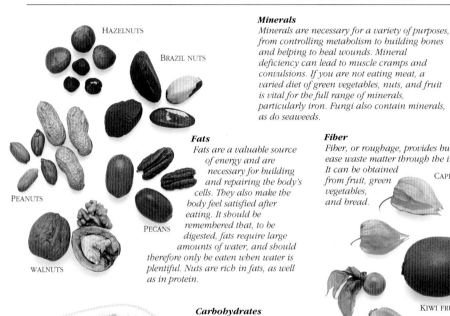

HAZELNUTS

BRAZIL NUTS

PEANUTS

PECANS

WALNUTS

Minerals
Minerals are necessary for a variety of purposes, from controlling metabolism to building bones and helping to heal wounds. Mineral deficiency can lead to muscle cramps and convulsions. If you are not eating meat, a varied diet of green vegetables, nuts, and fruit is vital for the full range of minerals, particularly iron. Fungi also contain minerals, as do seaweeds.

FUNGUS

Fats
Fats are a valuable source of energy and are necessary for building and repairing the body's cells. They also make the body feel satisfied after eating. It should be remembered that, to be digested, fats require large amounts of water, and should therefore only be eaten when water is plentiful. Nuts are rich in fats, as well as in protein.

Fiber
Fiber, or roughage, provides bulk to help ease waste matter through the intestines. It can be obtained from fruit, green vegetables, and bread.

CAPE GOOSEBERRIES

DATES

KIWI FRUIT

PERSIMMON

Carbohydrates
Carbohydrates play a vital role in nutrition by supplying the body with energy. They occur as either starches or sugars, and are broken down and stored in the liver until needed to provide energy in the form of glucose. Excess glucose not needed for energy is converted into fat. Honey is an excellent source of sugar.

HONEYCOMB

Vitamins
Vitamins control the growth and repair of the body's tissues and stimulate the production of energy. Fresh fruits are the best source of vitamins, but like most natural foods are seasonal. During long-term survival situations in temperate regions with clearly defined seasons, fruit must be collected and stored for the winter (see page 118).

PAPAYA

Protein
Protein is vital for building tissue and maintaining growth. Certain proteins must be obtained from food to provide essential amino acids that cannot be synthesized by the body. Meat and fish provide all the necessary amino acids, and many vitamins and minerals. Some protein can also be obtained from vegetable matter.

FISH

DAILY CALORIE REQUIREMENTS

The energy obtained from food is measured in calories. A human needs a certain number of calories to stay alive – even if staying in bed all day, one would burn off about 2,000 calories. The number of calories needed each day depends on factors such as age. Survivors should balance their calorie input and energy output.

Lumberjack
Heavy physical labor, such as logging, requires a higher daily caloric intake than a sedentary lifestyle, since more energy is needed to keep the body moving and the muscles in use. In logging camps, these calories are obtained from large, rich meals.

Tropical Scientist
People living in the tropics require fewer calories than those living in cold climates. High temperatures cause heavy sweating, resulting in the loss of minerals and salts, so diet must be well balanced and include plenty of water.

Mountaineer
Constant freezing temperatures and the need to be alert at all times make mountaineering a very calorie-costly activity. Well over 5,000 calories per day are needed in order for the body to maintain its core temperature. Extra calories may be needed for activities such as hauling a sled or snowshoeing.

ENERGY EXPENDED

Different activities require varying amounts of calories, depending on climate, physical condition, and the amount of exertion needed for a particular task. The following figures are a general guide for the "average" man and woman. You should bear in mind that your own calorie requirements and the amount of energy you expend on various tasks will change with the weather, as well as with the type of terrain in which you are working.

Activity	Cals per hour
Resting	70
Sitting	90
Lighting a fire	135
Walking	180
Cycling	240
Chopping wood	360
Sprinting	360
Running	400
Swimming	500

DAILY CALORIE NEEDS

Cals	18-35 Years			36-55 Years			Over 55 Years	
3,500								
3,000								
2,500								
2,000								
1,500								
1,000	Inactive	Active	Very Active	Inactive	Active	Very Active	Inactive	Active

Calorie Needs
The metabolism of men is less efficient than that of women, and they have less natural insulation, so they burn more calories. Young people burn more calories than older ones, partly because they are more active, but also because maturity tends to slow down the metabolism.

 MEN

 WOMEN

ADAPTING TO THE ENVIRONMENT

BECAUSE OF THEIR ingenuity, people are able to live in every type of environment on Earth and, over time, they adapt biologically and socially to the climate and terrain of their particular area. The so-called "primitive" peoples survive by living very closely within the environmental constraints of their region. Many of them have developed intricate social behavior, as well as adapting biologically. By contrast, in developing survival techniques for the concrete jungle, "civilized" urban dwellers have lost much of their ability to adapt to the land. Each person is an individual, dissociated from the cycle of nature, the seasons, and the natural world beyond the city or suburban streets. To survive in the wild, urban dwellers must relearn the skills practiced by their ancestors and by primitive peoples today.

Inuit
Forty years ago, Inuits still wore animal skins and built igloos as shelters during hunting trips. Their livers were large, enabling their bodies to convert the protein from their largely carnivorous diet into the carbohydrate that they lacked. Today, arctic settlements have modern technology, yet Inuits remain physically adapted to life in the extreme environment of the arctic.

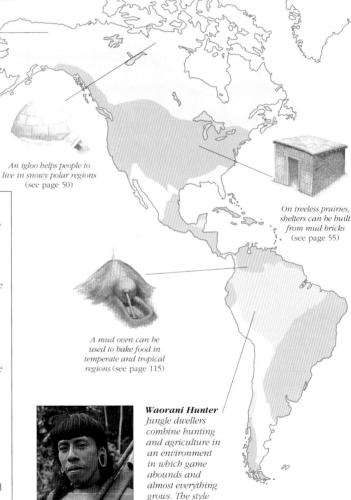

An igloo helps people to live in snowy polar regions (see page 50)

On treeless prairies, shelters can be built from mud bricks (see page 55)

A mud oven can be used to bake food in temperate and tropical regions (see page 115)

URBAN DWELLERS

Urban dwellers live in a very unnatural environment, totally dependent upon technology and free from the need to forage for food, allowing them to socialize for purely recreational reasons. They usually travel by vehicle, walking only short distances unless deliberately exercising. Central heating and air conditioning make the environment of one city very similar to that of another. Urban living requires its own set of reflexes and expertise, which are unrelated to those of the natural world. This leaves urban dwellers ill-prepared for the practicalities of surviving without the facilities of modern life. In the wild, a great deal of practical common sense is required, as well as the ability to apply basic scientific principles to everyday problems. Urban dwellers are not used to solving practical problems, largely because their pace of life does not allow them enough time, but also because there is no need. In the wild, however, time and necessity are both in plentiful supply.

Backpacker
Urban dwellers need special equipment to be able to survive in the wilderness.

Waorani Hunter
Jungle dwellers combine hunting and agriculture in an environment in which game abounds and almost everything grows. The style of cultivation employed by these people (burning jungle clearings in order to plant crops) frees them from constant food gathering, and so allows them plenty of time to socialize.

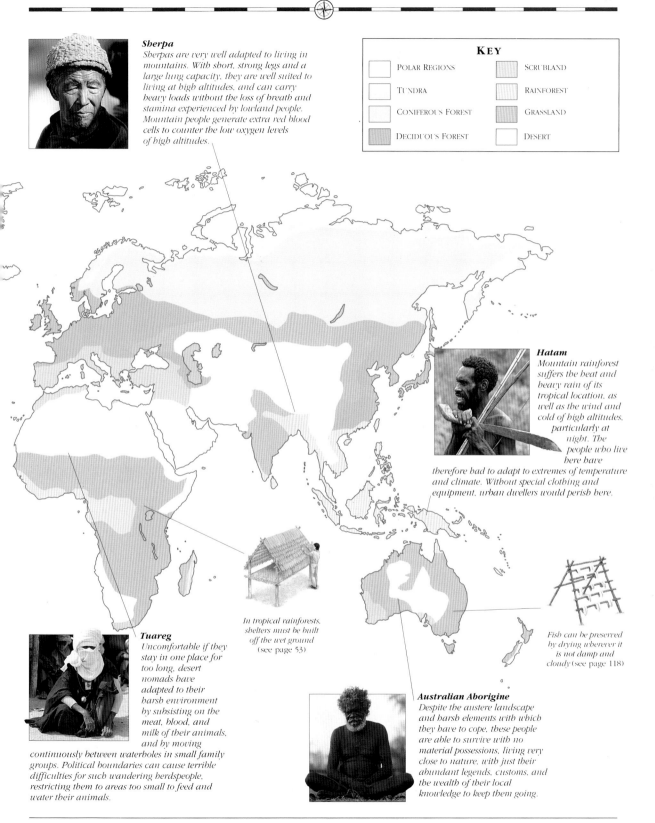

Sherpa
Sherpas are very well adapted to living in mountains. With short, strong legs and a large lung capacity, they are well suited to living at high altitudes, and can carry heavy loads without the loss of breath and stamina experienced by lowland people. Mountain people generate extra red blood cells to counter the low oxygen levels of high altitudes.

KEY

POLAR REGIONS	SCRUBLAND
TUNDRA	RAINFOREST
CONIFEROUS FOREST	GRASSLAND
DECIDUOUS FOREST	DESERT

Hatam
Mountain rainforest suffers the heat and heavy rain of its tropical location, as well as the wind and cold of high altitudes, particularly at night. The people who live here have therefore had to adapt to extremes of temperature and climate. Without special clothing and equipment, urban dwellers would perish here.

In tropical rainforests, shelters must be built off the wet ground (see page 53)

Fish can be preserved by drying wherever it is not damp and cloudy (see page 118)

Tuareg
Uncomfortable if they stay in one place for too long, desert nomads have adapted to their harsh environment by subsisting on the meat, blood, and milk of their animals, and by moving continuously between waterholes in small family groups. Political boundaries can cause terrible difficulties for such wandering herdspeople, restricting them to areas too small to feed and water their animals.

Australian Aborigine
Despite the austere landscape and harsh elements with which they have to cope, these people are able to survive with no material possessions, living very close to nature, with just their abundant legends, customs, and the wealth of their local knowledge to keep them going.

FITNESS

UNLESS WE WALK, run, and stretch regularly, our muscles become smaller and our heart-lung system less efficient, and we put on fat where we do not need it. Aerobic exercises are the most important ones to maintain fitness for long-term wilderness travel and endurance. They involve a lot of repeated movements using light weights to create general fitness, speed, and agility.

HOW FIT ARE YOU?

The Step Test
You can measure – and improve – your overall fitness by stepping on and off a box or step. The step should be about 8 in (20 cm) high to avoid excessive discomfort and breathlessness. Place the entire foot flat on the step each time, with the other foot flat on the ground. After about 24 step-ups per minute for three minutes, rest for 30 seconds and take your pulse at the wrist. Count the beats for 15 seconds, then multiply by four to get a heart rate per minute. Read off your fitness rating on the chart below.

1 Place your whole foot carefully on the box.

WARNING
When getting fit, start slowly, gradually building up your routine over several months. Seek expert instruction and, if suffering from any ailments, obtain medical advice first.

2 Straighten your leg and bring your other foot up to the step.

3 Maintain your balance, then step back down. Step up using the other leg.

MENTAL FITNESS
Physical fitness helps to create mental fitness. In the wild, you must survive without the props of urban life, and generate your own sense of satisfaction and self-worth from day-to-day living. Training helps to increase your self-confidence, and to improve your awareness of your abilities and limitations. Mental fitness also comes from within – from understanding who (and what) you are, and from coming to terms with where you stand in relation to the enormity of the rest of the universe. In a survival situation, you must believe in your own ability to cope. If you do not, you may not survive.

Fitness Rating
The fitter you are, the stronger your heart will be. A fit heart pumps slower, but more efficiently, than an unfit one. The hearts of children, women, and old people beat faster than those of young adult males, as the chart below left shows. When taken before getting up in the morning, the pulse can be an accurate measure of fitness – the "base rate." The chart below right shows the pulse rate after three minutes of exercise and 30 seconds of rest. The fitter you are, the quicker your heart will recover after exercise.

AGE (years)	20-29	30-39	40-49	50+
RATING	BEATS PER MINUTE AT REST			
Men				
Excellent	under 60	under 64	under 66	under 68
Good	60–69	64–71	66–73	68–75
Average	70–75	72–87	74–89	76–91
Poor	over 85	over 87	over 89	over 91
Women				
Excellent	under 70	under 72	under 74	under 76
Good	70–77	72–79	74–81	76–83
Average	78–94	80–96	82–98	84–100
Poor	over 94	over 96	over 98	over 100

AGE (years)	20-29	30-39	40-49	50+
RATING	BEATS PER MINUTE AFTER EXERCISE			
Men				
Excellent	under 76	under 80	under 82	under 84
Good	76–85	80–87	82–89	84–91
Average	86–101	88–103	90–105	92–107
Poor	over 101	over 103	over 105	over 107
Women				
Excellent	under 86	under 88	under 90	under 92
Good	86–93	88–95	90–97	92–99
Average	94–110	96–112	98–114	100–116
Poor	over 110	over 112	over 114	over 116

STRETCHING

Before exercising you should always stretch gently and mobilize every part of your body, starting at the top and working down. Never "bounce" against any resistance. It is just as important to stretch after exercise.

ARMS AND SHOULDERS

Rotate arms backward in half-circle

Bring arms forward past ears

Rotate arms in alternate directions

1 Swing both arms gently backward and upward.

2 Swing the arms forward together past your ears.

3 Next, rotate one arm forward. Repeat with the other arm.

4 Swing each arm alternately backward.

THE BENEFITS OF EXERCISE

The right kind of exercise makes your body more efficient, and you feel better and more alert than without exercise. Over time, changes such as weight loss occur, as well as improved posture, physique, strength, agility, and stamina. As a regular exercise regime develops, appetite and sleep patterns improve. A training schedule must have at least three sessions a week of 45 minutes of exercise, each of which puts the heart rate over 120 beats per minute.

Long-term Benefits
Regular exercise helps all organs in your body to function efficiently.

CHEST AND SHOULDERS

1 Lift elbows high and hold forearms horizontally.

2 Pull your elbows as far back as possible, twice.

3 On the third pull, straighten your arms out to your sides.

WAIST

1 Stand with your elbows high and forearms raised.

2 Twist at the waist to one side as far as possible, twice.

3 The third time, throw out leading arm. Repeat.

STOMACH

1 Lie with knees bent and hands touching ears.

2 Lift shoulder and point elbow at opposite knee.

ARMS

1 Lie face-down, keeping body straight and palms flat on floor.

2 Straighten elbows and thrust upward, keeping body rigid.

Stretching the Back
Lower back pain can result from carrying a heavy backpack or other exertion. These exercises re-establish the natural curve of the spine, easing back pain.

EASING BACK PAIN

1 Lie face-down, relaxing totally.

2 Rest on elbows and curve back.

3 Straighten arms and stretch.

Chapter Two

Basic Equipment

WITH THE CORRECT equipment for your particular activity and environment, you dramatically reduce the likelihood of accidents, and therefore of having to cope with a serious survival situation. Outdoor equipment suppliers are able to provide well-designed gear suitable for every extreme of climate and terrain. You can spend a lot of money buying glamorous items, but it is far more important to concentrate on obtaining the equipment you really need for survival. If you do not have first-hand experience, you should try to find out what other, more experienced, people have used in similar situations, rather than rely on glossy sales talk. Some items of equipment, for example a knife and a compass, are essential, and you should buy the best you can find. Other items, such as an inflatable pillow or a camp bed, are purely for comfort, and you can do without them. Having selected your equipment, you must be prepared to modify it to your precise requirements. Think about critical parts that could wear out or break, and about how you can secure tools and clothing – particularly gloves and hats – so that they do not get lost.

SURVIVAL GEAR
Backpacking has become a popular pastime around the world, and spawned numerous fashions in clothing and equipment. However, as long as you have the basic items, you can venture into the most awe-inspiring areas with safety and self-confidence.

THE RIGHT CLOTHING

WE RARELY WEAR clothing appropriate to the natural conditions in which we live. Urban life accustoms us to wearing clothes for comfort and fashion, rather than for the maintenance of body temperature, by cocooning us from the environment with artificial heating and air conditioning. Even if we buy clothes specially prepared for the outdoors, they often owe more to current fashion than to practicality. You can spend a lot of money on "designer" gear – or you can just buy the most essential items, and they will still do the job, even though they may not be in all the latest colors.

THE LAYERING PRINCIPLE

Several thin layers of clothing that trap air between them will keep you much warmer than a single, thick garment. If you get too hot, you can control your body temperature by removing layers or venting (opening zippers or buttons to allow warm air to escape and cool air to enter). This principle applies in both hot and cold weather.

The Core Layer
The first layer, which lies next to the skin, should consist of a wool or synthetic undershirt or a long-sleeved, thermal top, which should be close-fitting but not tight. It should be made of a material that will absorb perspiration and "wick" it away from the skin (move it to the outside of the material). This layer must be kept as clean as possible, to prevent dirt from clogging its pores.

The Second Layer
The second layer should be loose-fitting, but with the potential for keeping the blood vessels of the neck and wrists protected and warm. It can consist of a zip-up top with a polo neck, or a shirt with a collar, sleeves that can be rolled up, and cuffs that can be buttoned. In hot weather, this layer may be the outside one, with perhaps just a windproof shell (see opposite).

Underwear
Long, thermal underwear is usually necessary only in temperatures below freezing. In the arctic, a "groin patch" of impermeable material prevents windchill in that area, particularly when skiing. Wet pants dry out faster if long underwear is not worn, although you can combat this problem by wearing waterproof overpants. In mild weather, this layer can consist of cotton shorts.

The Third Layer
The third layer should be a woolen pullover or light, fleecy jacket. If you are on the move, even in the arctic, this layer is best removed to prevent you from becoming overheated. You can vent your insulated parka (see opposite) if you are still hot. When you stop to rest, you should replace the middle layer before you start to feel cold. This layer can act as the outside one in temperate regions when the weather is mild.

The Outer Layer
The outer layer should be a jacket that is either wind resistant or waterproof, or both, depending on the climate in which you are traveling. In the arctic, a padded, windproof parka is required for protection against cutting winds. You must be able to vent the jacket, to avoid becoming overheated. In temperate areas, rain is the main problem, although you can wear a waterproof shell over the jacket.

Pants
Pants must allow freedom of movement and should be made of a fabric that will dry quickly if it gets wet. In very wet conditions, using suspenders prevents a belt from chafing the waist. Waterproof overpants can be worn to protect your legs from driving rain (see opposite), but they may cause you to become overheated. In very cold conditions, quilted over-trousers should be zipped over pants and boots as added protection.

FEATURES OF CLOTHING FABRICS

Fabric	Advantages	Disadvantages
Wool	This natural fiber has insulating properties even when it is wet, remaining comfortable until it is soaked. It smolders, rather than burns, when exposed to flames.	Wool is heavy when wet and takes time to dry. Worn next to the skin, it can make the skin itch. It can shrink when it is washed.
Cotton	Cotton is hardwearing and able to "breathe," absorbing moisture. It is good for underwear and other clothing worn next to the skin in warm climates.	Heavy when wet, cotton can shrink if it is dried in high temperatures. It can also tear and burn easily. It is not windproof.
Fleece or pile	Used for the third layer to wick moisture away from the body while keeping it warm. Lightweight and hardwearing. Does not absorb moisture.	This manmade fabric is not windproof. It does not compress easily and can collect balls of fluff on the outside after long use.
Synthetic, breathable fabrics	These let sweat evaporate while keeping rain out. They are usually windproof, and are therefore used for the outer garments.	Seams in these fabrics can let in water. In very wet conditions their pores can become clogged, while condensation may form inside in cold conditions. The evaporation of sweat that is wicked to the outside can result in heat loss.

Choosing Fabrics
Outdoor clothing can be made from a variety of fabrics, from wool or cotton to synthetic material, some of which allows perspiration out, but prevents rainwater from entering. Manmade materials are not always as hardwearing as natural ones, however, and may retain body odor unless rinsed with vinegar. Natural fabrics, such as cotton and wool, may shrink if dried at high temperatures after washing.

EXTREME WEATHER CLOTHING

If you follow the layering system *(see opposite)* when choosing outdoor clothing, you should be able to equip yourself with the right garments for any type of weather. In a survival situation, you may not have garments manufactured for specific climates, but you can use the layering system in conjunction with shelters and fires as protection against the elements. In extreme climates and harsh terrain, clothing must give protection from conditions that can injure or cause death – for example, those encountered in deserts *(see page 142)*. Wind, cold, heat, sunshine, and rain are the main threats. Some clothing specific to particular climates – for example, jungle boots – may not be suitable for less extreme areas, but most types of clothing can be adapted to your needs.

Hat
A wide-brimmed hat protects the head and neck from the sun. Eyelet vents around the brim help to keep your head cool.

Core Layer
A light-colored, cotton T-shirt worn under the shirt absorbs sweat away from your skin, keeping you cool.

Second Layer
A lightweight shirt acts as the main layer. Sleeves should be rolled down in extreme heat, for example in the desert (see page 142).

Outer Layer
A lightweight, windproof jacket worn over the top will act as the final layer, protecting from the wind, and from the cold at night.

Keeping Cool
Clothing for hot weather should be lightweight and loose-fitting. Light colors reflect heat and help keep you cool. The layering principle applies here, just as much as in cold weather.

Head Protection
A balaclava covers the head, the sides of the face, and the neck, to prevent heat from being lost. An insulated hood can be worn on top for added warmth.

Core Layer
A thermal undershirt and long underwear make up the first layer. They should be able to absorb and wick away perspiration.

Middle Mitten
Wool mittens between the inner gloves and outer mittens allow you to grasp objects but still keep your hands warm.

Middle Layer
A fleece jacket should absorb sweat from the core layer, yet still trap a layer of warm air against your body.

Second Layer
A polo-necked shirt should overlap the balaclava at the neck and the gloves at the cuff.

Inner Gloves
Inner gloves prevent the skin from sticking to frozen objects, allowing use of the hands for short periods without the need for heavy mittens.

Outer Layer
A padded, hooded parka is essential. It should have overlapping front fastenings and a water-resistant shell in breathable fabric.

Pants
Pants should be loose-fitting and lightweight, and made of light material such as cotton.

Boots
Boots should be lightweight, but must have tough soles for walking (see page 24).

Pants
Mountain bibs overlap the waist where clothing can be disturbed during movement, while allowing venting at the shoulders and chest. They can be worn alone, or over pants or long underwear.

Outer Mittens
The layering system also applies to gloves, with heavy mittens worn on top of thinner ones.

Boots
Heavy snow boots have a plastic shell and thermal liners, which act as inner boots. Two pairs of socks should be worn underneath.

KEEPING DRY

Getting wet creates a serious survival problem. Waterproof clothes must be put on when rain starts, but they must be removed immediately when rain stops to prevent sweating. Impermeable rain gear is no good for walkers because it sweats – choose breathable materials. Wear waterproof pants only when it is both wet and cold. Gaiters will keep the feet and calves dry, even when you are crossing streams.

Wet-weather Gear
Waterproof clothing should cover the body from head to foot.

Keeping Warm
In extreme cold, all areas of skin must be covered, and it is vital to adhere to the layering system. Be prepared to vent or remove clothing if you become overheated when traveling or working. Trapped sweat reduces the insulating properties of clothes and can result in hypothermia (see page 163).

FOOTWEAR

HUMAN BODY WEIGHT is designed to be spread over four feet rather than two, so the feet are under constant pressure. With the added weight of heavy backpacks, crossing rough, wet ground makes protection for the feet the single most important equipment consideration. Footwear must always be broken in before being used. Break in leather boots by wetting them, then wearing them until they are dry. When hiking, keep your feet clean, washing them daily and dusting them with talcum powder. Always wear clean, dry socks, and tape up all hot spots before they turn into blisters.

LIGHTWEIGHT FOOTWEAR

Shock-absorbing sole for walking on roads

Fabric upper dries quickly when wet

Desert Boots
With tough soles and lightweight leather uppers, desert boots allow the feet to breathe while keeping hot sand out. High sides protect the ankles from thorny scrub, and give some support. In wet conditions, the porous nature of suede allows moisture to get in, so the boots take time to dry out.

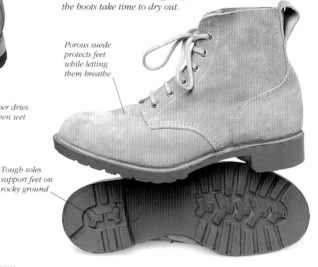

Porous suede protects feet while letting them breathe

Tough soles support feet on rocky ground

Fabric Boots
Many mountaineers wear lightweight trekking boots in camp or during the walk to a big mountain, saving their heavy, molded plastic climbing boots for the snow and ice. Lightweight boots can also be worn for light walking over short distances, as long as the terrain is not very rough. Although they offer less protection and support than leather boots, fabric boots do dry out quickly when wet, and give the feet a rest from hot, heavy footwear.

Molded foam sole for support and shock absorption

Light Hiking Boots
Light hiking boots provide comfort for sore feet around a camp, and are good for wearing in boats and in vehicles. However, while being comfortable and light, they do not offer as much protection to the feet as heavy walking boots. The constant wearing of light hiking boots may make the feet soft and susceptible to injury.

SOCKS

Thick socks, made either of wool or of fiber-pile cotton, are vital. Socks cushion the feet and prevent boots from rubbing the skin, as well as keeping the feet warm and dry by "wicking" away moisture (moving sweat to the outer layer of fibers, away from the skin). In very cold weather, you should wear two pairs of socks.

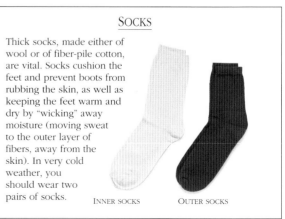

INNER SOCKS　　　OUTER SOCKS

HEAVY-DUTY FOOTWEAR

Hiking Boots

A compromise between weight, durability, and protection produces a good, all-around boot with a strong, cleated sole, water-resistant uppers, and ankle protection.

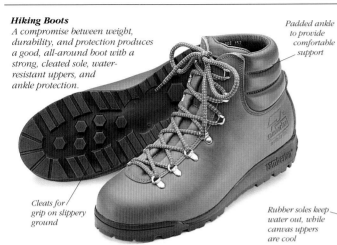

Padded ankle to provide comfortable support

Cleats for grip on slippery ground

Jungle Boots

Constant wetness is the main problem in the jungle, but boots must also provide ankle support and protection from sharp sticks and rocks. With rubber soles, these boots keep out water from damp ground while allowing the feet to breathe through the canvas uppers. After wading in a river, the action of walking squirts water out of vents in the instep. The cleats are wide and deep for good grip on wet ground.

Rubber soles keep water out, while canvas uppers are cool

Plastic Snow Boots

Designed to hold the foot rigid while using crampons for grip on ice, these boots are heavily insulated for use in the coldest of climates. Like ski boots, however, they make walking awkward. They have a thermal inner lining in the form of a separate boot, which may be worn on its own, for example inside a tent.

Non-slip cleats for walking in snow

Rigid sides give excellent support on rocky ground

GAITERS

Gaiters are essential, both in temperate areas for keeping the feet and the lower trouser leg dry, and in polar regions for keeping out deep snow. When crossing shallow rivers, gaiters will keep most, if not all, the water out of boots. They are better than rubber boots because they do not trap perspiration and overheat the feet.

MUD GAITERS   SNOW GAITERS

LOOKING AFTER YOUR BOOTS

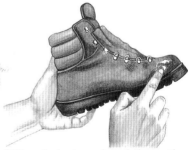

1 Remove laces and inner soles and wash off all mud from the boots. It is very important to remove peat, which has an acid content that can damage leather.

2 Allow the boots to dry thoroughly. If possible, keep the boots away from direct heat from a fire or the sun, since heat can cause the leather to crack.

3 When the boots are dry, rub them with waterproofing compound, using a finger. If you are not going to wear the boots at once, store them in a cool, dry place.

PERSONAL CAMP KIT

THE PERFECT COLLECTION of camping equipment is only created through trial and error. Before you embark on a journey, consider omitting from your kit any items that you did not use on your last trip. Modifications to the kit should be based on your previous experiences as well as the upcoming trip. Some items will more than earn their keep, and will become battered, well-worn friends. You will eventually become so attached to your gear that losing or breaking any item would be unthinkable.

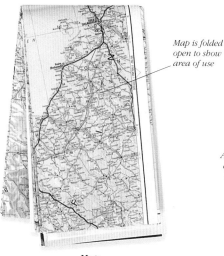

Map is folded open to show area of use

Compass
A compass is a vital piece of equipment, so it must be kept in a safe place.

Flashlight head can be twisted to turn on flashlight

Flashlight
A flashlight should be as small and waterproof as possible.

Binoculars
These should be as small and robust as possible. Even if they are waterproof, keep them in a plastic bag.

Map
A map must always be kept dry and folded neatly to show the area of use.

Fine screwdriver — Reamer
Chisel — Hook
Large blade — Corkscrew
Small blade
Magnifying glass
Phillips screwdriver — Can opener — Scissors
Wood saw
Nail file — Small screwdriver
Bottle opener

Swiss Army Knife
A knife with a good, solid blade is necessary. Additional tools on the knife are also useful but may break easily if used carelessly.

Mess Tin
A good mess tin is useful for cooking camping meals (see page 112). Wrap the metal handles with tape to avoid burns.

Water Bottle
A metal bottle may split if the water inside it freezes. A plastic one could melt if placed too close to a fire.

Water Purifier
This is used to purify natural water before drinking, in order to prevent infection with waterborne diseases (see page 75).

Stove
Choose a basic, but high-quality, stove (see page 114) and keep it clean, protecting it from knocks.

Stove Fuel
Ensure that your fuel bottle does not leak, and that your fuel is clean, filtering it if necessary.

PLATE   DISH

Plates and Dishes
Use plastic or wooden plates and dishes to prevent painful mouth burns that could get infected (see page 112). Never eat from a hot cooking pot.

Mug
A plastic mug can be used to hold both hot and cold drinks (see page 112).

SPOON   UTENSIL
SLEEVE

KNIFE   FORK

Utensils
Keep all utensils clean to avoid poisoning. If you lose or break eating utensils, you can carve new ones from wood (see page 113).

Lip Balm
Lip balm is vital in all climates, preventing lips from becoming chapped. Use throughout the day whenever lips feel dry.

Sunblock
Sunblock is essential in snow and bright sunshine, particularly at high altitudes.

Survival Kit
A survival kit contains vital items not found in the wild (see page 28).

Towel
A large towel can be cut into segments for use as sweatbands or washcloths. A towel can also be used as a scarf (see page 142).

First-aid Kit
This is essential for treating injuries (see page 174).

Waterproof Matches
These have waxed heads to keep them dry.

Sewing Kit
Use this for mending clothes and tents.

All-around zipper keeps out dirt and insects

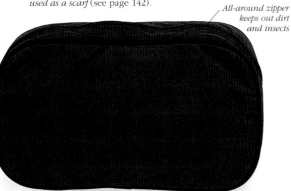

Wash Kit
Keep items for personal hygiene together in a special bag. Hang the bag on a tree while you wash to prevent individual items from getting lost (see page 57).

WARM AND DRY

Tents and sleeping bags represent your home comforts while in the wild, although you can survive without them. They must always be stored properly, and sleeping bags must never be allowed to get wet.

TENT   SLEEPING BAG

BASIC SURVIVAL KIT

IN SURVIVAL SITUATIONS, a few key items can make the difference between living and dying. These important items should be carried on the person at all times, preferably in a small tin that can be tucked into a pocket. Whenever you venture into the wild, you should secure other tools that are vital for survival separately about your person in order to minimize the chances of them being damaged or lost. Some can be hung on strong cords around your neck, then tucked inside your clothes so that they do not get pulled off if you brush through vegetation. Put each item between different layers of clothing so that the pieces do not clash together and break. You should assemble your own survival kit according to your personal needs.

Life-saving Equipment
The most important items of your survival equipment should be kept in a small tin with a tight-fitting lid.

Safety Pins
Use these for securing your clothing, or mending your sleeping bag or tent.

Fishing Line
Choose a strong line for catching fish and lashing tools.

Thin Wire
Wire can be put to many uses and may be reused over and over again. It should be thin enough to bend easily, yet not so thin that it will break.

Fishing Hooks and Sinkers
Pack plenty of small fishing hooks, floats, and split-shot weights. Small hooks can be used for catching both large and small fish.

Reflector
You can use the polished lid of your survival tin, or a specially made heliograph, to attract attention in a survival situation. Looking through the hole in the center of the heliograph, you can direct reflected sunlight toward an airplane.

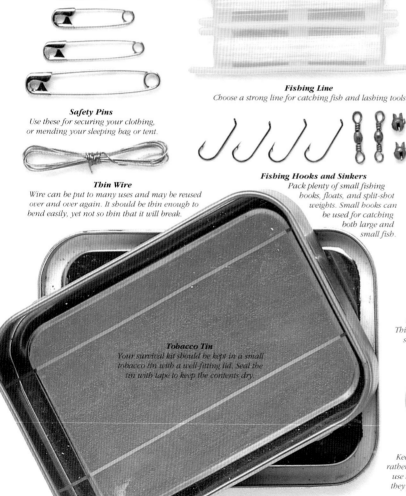

Tobacco Tin
Your survival kit should be kept in a small tobacco tin with a well-fitting lid. Seal the tin with tape to keep the contents dry.

Button Compass
This is essential. Ideally it should be luminous.

Candle
Keep this for firelighting, rather than as a lamp. Do not use tallow candles because they putrefy in hot weather.

Matches
Buy waterproof matches, or waterproof ordinary ones by dripping a thin layer of candle wax onto their heads and stems. Scrape off the wax before striking each match.

Needles, Thread, and Buttons
Keep several needles in your tin, all with large eyes, as well as plenty of thick, strong, preferably waterproof thread. Wrap the thread around the needles and store them in a plastic bag. Large buttons are useful for securing the flaps of tents.

Adhesive Bandages
You should have adhesive bandages in various sizes to prevent abrasions from becoming infected, or to pad blisters on your feet.

Wire Saw
A wire saw is easy, if slow, to use, and can cut most materials. Keep it covered with a film of grease, inside a plastic bag, so that it does not rust or break.

Antibiotic Tablets
These should be kept until you really need them.

Water Sterilizing Tablets
Keep these for emergencies, when you are unable to boil water that you believe is unsafe to drink.

Scalpel
This can be used for different purposes. Keep the blades in their original oiled package.

Magnifying Glass
A magnifying glass can focus sunlight on dry tinder, making it smolder, so that you can start a fire.

Pencil
A pencil is invaluable for making notes on where you have been and what is safe to eat, as well as for drawing maps.

Salt
This is essential for survival. If you do not replace the salt lost in sweat and urine, you may become very ill.

Plastic Bag
A strong plastic bag is useful for a variety of purposes, such as carrying water from a stream, or collecting water from vegetation in emergencies.

Potassium Permanganate
These crystals are useful for purifying water. Mixed with water to a deep red color, they can also be used to treat fungal infections, such as trench foot. Follow the instructions on the tin.

VITAL EQUIPMENT AROUND YOUR NECK

You should never be without your most valuable pieces of equipment, particularly in the wild. You should take great care not to lose or break them, since, away from civilization, they cannot be replaced or repaired. Each of these items should be attached to a separate strong cord and be hung around your neck, available for when you need it. Tuck the items inside your clothing when not in use, to prevent them from breaking.

Crucial Gear
Always keep your most important items of equipment where you can reach them.

Silva compass

Watch

Whistle

Pocketknife

SLEEPING BAGS AND BEDS

R EST IS AS essential for survival as eating. A good, uninterrupted night's sleep can counter all the worries and stress of a difficult situation, and turn pessimistic gloom into positive optimism. Being warm and dry makes you feel more secure than if you were sleeping on bare ground in the open air. Even in the humid heat of the jungle, shelter and insulation from the wet ground are required.

SLEEPING BAG FEATURES

Although there are many different shapes and styles of sleeping bag, a bag should always be padded well enough to keep you warm even if you do not have a tent. A sleeping bag must never be allowed to get wet. Always keep it inside a waterproof cover, such as a bivy sack made from porous fabric *(see page 43)*.

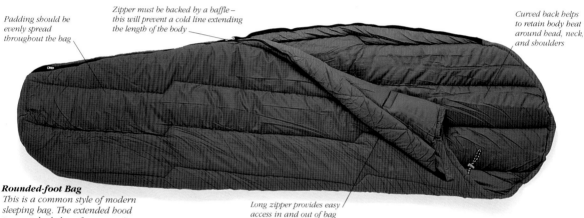

Padding should be evenly spread throughout the bag

Zipper must be backed by a baffle – this will prevent a cold line extending the length of the body

Curved back helps to retain body heat around head, neck, and shoulders

Long zipper provides easy access in and out of bag

Rounded-foot Bag
This is a common style of modern sleeping bag. The extended hood prevents body heat from escaping from head, chest, and shoulders.

Tapered foot helps to keep bag small and light

Mummy Bag
The neck of this bag can be closed with a drawstring to keep your head and neck insulated in cold weather. This is very important, since you can lose half your body heat through your head. With no zipper, it can be difficult to get out.

Attached pillow can be folded inside

Rectangle Bag
This bag is best for camping using vehicles, rather than for sleeping outdoors. It is very lightweight, and is therefore not suitable for very cold conditions like those of the polar regions.

SLEEPING BAG CONSTRUCTION

A down-filled sleeping bag is lightweight and warm. However, down can lose its insulation, compacting into balls when wet or tightly packed. Synthetic fillers are bulkier, heavier, and not as comfortable as down. They will, however, keep you warm if they get wet, and they dry quickly.

Boxwall
For cold-weather down bags, the filling is kept in fabric "boxes" to minimize bunching.

Shingle
These bags have slanted layers of overlapping fibers, which can fill with air for insulation.

Quilt
The filling is held in separate oval channels. However, heat is lost through the stitching.

Offset Quilt
Offset filling channels in a double layer prevent bunching and heat loss through the stitching.

SLEEPING ACCESSORIES

Liner
A cotton liner keeps a layer of insulating air between yourself and your sleeping bag. It can be washed more easily than the bag.

Camping Pad
This is essential for insulation from the wet and cold of the bare ground. It should be placed under your sleeping bag.

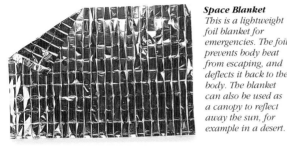

Space Blanket
This is a lightweight foil blanket for emergencies. The foil prevents body heat from escaping, and deflects it back to the body. The blanket can also be used as a canopy to reflect away the sun, for example in a desert.

Inflatable Pillow
Although a pillow is not strictly necessary, it provides extra comfort for long journeys.

CARE AND REPAIR

Shake your sleeping bag well before use to distribute the pile evenly, and air it well after using it. If your sleeping bag is torn, you should repair it immediately with a needle and thread, to prevent the damage from getting worse. A wide adhesive tape is useful for temporarily sealing tears. You can patch a torn sleeping-bag shell with pieces of its stuff sack *(see page 27)*, which is often made of the same type of material.

Sewing Kit
A sewing kit is essential for mending torn sleeping bags, tents, and clothes.

MAKING A BED

1 Without a sleeping bag, you must make a raised bed, to ensure adequate insulation and avoid insects and animals. Lay several logs longer than your height together on the ground to form the base of the bed.

2 Hold the log bed tightly together by hammering pegs made from sharpened sticks into the ground at the corners, to prevent the logs from rolling apart.

3 Cover the logs with a thick layer of grass to provide padding over irregularities in the logs such as rough bark and knots.

4 Add more layers of branches, ferns, and foliage mixed with grass and vegetation to create air space and a deep-pile effect. You should end up with a "mattress" into which you can sink in relative comfort.

5 Continue piling up layers of vegetation as a mattress until it is deep and comfortable. You can also make a pillow from a pile of grass.

TOOLS

WHETHER YOU ARE camping with all the latest gadgets, or surviving with minimal equipment after a disaster, you will need some tools with which to build a shelter and cut firewood. Broken or lost tools cannot be easily replaced in the wilderness, so you must take great care of them. Do not misuse them in ways that will either damage them or, more importantly, injure you. You can improvise some tools, but do not risk damaging or losing another precious tool in the process. Always work within the limitations of your tools, as well as within your own capabilities.

BASIC CUTTING TOOLS

The basic, essential tool for camping and survival is a good, strong knife. Although almost any other tool can be improvised, if you do not have a knife, making other items is very difficult. An ax is invaluable for heavy work, but you are unlikely to carry one because of its weight, unless you have a vehicle or pack animals.

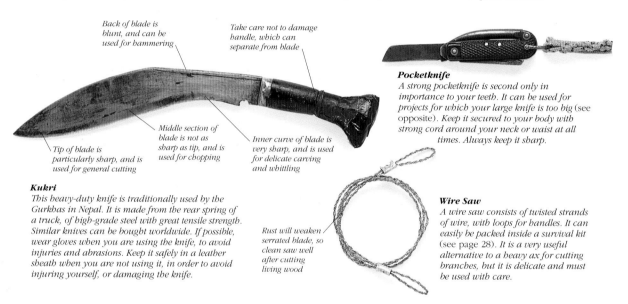

Back of blade is blunt, and can be used for hammering

Take care not to damage handle, which can separate from blade

Tip of blade is particularly sharp, and is used for general cutting

Middle section of blade is not as sharp as tip, and is used for chopping

Inner curve of blade is very sharp, and is used for delicate carving and whittling

Kukri
This heavy-duty knife is traditionally used by the Gurkhas in Nepal. It is made from the rear spring of a truck, of high-grade steel with great tensile strength. Similar knives can be bought worldwide. If possible, wear gloves when you are using the knife, to avoid injuries and abrasions. Keep it safely in a leather sheath when you are not using it, in order to avoid injuring yourself, or damaging the knife.

Pocketknife
A strong pocketknife is second only in importance to your teeth. It can be used for projects for which your large knife is too big (see opposite). Keep it secured to your body with strong cord around your neck or waist at all times. Always keep it sharp.

Rust will weaken serrated blade, so clean saw well after cutting living wood

Wire Saw
A wire saw consists of twisted strands of wire, with loops for handles. It can easily be packed inside a survival kit (see page 28). It is a very useful alternative to a heavy ax for cutting branches, but it is delicate and must be used with care.

SHARPENING A KNIFE

Lubricate sharpening stone before using it

Take care with the angle of the blade, visualizing the burr as you sharpen

1 Moisten the sharpening stone with water. Stroke the knife on the stone, away from the edge of the blade.

2 After sharpening the knife on one side, feel the other side for the burr of metal turned up by the abrasion.

3 Smooth the other side of the blade, realigning the burr to the center. More water may be needed.

4 Strop the knife (sweep it up and down) on a leather belt. This will help smooth off and strengthen the edge.

USING A KNIFE

Chopping
Chop with the main part of the blade, away from your limbs. Cut across the grain of the wood at 45 degrees to prevent the blade from glancing off and injuring you.

Cut away from yourself to prevent accidents

Whittling
Whittling is the carving of small, delicate objects, such as a sharp point on a harpoon for spearing fish (see page 104). For this type of carving, push the blade of the knife away from you with the ball of the thumb. You will probably find that your small pocketknife is better for this kind of carving than your heavy knife.

Carving
Carving or cutting must also be done away from the body, keeping all fingers and limbs out of the way. Cut with the grain of the wood, in shallow bites.

USING A WIRE SAW

String forms handles

1 The metal loops can cut your hands, so attach string or cloth as handles before using the saw.

Keep wire straight and taut

2 Use both hands to pull the saw back and forth through the wood. When cutting, it is best to keep the blade as straight as possible, although it will still work if it is curved around the wood. Maintain a steady movement, but go lightly.

CAUTION
Always keep your tools sharp, and take great care when using them. When pulling a knife from its sheath, hold the sheath by the blunt back of the blade. A sharp knife can cut through a sheath and slice the tendons of the hand. A wire saw could also injure you if you do not handle it with respect.

IMPROVISED TOOLS

1 You can create a natural blade by dropping a lump of flint on a rock. It will break open, leaving a sharp edge. Watch out for flying splinters.

Flint can act as knife or hammer

2 The sharp edge can be used as a crude cutting tool. You can use the reverse end as a hammer. When the edge becomes blunted with use, simply break open another flint.

OTHER MATERIALS

Bamboo Shovel
Bamboo can be cut to a very sharp, strong edge. Make a shovel by cutting a section of bamboo stem.

Glass Knife
A piece of broken glass provides a crude but effective blade. Before you use it, be sure to wrap the end in cloth to make a handle.

ROPES AND KNOTS

CORD, SUCH AS rope or string, is needed for almost all improvisation of equipment, unless you make wooden pegs or use glue for joining pieces of material together *(see page 77)*. If you do not have a manufactured rope or string, you can make cord from natural materials. Using the correct knots for the cord, specific to your purpose, is essential – for your own safety if you are using a rope for crossing a river, and for the success of improvised equipment, to ensure that whatever you have made stays together. If you can remember only one knot, learn the Square Knot *(see opposite)*.

CONSTRUCTION OF ROPES

There are two main methods of rope construction. Hawser-laid rope consists of three strands twisted together, while kernmantle rope has a central core surrounded by a woven mantle. Both kinds can be made from either natural or manmade fibers. The type of rope you choose will depend upon your intended use for it. A braided rope is less likely to kink than a laid, or twisted, one, while a rope made from natural materials may rot when wet. Natural-fiber ropes are more likely to break than ropes made from manmade fibers such as nylon or polyester.

Three separate branches of fiber strands are twisted together

Hawser-laid Rope
Hawser-laid rope is stronger than kernmantle rope, particularly if damaged. It consists of three strands of fibers twisted together. It may be made either of natural materials, such as sisal, hemp, or coconut husk, or of manmade fibers such as nylon. Hawser-laid ropes are often used for mooring and anchoring boats, because of their strength.

Thin nylon filaments are twisted into small, hawser-laid cords

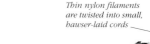

Kernmantle Rope
Climbers tend to use kernmantle rope, which is made of a core of thin, hawser-laid cords braided together (the kern), covered by a strong outer sheath (the mantle). Kernmantle rope is easy to handle, but can be hard to grip when wet or icy.

IMPROVISED CORD

To make cord from nettle stems, you must first soak them until they are pliable. Then pound them with a stone so that the fibers are separated from the pith, and leave the fibers to dry. You can twist the fibers together to form cords, which can be braided together. You can also make cord from willow or linden bark.

1 To braid fibers, first tie the ends of three strands to a branch. Bring the right-hand strand over the middle one.

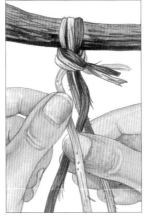

2 Next, bring the left-hand strand over the new middle strand, while keeping tight hold of all three.

3 Bring the new right-hand strand over the new middle strand. This step completes the first section of the braid.

Braid forms strong cord

4 Repeat the steps until the braid is the required length. Tie or bind the ends so that the strands do not unravel.

REEF KNOT

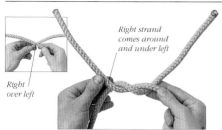
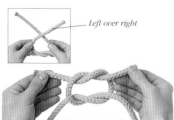
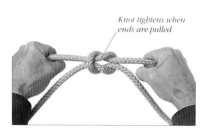

1 To begin the reef knot, first cross the right strand over and under the left one.

Right over left

Right strand comes around and under left

2 Take the left end over and under the right strand, keeping firm hold of both ends, as shown above.

Left over right

3 Pull both ends to tighten the knot. It can be made in reverse order (left over right, right over left), and can be easily undone.

Knot tightens when ends are pulled

BOWLINE

1 Used for making a loop, a bowline will neither tighten nor loosen. Make a small, overhand loop and bring the end up through it from behind.

The end (the "rabbit") comes up through the loop (the "hole")

2 Take the end of the rope around the main rope, then pass it back through the loop. This sequence can be easily remembered by "the rabbit comes out of the hole, goes around the tree, and then back down the hole again".

The "rabbit" goes around the "tree" and back into the "hole")

3 Pull the end and the main rope to tighten the knot. The bowline is useful, but many climbers prefer the figure-of-eight for lifelines *(see below)*.

Pull end of rope and main rope to tighten knot

4 For extra security, take the end over the right-hand side of the loop and through, then into the new small loop from the top. Tighten against the bowline.

Tie knot against bowline for extra security

SINGLE FIGURE-OF-EIGHT KNOT

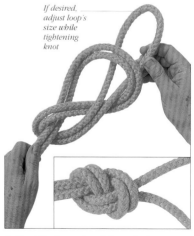

1 Here, the figure-of-eight knot is tied to create a loop in the rope. Form a doubled length of rope, about 3 ft (1 m) long. Bend the looped end back over and behind the doubled rope, forming a new, wide loop.

Fold looped end back over and behind doubled length of rope

2 Continue the figure-of-eight knot by bringing the looped end to the front of the knot. Pass the looped end over the front of the knot, then continue by passing it under the back of the wide loop.

Pass looped end under back of wide loop

3 Feed the looped end through the wide loop. Pull firmly to tighten the knot. The figure-of-eight knot is often used in climbing *(see page 149)*. It will not work loose, yet may be easily undone.

If desired, adjust loop's size while tightening knot

USING ROPES

A LENGTH OF ROPE may be used for a great many things, but it must be treated with care. Your climbing rope may be strong enough to tow a broken-down vehicle, but it will lose its ability to stretch, and get dirty and damaged in the process. It will therefore be less likely to save your life in the future when used for its intended purpose. Use your rope uniformly at both ends so as not to wear it out unevenly. Never apply a load to a rope that has a kink in it, since this will severely damage the rope. Keep your rope clean by washing it in fresh water, and coil it neatly when it is not in use.

CARING FOR ROPES

Damp conditions, strong sunlight, and gnawing insects may damage natural-fiber ropes. Manmade fibers may melt in high heat, or snap if snagged over an edge under tension, and are hard to grip when wet. Dirt particles in the fibers of a rope will cause damage, so keep your rope clean and dry. Rinse wet, dirty ropes in clean, fresh water, using a mild soap, rather than harsh detergent. Hang the ropes up to dry, shaded from the hot sun and fire.

Core damage
Even though it has no sheath damage, this rope is unsafe and should not be used.

Sheath damage
Cut out the damaged sections, using the remainder for lashings, slings, or other, non-vital purposes.

COILING A ROPE

1 As you begin to coil the rope, feel which way it wants to go and shake out any twists or kinks.

Lay each coil to about a 20-in (50-cm) diameter

2 Use your foot to hold the rope down while you coil it. On a dusty or dirty surface, you should form the coil in your hand.

Make sure the coils lie neatly, one beneath the next

Turn back end of first coil to form a loop 12–14 in (30–35 cm) long

3 Continue coiling until only the length of one coil remains. To secure the rope, make a loop by turning back the end of the first coil.

Gently pull loop under lashing to secure it

7 Pull the end of the rope that forms the loop. This will pull the the loop under the the lashing and secure it.

Lash end around coil to finish it off

4 Wrap the remaining long end around the coil. Go over the loop, but leave its end free.

Leave loop free of lashing

5 Finish off after lashing 4 in (10 cm), leaving 1 in (2.5 cm) of loop showing.

6 Pass the remaining end of the rope through the loop and pull it tight.

JOINING ROPES

1 If you need to join ropes together they must be properly tied to prevent them from slipping apart. Begin by making a loop in the end of each rope.

Keep firm hold of first loop

2 Thrust the two loops together, one inside the other. This sheetbend will join ropes of similar or different weight or material.

One loop goes inside the other

Leave long ends to prevent knot from becoming undone

3 Take the loose end of the outer loop and run it over itself, then through the inner loop. Do not let go of the first rope.

4 Pull the ends tight, holding the inner loop together. If possible, leave long ends to avoid slippage.

SHEAR LASHING

1 In lashing, cord is wound tightly around objects such as spars to join them together. To begin lashing, firmly tie the cord to the first spar.

2 After making several anchoring turns around the first spar, take the lashing firmly around the second one.

3 Wrap the cord tightly around the spars to about 1 in (2.5 cm) in depth, taking care not to overlap the strands of lashing, while keeping each new loop tight against the binding.

Binding is tight and neat

Binding is strong, secure, and flexible

Cord is tied to first spar to begin lashing

4 Bring the cord between the two spars and wind it tightly around the lashing several times to make it secure.

5 Finish off the lashing with a half-hitch (pass the end of the cord under a loop made around the spar). Pull the end tight to secure it.

6 When the lashing has been secured, pull the spars apart to the desired angle and use them to form various structures, such as an A-frame shelter *(see page 52).*

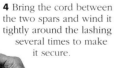

Pass end of cord under itself to secure lashing

CHAPTER THREE

LIVING IN THE WILD

ONCE YOU HAVE chosen an appropriate site, you will have to erect a shelter. This may be a manufactured tent, or a makeshift structure made from branches. In polar regions you may have to build a snow shelter such as an igloo, while in the jungle, constructing a bed above ground will be your priority. After the shelter is completed, you will need to build a fire for warmth or cooking. This will mean collecting dry wood and tinder, and perhaps even making your own method of creating a spark. Once your camp is established, you can dig a latrine, put up safety lanterns, and run a guide rope around the camp so that you do not get lost if you have to get up in the dark. When you decide to leave, you must make sure that you clear away every sign of your presence – unless you need to leave messages for possible rescuers.

Unlike city life, activities in the wild are determined by sunrise and sunset. Getting up before dawn offers opportunities to catch nature unaware - before she catches you. Adopt a routine that fits in with your environment, resting in the midday sun and making sure that you return to camp well before dark. Without the limitations imposed by deadlines, take the opportunity to slow down.

TEMPORARY HOME
Even though you can sleep under the stars in many areas, it is much more comfortable to live in a tent or shelter. You can carry a manufactured tent around with you, or you can build a shelter from the natural materials you find around you.

CHOOSING A CAMPSITE

MANY FACTORS AFFECT how you choose a campsite; safety is, of course, paramount. You may not be able to identify all the potential hazards or disadvantages of a particular spot, but in order to give yourself the best chance, you should allow plenty of time before dusk to look for a campsite. Time spent in reconnaissance is never wasted. Plan your schedule by thinking backward from the time of dusk. Your tent or shelter must be up and the cooking well underway by the time it gets dark, and you must allow an hour or more before that for settling in, and at least another hour for reconnaissance. Therefore, if it gets dark at 6 p.m., then by 3 p.m. you must be thinking about your campsite, and by 4 p.m. you should have stopped traveling and be actively looking for a suitable site.

Prevailing Wind
You should try to identify the direction from which the prevailing wind blows, and erect your tent so that the entrance faces away from it. You should dig your latrine downwind of your camp. Position your fire so that the smoke from it will not constantly blow into your tent.

TIPS FOR CAMP LIVING

■ In wet weather, dig a channel around the base of your tent, running away downhill, to prevent flooding. In high winds, keep tent guy ropes in place with large stones.
■ Keep everything packed until you need it. You will know where things are, be able to move quickly in an emergency, and stand less chance of losing irreplaceable equipment.
■ Never keep food inside a tent. Suspend your pack about 10 ft (3 m) above the ground, and about 3 ft (1 m) away from tree trunks, so that animals such as bears and monkeys cannot reach it.
■ Unpack your gear, do your repairs, and let your clothes and sleeping bag air in the sun before repacking.

Drying Boots
Leave your boots to dry on sticks stuck into the ground to prevent animals from crawling inside them.

Trees
Although you may want to camp near trees so that you have plenty of firewood, or wood for building a shelter, beware of dead trees that might fall on your tent, and the presence of dangerous animals.

River Bend
Avoid the inside bend of a river, since the land is often lower there than on the outside bend, and is vulnerable to flooding. Gravel bars build up on inside bends, where the water flows slowly, and these also contribute to flooding.

Avalanche Danger
If you are camping near mountains, do not pitch your tent in the path of a possible avalanche or rockfall. In addition, spring meltwater may rush down a mountain, causing a flood.

Collecting Water
Always collect water from upstream of your campsite. Collect drinking water upstream of places where you know animals drink.

OTHER SITES

When choosing a site, avoid cold air pockets and wet ground. Imagine how floodwater and cold air will flow, and choose a site above these flow lines. If you are bothered by biting insects, avoid wet ground and seek high, windswept areas.

Dishes
Do not wash cooking pots directly in your water source. Instead, scrape the food residue away with sand or a cloth. You can then rinse off the sand in the river, as long as there are no food remnants to pollute the water and attract animals. Do not use detergent, since this can poison fish.

Tent
Site the tent away from the sound of the river, which can mask the noise of animals. Make sure the entrance faces away from the wind, as well as the latrine.

Latrine
Locate the latrine downstream and downwind of the tent. Ensure that it is far enough away from the river to avoid contamination of the water.

Fire
Smoke from the fire should help to keep insects away from the tent, but the flames should not close be enough to set it on fire.

An Ideal Campsite
In the shelter of trees but away from any dead trees that might fall on the tent, the ideal campsite is close to water but well away from the danger of flooding, and from evidence of animal use. On the side of a valley, but not at the bottom, the site is level, well drained, and protected from the prevailing winds of the area.

Clothes
Wash your clothes downstream of your tent and the place where you collect drinking water. First wet them in the water, then use soap on land. Rinse them in a bucket, and empty the bucket well away from the river.

CHOOSING A TENT

TENTS KEEP RAIN and wind out, while keeping warmth in. The outer flysheet should be strong, impermeable, and taut, able to deflect even driving rain and high winds. The inner tent – which may be attached to the flysheet – is loose, made of permeable material to minimize condensation but retain heat, with air vents. The inner and outer parts of the tent must not touch each other – if they do, heat may be lost and condensation may form on the underside of the flysheet and seep through the inner tent. An impermeable groundsheet is sewn into the bottom of the inner tent to keep water out.

FEATURES OF A TENT

There are many different styles of tent, but most are constructed along the same lines as a basic sloping-ridge tent. The tent is held up by poles, and is pegged down through eyelets along its bottom edges. It is held steady by adjustable guylines attached to pegs in the ground. The tent may have a flysheet over the top.

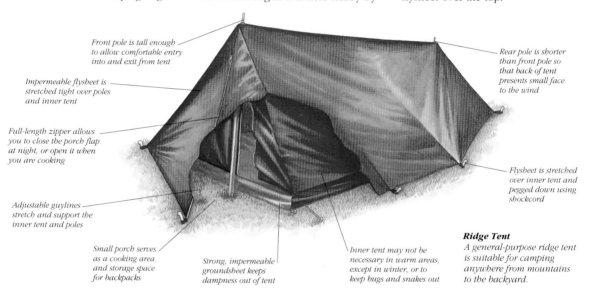

Front pole is tall enough to allow comfortable entry into and exit from tent

Rear pole is shorter than front pole so that back of tent presents small face to the wind

Impermeable flysheet is stretched tight over poles and inner tent

Full-length zipper allows you to close the porch flap at night, or open it when you are cooking

Flysheet is stretched over inner tent and pegged down using shockcord

Adjustable guylines stretch and support the inner tent and poles

Small porch serves as a cooking area and storage space for backpacks

Strong, impermeable groundsheet keeps dampness out of tent

Inner tent may not be necessary in warm areas, except in winter, or to keep bugs and snakes out

Ridge Tent
A general-purpose ridge tent is suitable for camping anywhere from mountains to the backyard.

SELECTING THE RIGHT TENT

There are many different styles of tent, but they are all variations on a theme. Your precise purpose, as well as the climate and terrain of your destination, will determine the type of tent you buy. You should also take into consideration the tent's weight and size – you will have to carry it if you are not using a vehicle. The privacy of a one-person tent may seem appealing. However, in cold climates the warmth of two bodies increases each person's comfort.

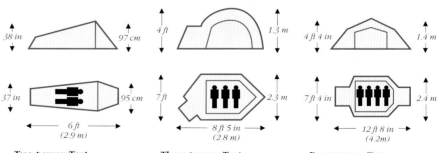

38 in / 97 cm

37 in / 95 cm

6 ft (2.9 m)

4 ft / 1.3 m

7 ft / 2.3 m

8 ft 5 in (2.8 m)

4 ft 4 in / 1.4 m

7 ft 4 in / 2.4 m

12 ft 8 in (4.2m)

Two-person Tent
A two-person, wedge-shaped ridge tent is lightweight, but has space for storage and cooking under the flysheet, and just enough room for two people to sleep in it side by side.

Three-person Tent
There is quite a lot of room inside this dome tent, both for storage of gear and for sitting up comfortably. Three flexible poles give the structure great strength against high winds.

Four-person Tent
Four people can fit into this tent, although they will make it very cozy. In a shared tent, you must ensure that ventilation is good, and that gear is kept neatly packed to avoid conflict.

TENTS FOR ALL TERRAINS

Certain styles of tent are more suitable for a particular terrain than others. A basic, traditional ridge tent can be used almost anywhere, but some modern styles, such as geodesic dome tents, can better withstand harsh terrain and extreme climate – for example, the high winds and heavy snow of mountainous areas. Tents with external poles are easier to pitch in high winds than those with internal poles. Two-hooped tents are unstable in extreme weather.

Dome Tent
This is ideal for extreme conditions, like those found in mountains or polar regions, since it can be stabilized by being buried in snow. It must be dug out, however, before the snowfall gets too heavy. Being dug into a snowbank is an ideal way to shelter from the wind.

Tunnel Tent
A tunnel tent is a cross between a dome tent and a ridge tent. One-person versions of this type of tent are ideal for backpackers, since they are lightweight and easy to erect. They can be used on grass or in rocky river valleys, and can deflect high winds.

Three-hooped Tunnel Tent
Tunnel tents can have a frame of up to three hoops, with small hoops at the ends and a large one in the center. Three-hooped tunnels can sleep two or three people. They are quite stable, and their shape allows rain to run off. They often have two entrances.

Horizontal-ridge Tent
A traditional horizontal-ridge tent can be set up almost anywhere. It has a central, horizontal roof pole, and two ends of the same height. This style of tent can come in virtually any size, from a one-person tent to one that will accommodate several people.

Geodesic Dome Tent
Geodesic dome tents are strong, light to carry, easy to erect, and equally simple to take down again. In high winds they must be firmly tied down, but the arrangement of their curved, interlocking poles makes them sturdy. Geodesic dome tents are supported by flexible poles that cross at different intervals to hold the tent material taut instead of guylines. Their shape provides quite a lot of valuable headroom.

BIVY SACK

A bivy sack can be either a simple, waterproof cover for a sleeping bag, or it can have short poles at its entrance that form a porch, to make the bag a small tent. It should be made of breathable material to minimize condensation, and may be used even in heavy rain out in the open – although this is very noisy. A bivy sack can also be used on its own as a waterproof survival bag.

Sleeping Bag Cover
A bivy sack makes a good waterproof cover for a sleeping bag, or it can be used on its own instead of a tent.

ERECTING A TENT

CHOOSING A CAMPSITE entails selecting the right spot for your tent in relation to everything else in your camp, and with regard to safety and shelter. You must decide which way the entrance will face and how the guylines will be secured, and consider any potential hazards *(see page 40)*. You must then clear and level the site, removing or flattening all uncomfortable bumps. Get your tent up before you do anything else. As with all camp craft, try to establish a routine, doing everything in the same order each time, so that it becomes a habit. This will enable you to erect your tent in darkness, or in a blizzard or heavy rainstorm. Make sure you know exactly where to find each piece of the tent when you come to put it up. You should pack it away systematically *(see page 46)*.

1 Get used to putting up your tent as if there were a howling blizzard. First lay the inner tent on the ground and immediately peg down the corners.

Peg corner eyelet straight and taut

2 Assemble the tent poles. Take care to screw the right pieces together, or you may not be able to take them apart again. Hook the back tent eyelet over the short pole.

3 Hold the short pole upright and peg its guyline into the ground, adjusting it so that the pole will stand up by itself. Make sure that the back wall of the tent will face into the wind.

4 Insert the other pole into the front roof eyelet. Stand the pole upright and tighten its guyline. Work quickly – if it is windy, the tent will be unstable, and in rainy weather, it will get wet.

5 Slip the flysheet over the short tent pole down at the small end of the tent, then peg it down securely.

6 Pull the flysheet over the top of the tent, slipping the eyelet over the main pole at the tall end of the tent. Peg down the flysheet at the tall end. You may have to move the inner tent's guyline toward the pole to make the flysheet fit.

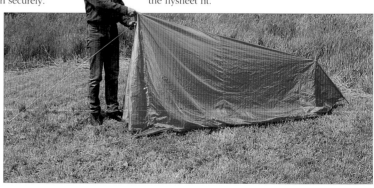

CAUTION

Do not use tent tapes for pulling out pegs that you have pushed into the wrong place. If you do, the tapes will break. To remove pegs from hard ground, use another tent peg, or a special tent-peg hook.

Tighten guylines going into pegs

7 Zip up the flysheet door flap over the inner tent's front guyline. The space between the inner tent and flysheet provides a porch that can be used as a storage area for gear.

8 Peg the guylines around the inner tent, taking care to tension and balance both sides equally.

9 Peg the sides of the flysheet so that it is stretched quite tightly over the inner tent. Make sure that the flysheet does not touch the inner tent *(see below)*.

10 Unzip the front flaps and, using the guys, adjust the balance of the whole tent until it is tight and secure. Take care not to pull the tent over by overtightening the guylines.

11 The short end of the tent (the back) should ideally face into the wind. The tent must be stretched tightly, streamlined against the wind and the rain. Backpacks may be stored in the front porch, but never leave unwrapped food in the tent *(see page 40)*.

USING TENTS

■ In winter, you must use both the inner tent and the flysheet, but at other times of the year, or in warm climates, the inner tent is unnecessary. Using just the flysheet gives much more space inside the tent.

■ Ventilation is essential. Never cook inside a tent, although you can cook inside the porch with the door flap half unzipped.

■ Tent pegs can be damaged by very hard or rocky ground, so you may have to tie the guylines around large rocks.

■ There should be a layer of air between the inner tent and the flysheet that serves as insulation. Take care to pitch the flysheet taut enough to avoid touching the inner tent. If it does, condensation may form on the inside of the inner tent and run down the walls and into your sleeping bag and other equipment.

DISMANTLING A TENT

WHEN DISMANTLING A tent, you should pack every component neatly, so that it can be found quickly when needed again. If it is raining, once the flysheet is down, stow all other parts of the tent as rapidly as possible. The inner tent in particular must be packed quickly. In addition, you are vulnerable without shelter, and need to move on to your next campsite as soon as possible, so that you can re-erect your tent before it gets dark. If the weather is fine, before packing the tent, lay all the parts out in the open air to allow the wind and sunshine to dry moisture from both the flysheet and the inner tent. This will prevent them from becoming moldy when packed away.

1 First remove all pegs securing the flysheet and inner tent. In high winds, keep hold of some part of the structure to prevent it from blowing away. Take special care with tent pegs – never use guylines or tapes to pull them from the ground, and always keep count of them.

Pull pegs from ground without bending them

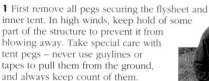

2 Unzip the door of the flysheet and remove the front pole.

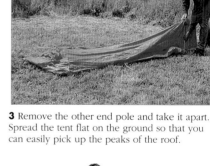

3 Remove the other end pole and take it apart. Spread the tent flat on the ground so that you can easily pick up the peaks of the roof.

4 The inner tent and the flysheet must be rolled and packed separately so that you can easily tell them apart when you next want to erect the tent. To stow the flysheet, first lift it from the inner tent, holding it by the eyelets in its roof peaks. Take care not to lift the inner tent, too.

5 Still holding the flysheet by the eyelets, lift it so that it falls into its natural shape. Then carefully fold it in half, to form a long "V" shape. Make sure that there is no moisture on it before folding it.

6 Lay the flysheet on a dry patch of ground and begin rolling it as tightly as possible. Fold in the flysheet's sides as you roll it, making sure that the guylines are not tangled.

7 Shake out the inner tent so that the guylines hang down freely, then lay the inner tent on the ground and roll it as tightly as possible. Fold in the sides of the tent as you go.

8 Tuck the guylines carefully into the roll before it is finished, ensuring that they are not knotted or tangled. If they are, they must be untangled first.

9 Store the pegs in a tough bag so that they will not damage the tent. Keep the peg bag in the main tent bag. Mud or moisture left on the pegs may cause corrosion or damage.

10 Wipe the poles clean and put them in a strong bag, then into the tent bag. If you keep the poles clean, they will fit together easily when you use them.

11 Put both the flysheet and the inner tent into the tent bag. It is a good idea to place each item in a separate plastic bag for protection.

12 Before drawing the strings tight on the tent bag, check that everything is packed, and that you have not omitted any tent pegs or poles. In long grass, it is easy to mislay these items.

CAUTION

Make sure that you do not lose any pegs, guylines, or poles when you dismantle your tent. You should also take care not to damage any part of the tent – if you do, it will have to be repaired before you can use it again.

CARE AND REPAIR OF A TENT

- Your tent should be totally dry when it is stowed – apart from being lighter to carry, the fabric will be less likely to rot than if it is packed when wet.
- Avoid leaving your tent up in really hot sunshine, or packing it up when it is hot. The rubberized waterproofing may melt in excessive heat and stick other tent materials together.
- Check all parts of the tent regularly. Repair them immediately, if necessary.
- Before storing a tent, wash it in fresh water, then rinse it in clean water. Hang it up to dry before packing it.

Repair Patches
You can buy special vinyl patches with which you can make temporary repairs to a tent.

BUILDING A SHELTER

GETTING OUT OF the wind, rain, and sun, and being able to rest and sleep, are vital for survival. The better you build your shelter, the more comfortable you will be – and the more rest you will be able to get. Being rested is essential for your physical health, as well as for your psychological well-being, which determines how sensibly and logically you think and how strongly you are resolved to survive. A lean-to shelter is probably the easiest and quickest type of shelter to build and is suitable for most terrain. It should be erected on a sheltered, safe, level site *(see page 40)*, and built so that the roof faces into the wind. The construction of your shelter will depend entirely upon the materials at your disposal. If you have a tarpaulin or plastic sheeting, you should use that to make the roof of your shelter, but otherwise you will have to improvise with whatever items you find.

Ridge pole should be taller than you can reach

1 To make a lean-to shelter, first cut a long branch as a ridge pole. Measure the correct length of the ridge pole by reaching up as high as possible and cutting it another 2 ft (60 cm) or so above that. Try to get as straight a branch as possible for the ridge pole, and trim off all projecting twigs. Do not use a dead branch, which may snap and break in a high wind.

2 Cut two Y-shaped supports to about chest height, each with an extra 1 ft (30 cm) that will be hammered into the ground. Sharpen the bottom ends.

Sharpen post ends so that they can be hammered into the ground

3 Hammer both the supports into the ground with a heavy rock until they are secure and will not fall over. The distance between them should be about 2 ft (60 cm) less than the length of the ridge pole.

4 Lay the ridge pole between the two forks of the support posts, allowing equal overlap at the ends. The ridge pole must be fairly light, but sturdy enough to take the weight of the finished roof and withstand heavy rain and strong winds without collapsing.

5 Cut several fairly strong branches long enough to lean against the ridge pole at an angle of about 45 degrees to the ground. This will allow maximum rainwater runoff from the roof. Space them 8 in (20 cm) apart. They should overhang the ridge pole by about 4 in (10 cm).

6 Cut plenty of straight, fairly sturdy saplings. Weave the saplings over and under alternate sloping roof branches, until all the branches are joined fairly firmly together in a lattice. Weave a row of saplings over and under the ridge pole, as well, to hold it in place.

Weave the top saplings over and under the ridge pole to hold it in place, thus giving the structure tensile strength

7 Weave whole branches, complete with foliage to keep out the wind and rain, into the roof lattice. Using whole branches will make the roof strong and keep the foliage alive longer, especially if it is deciduous.

8 Continue weaving the foliage into the lattice until you are content with the density of your roof. Some types of foliage die faster than others, and may have to be replaced after a few days. It is best to weave new branches over the old ones to build up the layers of the roof. Branches from small-leaved trees are preferable, since large leaves tear, die quickly, and are hard to weave into a flat mat.

9 The finished shelter may require further improvement – for example, you may want to place large rocks along the back to hold down the bottom of the roof in high winds, or to add side walls. Light your camp fire in front of the shelter, but keep the flames away from the thatch. Rethatch as the roof foliage withers.

USING MANMADE MATERIALS

Manmade materials should be used if available, and augmented by natural ones where necessary. Plastic bags and sheets of polyethylene are common forms of rural litter. Wooden boxes, plywood, cardboard, and galvanized metal sheets can also be used.

Other Materials
Shelters can be made from all kinds of discarded manmade materials.

SNOW SHELTERS

PROVIDED TEMPERATURES REMAIN below 32°F (0°C), constructing snow shelters is relatively easy. Sheltering from the wind is the first priority, since the wind can drastically decrease the air temperature *(see page 141)*. Temperatures below 14°F (–10°C) become increasingly unpleasant, so that it becomes necessary to construct shelters in which heat can be retained extremely well. These can range from a simple, hollowed-out heap of snow to an igloo, which can take a few hours to construct. In a long-term shelter, such as an igloo, heavy, cold air can be diverted away from the occupants by digging a cold sink to channel the air down and away from the shelter. It is important to allow for adequate ventilation in all snow shelters in order to prevent suffocation.

BUILDING AN IGLOO

1 Cut blocks from dry, hard snow, using a snow saw or large knife. Each block should be about 3 ft (1 m) long, 15 in (40 cm) high, and 8 in (20 cm) deep.

2 Form a circle with blocks around the hole created where you cut the blocks. Cut the circle in a spiral from the top of the last block to the ground ahead of the first block. This will make it easy to construct a dome.

3 Build up the walls, overlapping the blocks and shaping them so that they lean inward. Cut a hole under the wall for the cold sink and entrance. Put several blocks along one wall as a sleeping platform.

4 The last block must initially be larger than the hole. Place the block on top of the igloo, then, from inside, shape and wiggle it to slot exactly into the hole.

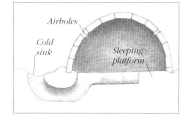

Airholes

Cold sink

Sleeping platform

5 Hot air from your body and stove rises, and is trapped inside the dome. Cold air falls into the sink and flows away to the outside. It is essential to cut ventilation holes in the walls with an ice ax.

Finished Igloo
With warmth inside the igloo, the surface of the walls will melt and freeze over, to form a smooth, airtight ice surface.

Roof over entrance tunnel prevents snow from blowing into igloo

BUILDING A QUINZE

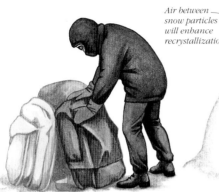

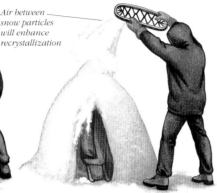

Air between snow particles will enhance recrystallization

Smooth dome to help snow harden

1 Place backpacks and other equipment in a tight cone. The equipment will form the inside core of the shelter, and will reduce the amount of snow needed to build the quinze (pronounced "kwinzee").

2 Using a snowshoe or a shovel, pile snow over the backpacks, compacting it. Wait at least 30 minutes for the snow to freeze before adding more snow to build up the thickness of the dome.

3 When the snow in the pile is about 3 ft (1 m) thick, smooth the dome and leave it for about an hour to harden. This period is important, since it allows the snow to recrystallize, bonding the particles together.

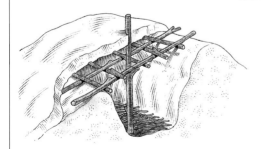

4 Gather several sticks about 2 ft (60 cm) long. Push them into the snow all over the dome as depth guides, pointing to the center of the quinze.

5 Dig down beside the quinze and burrow under the wall until you can carefully remove the backpacks. Then excavate inside with a cooking pot until the ends of the sticks appear.

OTHER SNOW SHELTERS

Trench
Dig a trench and make a roof by weaving together sturdy branches. Take care to leave a branch poking through any snow that falls on the roof, so that you get adequate ventilation inside the trench.

Snow cave
Hollow out a shelter in a snow bank. Block up the entrance and poke a ventilation hole in the wall.

Natural hollow
A snug, almost ready-made shelter can be found under an overhanging conifer. Take care not to dislodge snow from the branches.

TROPICAL SHELTERS

THE REGION BETWEEN the Tropic of Cancer and the Tropic of Capricorn, about 23 degrees north and south of the equator, is known as the tropics. Within this region are rainforests, swamps, and savannah (grasslands), and all are characterized by lush vegetation, torrential rain, and abundant animal life. Shelter from the rain, wind, and sun is very important in every kind of tropical area. In the mountain rainforests, it can get quite cold at night. In jungles and swamps, you must sleep off the ground – preferably high enough to allow small animals to pass beneath you and to ensure that torrential rain does not constantly splash you as it hits the ground. A waterproof roof and mosquito net are vital. Sleeping above the ground is not as important in tropical grasslands as in jungle areas.

A-FRAME SHELTER

1 An A-frame shelter is the easiest type of shelter to construct. Cut seven long branches and lash two of them to a tree.

2 Make a second A-frame and set it at a distance of about 2 ft (60 cm) longer than your height from the first one.

3 Place a lightweight branch across the two top V's of the A-frames. This will act as a ridge pole to support the roof.

4 Tie the sides of a groundsheet together to make a tube. Insert two long poles and pull them apart to make a stretcher. Wedge the stretcher between the A-frames with the poles on the outside.

5 Stretch a waterproof tarpaulin across the ridge pole to make a roof. Pull it tight on either side and tie it to trees. The roof should keep off rain, yet still allow air to circulate around your head.

BAMBOO SHELTER

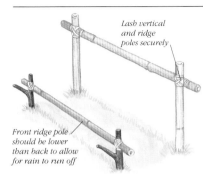

Lash vertical and ridge poles securely

Front ridge pole should be lower than back to allow for rain to run off

1 This shelter can be made wherever bamboo grows. Set four thick, vertical posts in the ground a distance of your height plus one arm's length apart. The front posts should be about 1 ft (30 cm) shorter than the back ones. Place horizontal ridge poles in between the vertical posts as shown.

2 Using a knife, split a bamboo stem lengthwise and lay it between the short vertical posts as a gutter. Block one end with leaves and set a billycan under the other end to catch rain dripping off the roof. Lay split bamboo stems between the ridge poles, with their open sides uppermost and their lower ends supported by the gutter. Place more stems on top, round side uppermost, so that they interlock with the bottom layer as shown.

Bamboo sections interlock to shed rainwater into gutter

Billycan catches water from gutter

JUNGLE SHELTER

1 To make the shelter frame, hammer four solid logs into the ground as corner posts, spaced just over your height apart. Attach four branches between the posts, lashing them into notches on the outsides of the posts, to make a bed frame. Weave smaller branches across the frame to make a bed *(see page 48)*.

Notch upright poles so that frame fits securely

Ridge pole should be longer than your height

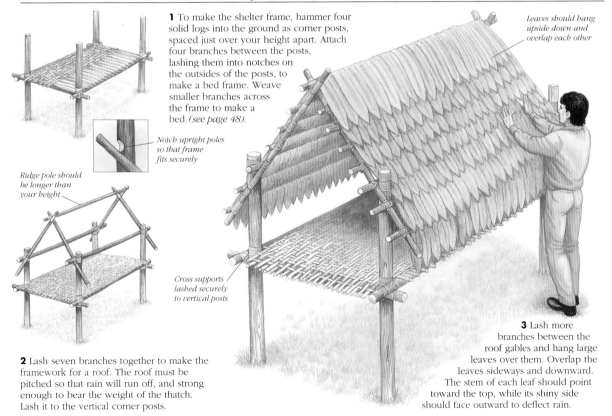

Leaves should hang upside down and overlap each other

Cross supports lashed securely to vertical posts

2 Lash seven branches together to make the framework for a roof. The roof must be pitched so that rain will run off, and strong enough to bear the weight of the thatch. Lash it to the vertical corner posts.

3 Lash more branches between the roof gables and hang large leaves over them. Overlap the leaves sideways and downward. The stem of each leaf should point toward the top, while its shiny side should face outward to deflect rain.

LONG-TERM SHELTERS

IN A SURVIVAL situation, you do not know how long you are likely to be marooned, or how long you will be in one place. Therefore, you should try to make the best shelter possible. If you are forced to spend a winter in the wilderness, for example, you will need a sturdy shelter such as a log cabin.

Before you spend days, or even weeks, building a permanent shelter, you must be certain you have the right location for it. Food, fuel, and fresh, reliable water must be nearby, the ground must be well drained and solid, and the site sheltered from natural hazards *(see page 40)*.

LOG CABIN

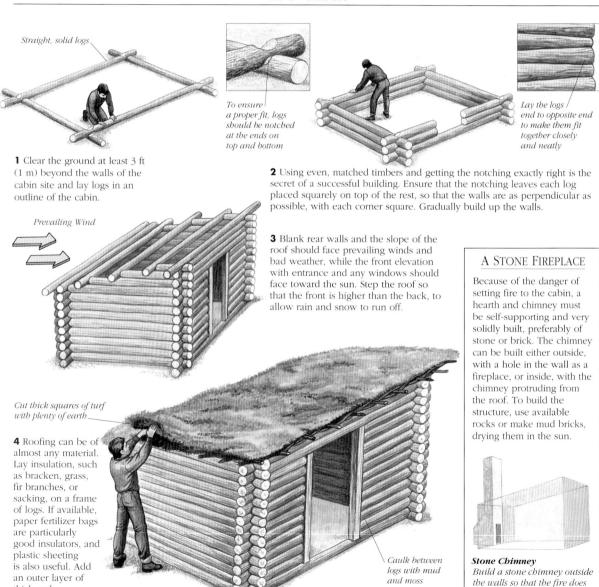

Straight, solid logs

To ensure a proper fit, logs should be notched at the ends on top and bottom

Lay the logs end to opposite end to make them fit together closely and neatly

1 Clear the ground at least 3 ft (1 m) beyond the walls of the cabin site and lay logs in an outline of the cabin.

2 Using even, matched timbers and getting the notching exactly right is the secret of a successful building. Ensure that the notching leaves each log placed squarely on top of the rest, so that the walls are as perpendicular as possible, with each corner square. Gradually build up the walls.

Prevailing Wind

3 Blank rear walls and the slope of the roof should face prevailing winds and bad weather, while the front elevation with entrance and any windows should face toward the sun. Step the roof so that the front is higher than the back, to allow rain and snow to run off.

Cut thick squares of turf with plenty of earth

4 Roofing can be of almost any material. Lay insulation, such as bracken, grass, fir branches, or sacking, on a frame of logs. If available, paper fertilizer bags are particularly good insulators, and plastic sheeting is also useful. Add an outer layer of thick sods.

Caulk between logs with mud and moss

A STONE FIREPLACE

Because of the danger of setting fire to the cabin, a hearth and chimney must be self-supporting and very solidly built, preferably of stone or brick. The chimney can be built either outside, with a hole in the wall as a fireplace, or inside, with the chimney protruding from the roof. To build the structure, use available rocks or make mud bricks, drying them in the sun.

Stone Chimney
Build a stone chimney outside the walls so that the fire does not burn down the cabin.

SOD HOUSE

Sod should be cut in brick shapes

1 Turf blocks (sod) can be used for building as if they were undried bricks, cut and laid without mortar. Begin by cutting a selection of sod from the ground.

2 Lay an outline of the cabin on a clear piece of ground, leaving a hole for a door. The ground below must be flat and solid, and capable of taking the considerable weight of the walls and roof without subsiding. Begin building up the walls.

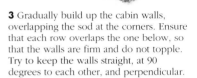

Place each sod over the join of the two below it

3 Gradually build up the cabin walls, overlapping the sod at the corners. Ensure that each row overlaps the one below, so that the walls are firm and do not topple. Try to keep the walls straight, at 90 degrees to each other, and perpendicular.

Add a door frame of wood, the lintel of which must be strong enough to carry the weight of several rows of sod

4 Build the front higher than the back, sloping the roof into the wind to allow rain to run off. Construct a roof framework of branches, if available.

5 Lay a roof of sods with the grass facing upward. Repair any cracks in the walls with mud. After weathering, the walls will become hard and smooth.

OTHER LONG-TERM SHELTERS

Caves
When using caves, explore their full extent first. The fire should be built at the back of the cave, so that the smoke will escape and not blow back inside. You can build a rock or log wall on the other side of the fire to deflect the heat back into the cave.

Natural Hollows
Natural shelters can sometimes be found under large rock formations, but you should take great care to ensure that the entire structure is solid and immovable. If digging into the underlying ground, do not disturb the structure's foundations.

RUNNING A SAFE CAMP

HAVING CHOSEN AS safe a campsite as possible, certain basic safety rules must always be observed. There is potential danger in many things, from fires and unventilated stoves to lack of basic hygiene. Never cook inside a tent, since it can easily catch fire and will burn fiercely. Any sort of flame inside a tent also reduces the amount of oxygen and may create poisonous gases such as carbon monoxide. Tents and other kinds of shelter must therefore be well ventilated *(see page 114)*. Without refrigerators and flushing toilets, food poisoning and other illnesses can occur very quickly in camp.

SAFETY AROUND THE CAMP

If you are camping for more than one night, you should make your camp as safe as possible. Accidents often occur at night – for example when individuals stumble from their tents to the latrine and trip and fall into the remains of the fire, or into the river, or get lost in the darkness and are unable to relocate their tent.

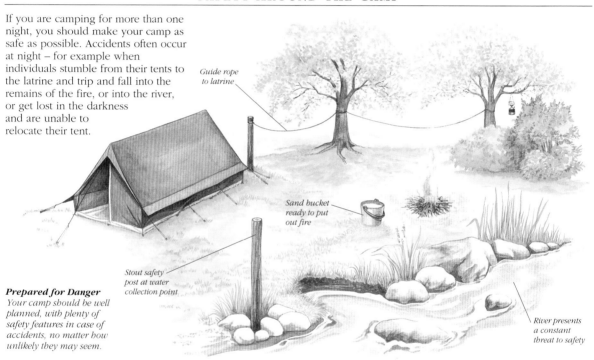

Guide rope to latrine

Sand bucket ready to put out fire

Stout safety post at water collection point

River presents a constant threat to safety

Prepared for Danger
Your camp should be well planned, with plenty of safety features in case of accidents, no matter how unlikely they may seem.

BUILDING A LATRINE

A latrine should be located downwind of your tent. Sprinkle earth into it whenever it is used. Never add chemicals to a latrine, since they will prevent the natural breaking down of fecal material and make it smell much worse than it naturally would. Have a separate urination point, marked by a stake, over to one side. Fill in the latrine when you leave *(see page 64)*.

Camp Toilet
Dig a latrine only in a long-term camp, or if there are a lot of people in your party. Use it for solid waste.

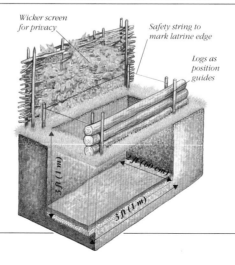

Wicker screen for privacy

Safety string to mark latrine edge

Logs as position guides

3 ft (1 m)

2 ft (60 cm)

3 ft (1 m)

TOILET CAN

Where it is impractical or illegal to bury human waste, make a portable toilet by lining a lidded coffee can with a plastic bag. Put bleach in the bag to reduce odor. Use the can only for solid waste.

PORTABLE TOILET

WASHING CLOTHES

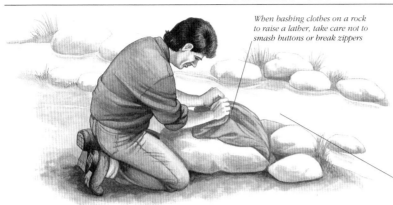

When bashing clothes on a rock to raise a lather, take care not to smash buttons or break zippers

Keeping clothes clean maintains their ability to insulate, as well as preserving hygiene. In the tropics, clothes must be washed every day, with a clean, dry set kept for wearing at night. In cold climates, only socks and underclothing need to be washed regularly. Do not wash or rinse clothes directly in your water source. Clothes should be repaired as soon as they get torn *(see page 31)*, so that the damage does not get worse and make the clothes unwearable.

Do not let any detergent suds get into your water supply

PERSONAL HYGIENE

Keep your washing and personal gear in a waterproof holdall so that you do not lose items. Using a bag will also keep the items clean. While you are using the wash kit, have it hanging on a tree for easy access to the items inside. A large towel can be used for many purposes. It can also be cut up and reused in various ways *(see page 27)*.

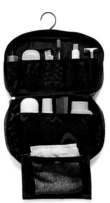 

WASH KIT   TOWEL

IMPROVISED CLEANERS

Horse Chestnut Leaf
Horse chestnut leaves crushed in warm water can be used as soap. They also have a mild antiseptic effect.

Strawberry
Strawberries can remove stains from teeth if rubbed on them. Wood ash can also be used as toothpaste, or as soap.

PROTECTING THE ENVIRONMENT

■ Keep soap suds, food debris, and other pollutants out of your water supply, washing and rinsing clothes and dishes in a bucket, and emptying the wash water well away from the river. Bear in mind that there may be other campsites downstream from you.
■ Avoid keeping a tent pitched in the same place for too long, so that the grass can have a chance to grow back.
■ Do not mutilate trees and plants unless you need to build a shelter.
■ Use existing fire pits when possible, rather than making new ones, and be careful not to start a forest or brush fire.
■ Burn all garbage and take the residue with you when you leave.
■ Always fill in the latrine and fire pit, and remove all traces of your camp when you leave *(see page 64)*.

KEEPING FOOD SAFE

1 While you are cooking a meal, you may want to keep some items of prepared food cool and fresh, away from insects and animals. Make a temporary holder from a roll of cloth, tying the ends to close it. Put a plate inside to act as a base.

Plate of food kept safe from insects

2 Hang the cloth roll from a branch. Keep food inside the holder only for short periods. Food in cans can be kept cool by being placed in river shallows.

CAMPFIRES

Having a campfire will determine whether or not you survive, providing warmth and a way of cooking food, as well as an enormous boost to morale. Fire keeps wild animals and insects away, provides heat that conserves precious body calories, turns inedible food into a cheering meal, and dries clothing and boots. You will need three ingredients for a fire – tinder, kindling, and main fuel. A fire also needs oxygen in which to burn. The best source of dry fuel is standing deadwood of all sizes. If you have to use fallen wood, leave any in contact with the ground, and take branches overlaying it.

TYPES OF TINDER

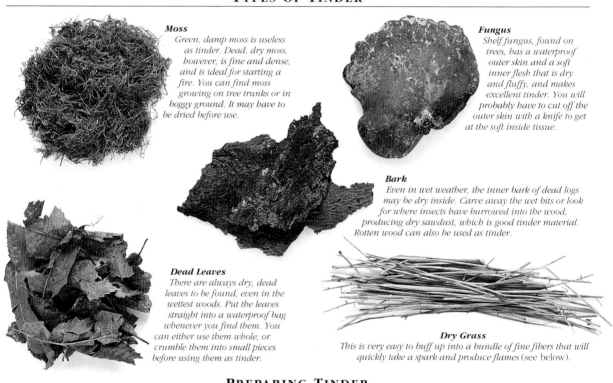

Moss
Green, damp moss is useless as tinder. Dead, dry moss, however, is fine and dense, and is ideal for starting a fire. You can find moss growing on tree trunks or in boggy ground. It may have to be dried before use.

Fungus
Shelf fungus, found on trees, has a waterproof outer skin and a soft inner flesh that is dry and fluffy, and makes excellent tinder. You will probably have to cut off the outer skin with a knife to get at the soft inside tissue.

Bark
Even in wet weather, the inner bark of dead logs may be dry inside. Carve away the wet bits or look for where insects have burrowed into the wood, producing dry sawdust, which is good tinder material. Rotten wood can also be used as tinder.

Dead Leaves
There are always dry, dead leaves to be found, even in the wettest woods. Put the leaves straight into a waterproof bag whenever you find them. You can either use them whole, or crumble them into small pieces before using them as tinder.

Dry Grass
This is very easy to buff up into a bundle of fine fibers that will quickly take a spark and produce flames (see below).

PREPARING TINDER

Powdering
You can turn dry sticks and pieces of bark into powdery tinder by trimming them into tiny pieces with a knife. Make the pieces as fine as possible, and keep them in a bag.

Nicking
Make a small depression in the surface of the tinder – for example in a piece of shelf fungus. A glowing ember dropped in the niche will have a large surface area to heat.

Buffing
To take the smallest spark, tinder must be as fine as cotton wool. Rub and twist the material in your fingers, or against a rock, in order to break up the fibers.

FUELS

Fuels for Warmth
Soft woods, such as fir, apple, hazel, and holly, burn quickly and brightly, and give off good heat. However, they also produce sparks. The woods that give off the most sparks when heated are cedar and hemlock. Because they burn so quickly, soft woods are good for getting a fire going, and can be useful for fast cooking, for instance boiling water. However, they are soon used up, and leave a lot of ash, rather than embers that can be used for baking and other forms of slow cooking.

HOLLY

FIR

Fuels for Cooking
Dense, hard woods, such as oak, ash, beech, birch, maple, hickory, and sycamore, burn slowly and evenly, giving off great heat and producing coals that can be used for slow cooking (see page 117). The taste of the food you cook over a fire can be affected by the smell of the smoke. Different woods produce different smells when burning. For example, pine tends to make food taste of resin, while apple and sycamore can add richness to its flavor. Experiment with different kinds of wood.

OAK

BEECH

Emergency Fuels
In a survival situation, you may have to use whatever you can find that will burn. Emergency fuels can include animal dung, dry lichen, moss, heather, and even blocks of peat, all of which have to be dried in the sun before use. On a seashore, you can use dried seaweed. Lumps of coal can sometimes be found and burned, while oil occasionally seeps into pools on the surface of the ground. Sand may contain oil and, if so, can be burned. You can also use animal fat as fuel.

DRIED DUNG

SEAWEED

WOODS TO AVOID USING

Some resinous woods spit quite fiercely in a fire, and should be avoided when possible. These include pine and blackthorn. Other woods, such as alder, chestnut, poplar, and willow, do not burn well, but merely smolder. Bamboo may explode when heated, unless it is split open first.

POPLAR

WILLOW

INGREDIENTS FOR A FIRE

The secret of making a good fire is to build it up gradually, beginning with small pieces of wood, then progressing to larger branches and logs as the fire gets going. Your wood should be graded into tinder, dry kindling, and lots of small sticks, large sticks, and logs. Get each grade of wood burning well before adding larger pieces.

Tinder
You will need a ball of tinder at least the size of a grapefruit, buffed to its finest consistency (see opposite). Tinder is the most important part of a fire, since you cannot start a fire by lighting thick sticks, unless you have a manufactured firelighter that takes the place of the tinder (see page 62).

Kindling
Once the tinder has begun to burn, you can add dry kindling in the form of small sticks and leaves. Make sure that the kindling is bone dry. The sticks should be about the thickness of a pencil.

Small Fuel
When the kindling is burning well, you can add sticks about the thickness of a finger. The sticks take the flames from the initial stages to a fully burning fire.

Main Fuel
Large sticks act as the main fuel. They should be thicker than your finger, but easy to break into manageable pieces. You will use mainly this size fuel for your campfires.

Large Fuel
Thick logs are for keeping an established fire going all night, or in a semi-permanent camp. Make sure that they are completely burned when you put out the fire.

BUILDING A FIRE

THE SECRET OF making a fire is having dry fuel and building up the fire steadily from a small beginning. You must choose and construct your fireplace with care, and build the right type of fire for your purposes, in keeping with local conditions *(see opposite)*. Safety is an essential consideration.

Fires are potentially dangerous – they can get out of control, setting dry vegetation, tents, or clothing alight. They can also use up all the oxygen in an enclosed shelter, asphyxiating the inhabitants. A fire can scar the landscape if not properly put out and cleaned up *(see page 65)*.

SIMPLE TEPEE FIRE

1 Remove a square of turf and put it to one side. Lay a platform of green sticks in the hole.

2 Begin building a tepee shape by balancing four upright sticks against each other, their top ends meeting in a point. The tepee does not need to be very big.

CAUTION

Do not build a fire:
■ where vegetation is dry because of drought
■ under overhanging branches that may catch fire
■ larger than you can control
■ on private land without special permission

3 Build up the tepee gradually, trying to make it as sturdy as possible. Make sure you leave enough space underneath the tepee in which to put your tinder, as well as an opening to one side.

4 Put your tinder inside the finished tepee. Ignite the tinder *(see page 58)*, then add dry leaves and twigs, building up the flames within the tepee. As the heat builds up, the tepee will catch fire, creating a surge of flame. The tepee will eventually collapse in on itself and create a hot bed of embers that can either be fed more fuel, or used for cooking. The wood platform will also eventually burn, creating more hot embers.

Keep kindling close at hand for feeding the fire

FIRES FOR ALL CONDITIONS

Although you can use the basic tepee fire for almost all areas, you may find that you have to adjust it under certain conditions. For example, in a strong wind, you can build your fire in a trench so that it is sheltered and will still burn. In snow, you may have to scrape down to bare ground and lay a platform on which to build your fire.

Trench Fire
In very windy conditions, dig a trench about 1 ft (30 cm) deep. Trench fires are excellent for cooking, and conserve fuel. The flames are prevented from flaring too fiercely in the wind, yet still have enough air for burning.

Rock Wall Fire
A rock wall will shelter a fire from the wind, preventing dangerous swirls of flame and conserving fuel. Select dry, nonporous rocks, and avoid slate, which can explode when heated. Use the largest, most stable rocks you can find. You can fill the gaps with mud or clay to form a functional area for cooking.

Rock wall shelters fire from wind

Star Fire
Rather than having to constantly collect fresh wood, once your fire has a good bed of embers, feed four long logs, each at least 6 in (15 cm) in diameter, into the center of it. As the logs burn, you can push them in farther. Only use this fire in a long-term camp, so that you can be sure that the logs are fully burned when you clean up the fire (see page 64).

LONG-LASTING FIRE

To keep a fire going all night or all day, lay three thick logs close together over a deep bed of hot coals. For added warmth, you can build a wooden wall behind the fire to reflect the heat back to you. Do not sleep so close that you might catch fire.

All-night Fire
A long log fire can burn all night.

CARRYING FIRE

1 You can keep smoldering embers alive for several days so that you can start a fire wherever you are. Attach a handle of string or wire to a can.

Driest moss goes on top

2 Fill the can with dry moss. If you can only find damp moss, you can still use it, as long as you place it at the bottom, with drier moss or grass on top. The damp moss will soon dry out.

3 Place healthy, glowing embers into the nest of moss, then cover them with more moss. You can blow gently on the embers whenever they appear to be going out.

Smoldering embers set moss on fire

LIGHTING A FIRE

NEXT TO FIRST AID, fire lighting is the most vital survival skill, separating us from the rest of the animal kingdom. When wood or other fuel is heated, it gives off gases that ignite to create flames. Fires must start very small – as just a few wisps of bone-dry tinder coaxed into flame – and be built up gradually. Having dry fuel is important, since wet wood will kill all but the very hottest fire. As well as heat and dry fuel, fires also need plenty of oxygen, particularly when being lit. A fire can be put out by being smothered with soil so that the flames cannot get enough oxygen to continue burning.

FIRE-LIGHTING METHODS

Flint and Steel
Make a tinder nest just outside the tepee. Strike the flint with the steel, over the tinder. Blow on the sparks, coaxing them into flame. Once the tinder catches fire, push it into the tepee.

Strike flint with steel saw, aiming sparks onto tinder

TIPS FOR FIRE LIGHTING

■ Ensure that the fire is sheltered from the wind (*see page 60*), but remember that fire needs oxygen to burn.
■ Always keep a supply of dry tinder.
■ Gather together all the materials you need before lighting the fire.
■ Waterproof matches by dripping candle wax onto their heads. Scrape off the wax before striking them.

Matches
Strike a match inside your cupped hands, allowing the flame to burn the stem. Hold the match to the tinder until the tinder is burning. Leave the match in place, and add more tinder, then kindling.

Cup hands around match

Magnifying Glass
Place a nest of tinder inside your tepee, then focus the rays of the sun through the magnifying glass so that the strongest point of light plays on the tinder. As the tinder smolders, blow gently until it glows.

Focus sunlight on to tinder through magnifying glass

SHORTCUTS TO LIGHTING A FIRE

There are many different ways to light a fire, using a great many tools. They range from the traditional flint block and steel saw, to modern paraffin blocks and sticks of wood chips treated with various chemicals. Choose the method you find easiest to use.

Waterproof Matches
Scrape the wax from the heads of the matches before you use them.

Flint and Steel
This steel saw and magnesium alloy "flint" produce larger sparks than natural flint.

Magnifying Glass
The larger the magnifying glass, the better, particularly in the weak sunshine of northern latitudes.

Cotton Wool
Cotton wool soaked in kerosene is available as a light alternative to natural tinder.

Paraffin Blocks
These can be used to ignite large sticks without tinder.

Fire Sticks
These sticks of wood shavings treated with chemicals can be lit with a match to easily start a fire without tinder.

BOW DRILL

1 Cut a stick for the drill from hard wood *(see page 59)*. It should be about 15 in (38 cm) long and 2 in (4 cm) thick. Round the ends, carving one to a point.

2 Choose a piece of soft wood, such as pine or balsa, for a hearth and cut a V-shaped notch in the side. Friction between the drill and hearth will create ash.

3 Dig out a small hole beside the notch for the drill point to fit into. Hot black ash created by the drill spinning in the hole will fall through the notch onto the tinder.

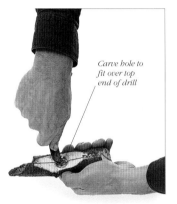

Carve hole to fit over top end of drill

4 Use a piece of hard wood as a bearing block with which to press down on the drill. Carve a hole for the top of the drill in the center.

5 Cut a strong, hardwood stick for the bow, about 2 ft (60 cm) long and 1 in (2 cm) thick. Loosely tie string or natural cord to both ends, making sure it is slack enough to wind around the drill.

Hand pushes down on bearing block to exert pressure on drill

Drill center is notched so that bow string does not slip

Hot black dust caused by friction

Pull and push bow to rotate the drill

HAND DRILL

A simpler method of fire lighting than the bow drill involves rotating a pointed stick between your hands in a hearth. However, since hands can create less friction than the bow drill, this method only works effectively in hot climates, where the wood is really dry. Push the drill down into the hearth as you turn it, making it spin in short bursts.

Using a Hand Drill
A hand drill is simpler to use but not as effective as a bow drill.

6 Notch the center of the drill and wind the bow string around it. Place tinder beside the notch in the hearth. Set the drill point in the hearth and place the bearing block on its top end. Rotate the drill by pulling and pushing the bow, while pushing down on the drill with the other hand. Smoke will soon be produced, along with hot ash and sparks, which will fall from the notch onto the tinder.

STRIKING CAMP

STRIKING CAMP MUST be a routine, with everyone working toward an agreed time by which the party hits the trail. In extreme cold and heavy rain, waiting for one person to get ready is irritating, and can be dangerous. The second-in-command – who should walk at the rear of the party (*see page 136*) – must check the campsite before setting off. It is important to clean up your campsite so that it looks as if you have never been there – unless you are in a survival situation and must leave signs for possible rescuers. Dismantle your tent or shelter last, so that you can benefit from it as long as possible.

CLEANING UP THE CAMPSITE

You must leave your campsite exactly as if you had never passed through, taking all garbage with you, replacing any sod you removed, and obeying local rules. Not only will this ensure that the wilderness remains unspoiled, but it will also contribute to the enjoyment of future visitors to the area. In a survival situation, if you need to leave messages for possible rescuers, you can do so without damaging the environment (*see opposite*).

Tent
Tents should be dismantled last, so that in bad weather you can shelter until the last possible moment. "Pull Pole" is the time toward which everyone should be working, with everything else completely packed and ready to go. Having packed the tents, leave the site immediately.

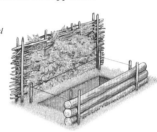

Latrine
The latrine must be filled in and resodded, and labeled with the date of your departure for the benefit of future campers. In areas where the environment was too sensitive for you to have dug a latrine, you must take all your waste with you in plastic bags.

Site of fire pit must be resodded and scattered with leaves

Pack garbage in plastic bags and take them with you

Erasing Your Presence
It is very important to leave your campsite looking as if you had never been there. Dismantle your fire and camouflage the fire pit, take away all waste, garbage, and food residue, and fill in the latrine. If you always do this when you strike camp, you will leave the wilderness undamaged for the wildlife that lives there, as well as for other campers.

Fire
Your fire must be completely out. Its ashes should be scattered and dug well into the ground. Any unburned debris should be collected and taken away to be disposed of.

CLEANING UP THE FIRE

You must make sure that the fire is fully out when you finally strike camp. Even if you have filled in the fire pit, it may contain embers that are still smoldering – these can cause a forest fire. Use as little wood as possible to cook breakfast on the day of your departure, and make sure that every piece of wood has been consumed.

1 When the fire has burned down, rake the remains into the center until they have all crumbled to ash. When the ashes are cold, spread them out and dig them into the ground to disperse them.

2 Making sure that there are no ashes on the surface to kill the grass, fill in the fire pit with soil. Smooth it down with your hands. Then lay the sod that you cut to dig the fire pit back over the site. If you used any rocks, scatter them and camouflage them.

3 Fill in the edges of the cut sod with dirt and grass so that there is no trace of the joint. Scatter leaves and grass on the site so that it resembles the surrounding area. Pack any unburned debris in plastic bags and take it with you until you can burn it or dispose of it.

LEAVING NO TRACE

Many wilderness areas suffer damage because visitors leave garbage that despoils the landscape and can kill animals, damage trees and other vegetation, cause forest fires, and pollute watercourses. You should leave all wild areas looking as if you had never passed through, paying particular attention to your campsite. In some managed wilderness areas, building a fire or digging a latrine is forbidden, and you must respect these rules – for the benefit of the environment and for the enjoyment of campers who may use the same site after you. If you leave food remains animals may become a nuisance to campers, perhaps endangering themselves and people.

LEAVING MESSAGES FOR RESCUERS

Anything out of the ordinary will be noticed by people who come behind, especially if they are looking for you. Indicate your direction, as well as the time and date, on any signs you leave for rescuers. These signs will also help you to retrace your route, if necessary. Place signs as high as you can reach, so that they are secure against animals.

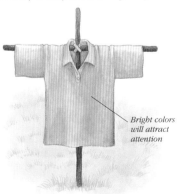

Bright colors will attract attention

Light-colored stones stand out against background

Flag
Lash two sticks together to form a cross and hang a brightly colored T-shirt on top. Set the cross upright in a clearing. If you use two or more of these signs, they can be set so that they lead in the direction you have taken.

Pinecone
Wedge a pinecone into a split branch at the side of the trail you have taken. Something that never occurs naturally will be noticed by anyone looking for you. Be careful not to use anything that animals might eat.

Arrows
Laid in clearings, large stones in the shape of an arrow will indicate your direction of travel. The arrow will also be visible from the air. Make new arrows every so often, and where your trail divides into separate forks.

CHAPTER FOUR

FINDING WATER

ALL LIVING THINGS consist largely of water, without which they die. In a survival situation, after finding shelter, your first priority must be to locate an adequate supply of clean water. Not even food is this important. Water is the basis of all human settlement and social organization. Rivers provided the rich soils from which ancient civilizations grew, their constant supply of water giving mankind surplus food. This allowed the development of commerce and culture, and gave people time to step away from the thin line of harvest-to-harvest survival. Water has also brought death to human civilizations, spreading lethal epidemics of cholera and typhoid, or killing whole cities as rivers changed course and flooded or dried up. Today, urban dwellers take fresh, clean water for granted. However, this is a fundamental delusion of Western life, which seems likely to be shattered as our groundwater resources are used up, bleeding the rivers dry. To survive you should not take either life or water for granted.

ESSENCE OF LIFE
Water is the most important element in our lives. Although we can live without food for several days, without water, our bodies soon cease to function properly, and we die. Finding water is probably the most important thing you should learn before venturing into the wilderness.

THE IMPORTANCE OF WATER

HUMANS MUST DRINK a bare minimum of 6 pints (3 liters) of water every day. Having a constant supply of good water is thus vital for life. Traveling is usually determined by the availability of water, since even vehicles cannot carry more than a few days' supply. On foot, you should always carry enough water to last at least one day, as well as an emergency reserve. It is vital to reach a waterhole at least once every day. Knowing where to find water and how to obtain it is, therefore, essential.

WHERE TO LOOK FOR WATER

When rain falls in mountains, it gathers in small streams, which join together in larger torrents. By the time water reaches the lowlands, these torrents have become large, slow-moving rivers, which eventually flow into the sea. Drinkable water may be found anywhere within this system. All water should be purified before being drunk, to avoid waterborne diseases *(see page 75).*

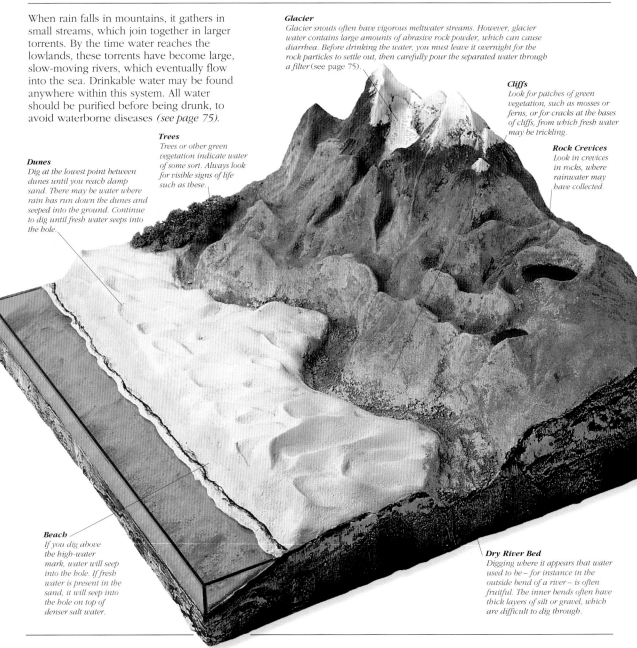

Glacier
Glacier snouts often have vigorous meltwater streams. However, glacier water contains large amounts of abrasive rock powder, which can cause diarrhea. Before drinking the water, you must leave it overnight for the rock particles to settle out, then carefully pour the separated water through a filter (see page 75).

Cliffs
Look for patches of green vegetation, such as mosses or ferns, or for cracks at the bases of cliffs, from which fresh water may be trickling.

Rock Crevices
Look in crevices in rocks, where rainwater may have collected.

Trees
Trees or other green vegetation indicate water of some sort. Always look for visible signs of life such as these.

Dunes
Dig at the lowest point between dunes until you reach damp sand. There may be water where rain has run down the dunes and seeped into the ground. Continue to dig until fresh water seeps into the hole.

Beach
If you dig above the high-water mark, water will seep into the hole. If fresh water is present in the sand, it will seep into the hole on top of denser salt water.

Dry River Bed
Digging where it appears that water used to be – for instance in the outside bend of a river – is often fruitful. The inner bends often have thick layers of silt or gravel, which are difficult to dig through.

SIGNS OF WATER

The presence of water is usually indicated by signs of life such as green vegetation, animal tracks, or human habitation. However, there are other natural signs indicating hidden water. In an otherwise lifeless terrain, look out for living things, although certain birds, such as vultures, can travel large distances from water.

Trees and Other Vegetation
All trees need water to live, although some drive very long taproots into the ground in search of it. Palm trees usually grow where there is some kind of water close to the surface, and some varieties store water in their trunks or roots (see page 72).

Animal Tracks
Grazing animals need to drink at least twice daily, at dawn and at dusk, so at those times they are usually heading to or from water. Look for places where animal tracks converge; this may mean that a water source is nearby. If using a waterhole, take care to avoid predators that may also be using it.

Bees and Flies
Bees do not usually fly more than about 3 miles (5 km) from their nests and must have a constant supply of water. Watch the direction in which they fly upon leaving the nest. Flies stay even closer to water – about 110 yards (100 m) or so. Nevertheless, in the desert they seem to arrive from nowhere, regardless of the nearest source of water.

Ants on the Move
Ants are dependent on having a constant water supply. If you see any marching up a tree, they are probably heading for a reservoir of rainwater.

DEHYDRATION AND THE BODY'S WATER NEEDS

Water is a vital constituent of the human body. However, we have no method of storing water in our bodies as we do with food fats. We therefore need a constant supply for control of body temperature (perspiration), the elimination of waste products through the kidneys, and the operation of our nervous systems. Without food we can survive on our bodily reserve Ifor about three weeks, but if lost water is not replaced within five days, we will die.

Water Needs
About 75 percent of the human body is water, which is vital for life. As this water is lost from the body through sweating and urination, it must be replaced. If it is not, health problems begin to occur. These become more serious until they result in death.

THE EFFECTS OF WATER LOSS		
1-5% Lost	**6-10% Lost**	**11-12% Lost**
Thirst	Headache	Delirium
Discomfort	Dizziness	Swollen tongue
Lethargy	Dry mouth	Twitching
Impatience	Tingling in limbs	Deafness
Lack of appetite	Blue shade to skin	Darkening vision
Flushed skin	Slurred speech	Lack of feeling in skin
Increased pulse	Difficulty in breathing	Skin starts to shrivel
Nausea	Inability to walk	Inability to swallow
Weakness	Blurred vision	Death

PREVENTING WATER LOSS

Even when resting in the shade, the average person loses over 1½ pints (1 liter) of water each day through breathing and urination. Exertion increases water loss through perspiration, especially in hot weather, so if you are short of water, you should rest, working only at night. Try to stay cool and in the shade. Breathe through your nose to reduce water loss, and do not smoke. Do not lie on the hot ground. Eat the minimum amount to keep you alive. Omit fatty foods from your diet and do not drink alcohol – both require large amounts of water for digestion. Do not wait until you have run out of water before going to search for more.

COLLECTING WATER

IN A SURVIVAL situation, after finding shelter, the collection of water is your next most important task, since without water you cannot survive for more than a few days. You may not always be fortunate enough to be camped beside a safe, reliable water supply *(see page 40)*. However, you can sustain yourself in an emergency by collecting rain or dew. Water collected from the atmosphere, or from plants or ground stills, has the enormous advantage over other natural water sources of always being pure *(see page 74)*. Dawn is the best time for the collection of water.

COLLECTING RAIN

While you are in camp, you should set out containers to collect any rain that may fall. You should also collect the flow from the roof of your shelter, using improvised guttering to channel the rain into containers *(see page 53)* or into a pond *(see page 77)*. Even if there is a river or stream nearby, you should still collect rainwater, since it will be pure, allowing you to dispense with chemical purification or boiling *(see page 75)*. To collect rainwater, stretch a waterproof sheet tightly over a wide area, preferably on a slope. Peg down its corners with sticks and collect the rain in a container.

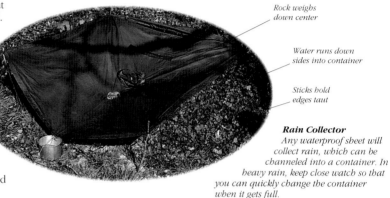

Rock weighs down center

Water runs down sides into container

Sticks hold edges taut

Rain Collector
Any waterproof sheet will collect rain, which can be channeled into a container. In heavy rain, keep close watch so that you can quickly change the container when it gets full.

COLLECTING DEW

As air cools at night, the water vapor it contains condenses as dew on low-lying ground, vegetation, and vehicles. This water rapidly evaporates as the sun rises. Many plants, insects, and animals depend upon dew to survive, and humans can also make use of this natural water supply.

1 You can collect dew by soaking a cloth in long, wet grass. The best time for collection is around dawn, since dew quickly evaporates after sunrise. Indigenous people in arid lands regularly use this method of obtaining pure water.

2 When the cloth is soaked, wring it out into a container. Repeat.

DIGGING FOR WATER

Water will often seep into a hole dug in boggy ground. Dig a hole about 1 ft (30 cm) deep. Scoop up the water that rises in the hole. The water will be silty for the first few times the hole fills, but clear water will eventually rise and can be purified and drunk.

Water from Mud
Scoop muddy water from a hole in boggy ground until freshwater rises to the surface.

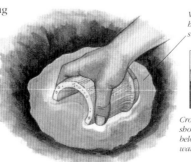

Water seeps into hole from surrounding soil

Cross-section shows hole dug below where water fills soil

WARNING

Before you dig a waterhole, note your surroundings. Never dig where the mud has a potent smell, or has green slime on its surface – any water there is probably contaminated. Do not collect water where there are dead animals. Always purify the water before drinking it *(see page 74)*.

WATER FROM VEGETATION

Plants give off water vapor through their leaves. This water can easily be collected by enclosing foliage in a plastic bag so that the vapor condenses into droplets on the bag.

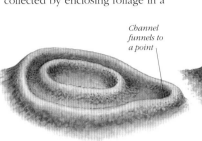

Channel funnels to a point

1 Dig a shallow crater on a slope, with a larger crater outside that forms a channel to a collection point. The craters should be separated with a raised ridge of earth.

2 Place a large plastic bag over the craters, held up with a stick and weighed down with stones around the inside. Put green leaves and grass inside the central crater.

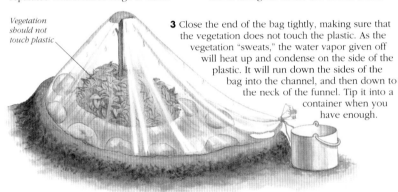

Vegetation should not touch plastic

3 Close the end of the bag tightly, making sure that the vegetation does not touch the plastic. As the vegetation "sweats," the water vapor given off will heat up and condense on the side of the plastic. It will run down the sides of the bag into the channel, and then down to the neck of the funnel. Tip it into a container when you have enough.

OTHER METHODS

You can sometimes collect water droplets from fog or a heavy ground mist by laying out a cloth on the ground, or hanging it up between trees. In an emergency, you can lay out a plastic sheet on grass overnight. As the night air cools, the warm air from the ground will condense into water droplets on the underside of the sheet. Although this method will not provide much water, it may be enough to keep you going until you find a more reliable supply.

Using a Branch
Tie a plastic bag over a growing branch or a whole plant. The water vapor given off by the foliage will heat up inside the plastic and condense as water on the inside surface of the bag.

Condensation forms on inside of plastic bag

EXTRACTING WATER FROM SOIL

Water can be extracted from soil using a solar still. As long as there is a difference in temperature between two surfaces, air between them will heat up and become saturated, condensing as droplets on the cooler surface.

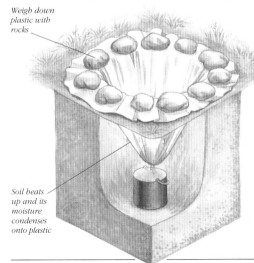

Weigh down plastic with rocks

Soil heats up and its moisture condenses onto plastic

Constructing a Solar Still
Dig a hole about 3 ft (1 m) wide and 2 ft (60 cm) deep. Put a container at the bottom. Spread a plastic sheet across the hole and hold it in place with rocks. Weigh down the center of the sheet over the container with a fist-sized rock. As the air in the hole heats up, water vapor will condense on the underside of the cooler sheet, then run into the container. This still works very well in the desert – by night, as well as by day. At night, the outside air cools the sheet, and because the air in the hole is warmer, you still get condensation on the sheet. Dig another hole when the moisture in the still has been used up.

CONDENSING SEAWATER

Seawater or urine can be condensed into freshwater by employing the same principle as the solar still. Put seawater in a bowl, with a mug in the center. Drape a piece of plastic over the bowl and tie it down. Place a stone in the center so that a cone is formed over the mug. The air under the plastic heats up, and as the seawater warms, it condenses as freshwater on the underside of the sheet.

SEAWATER STILL

NATURAL WATER SOURCES

THERE ARE MANY natural sources of water. For example, you can obtain water from plants, from the blood and eyes of animals, and from some frogs that retain moisture in their skins while they hibernate baked in the mud of dried-up waterholes. Local people know where to find water, which is their most precious resource. In taking natural water supplies, you could be destroying a carefully maintained lifeline, to which the local people may strongly object. You must therefore be careful not to damage waterholes or wells, and must ensure that you can collect the water so that none is wasted.

EXAMPLES OF WATERBEARING PLANTS

There are many different kinds of plant that store water, either in their roots or in their leaves. Some collect rainwater in order to trap insects for food, while others secrete special fluids for their own use, which can be tapped and drunk by humans in emergencies. Below are a few examples of plants around the world that store water.

Carrion Flower (Stapelia *spp.*)
Like other succulent plants, the carrion flower retains water in its stem. You can also chew the fleshy leaves to obtain moisture.

Pitcher Plant
(Nepenthes *spp.*)
This plant catches insects in a watery fluid in its "pitcher." You can extract the water, but it must then be strained to remove any insects (which you can eat).

Acacia Tree (Acacia *spp.*)
Like some other types of desert tree, the acacia stores water in its roots, just below ground surface.

Neoregelia
Bromeliads often collect rainwater in their centers, and have edible leaves that can be chewed for water.

Prickly Pear
(Opuntia *spp.*)
Some cacti, such as prickly pears, have fleshy leaves that can yield moisture when chewed.

OTHER SOURCES OF WATER

Many palm trees contain a sugary liquid that can be drained from flowering stalks. The roots of desert plants store water, but are hard to locate and dig up. Some Australian and African frogs store water in their bodies when they spend dry seasons underground. In a dire emergency, this water can be squeezed out.

Barrel Cactus (Ferocactus *and* Echinocactus *spp.*)
These barrel-shaped cacti are the only exception to the rule about not drinking milky plant fluid (see opposite). The various species of barrel cactus grow to about 3 ft (1 m).

WATER FROM A CACTUS

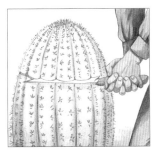

3 Suck out the juice from the pulp through a hollow grass stem or reed. You should only use cacti for water in an emergency, since they are very slow-growing, and some species could easily become extinct in certain areas if overused.

Suck up moisture from pulp with hollow reed

1 To extract moisture from a large barrel cactus, carefully cut off the top with a sharp knife or machete, avoiding the spines.

2 Mash up the flesh inside the cactus with a stick to make a pulp. This will release the moisture from the flesh.

WATER FROM A VINE

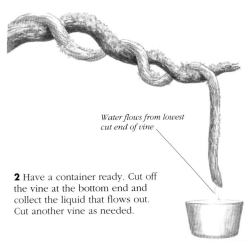

Water flows from lowest cut end of vine

1 Cut through a vine as high as you can reach with a large knife or machete. Do not cut the bottom first, since liquid will flow upward through capillary action.

2 Have a container ready. Cut off the vine at the bottom end and collect the liquid that flows out. Cut another vine as needed.

WARNING

Milky plant sap is usually poisonous, as is the fluid from the giant saguaro cactus (*Carnegiea*) of the American Southwest. Coconut milk and animal fluids contain protein, which requires extra water to be digested by the body. In addition, thick, rich, mature coconut milk is a strong laxative, so it can cause diarrhea. This can result in weakness and dehydration.

WATER FROM TREE ROOTS

Cut trunk to just above the ground

1 Cut down a young banana or plantain tree to about 3 in (8 cm) above the ground.

2 Hollow out the center of the trunk. Water will seep into the hollow from the roots, and can be scooped out.

WATER FROM ICE AND SNOW

Melting Snow
Use dense snow dug from as far below the surface as possible. Hang it in a cloth over a container close to a fire and it will gradually melt. Do not melt snow in a pot over a fire, since any water produced will be quickly soaked up by the remaining snow and the pan will burn. About 16 in (41 cm) of compact snow yields only 1 in (2.5 cm) of fresh water.

Melting Ice
Melt ice slowly on a tilted rock over a fire. Do not use recently frozen sea ice, since it contains salt. Old sea ice, such as Arctic pack ice, has a blue color and contains much less salt.

WATER PURIFICATION

IN THE WILD, water is seldom pure, and should always be purified before being drunk, since it can contain harmful microorganisms that transmit disease. Particles of silt and other contaminants should be filtered out. In Western countries, people assume that water is always drinkable, especially if it comes from a tap. However, in many areas, even tap water is not pure. Some people acquire a tolerance for slightly impure water, but they also become used to suffering, as a matter of course, from a wide range of gastroenteritic problems.

Drinking Water
Wild water should be filtered, even if only through a sock or handkerchief. It should always be purified, as well, to eliminate harmful organisms.

METHODS OF PURIFYING WATER

Except for rain, even the purest-looking wild water is never just H_2O, but contains salts, minerals, and harmful organisms. Wild water must first be filtered to remove particles, then purified to remove harmful organisms by being boiled for at least five minutes, or treated with chemicals. Seawater and urine must never be drunk in their natural state, but they can be distilled in an emergency *(see opposite)*. There are many purifiers available, most of which filter water, then purify it with chemicals. Alternatively, you can use purifying tablets, or boil the water after filtering it *(see opposite)*.

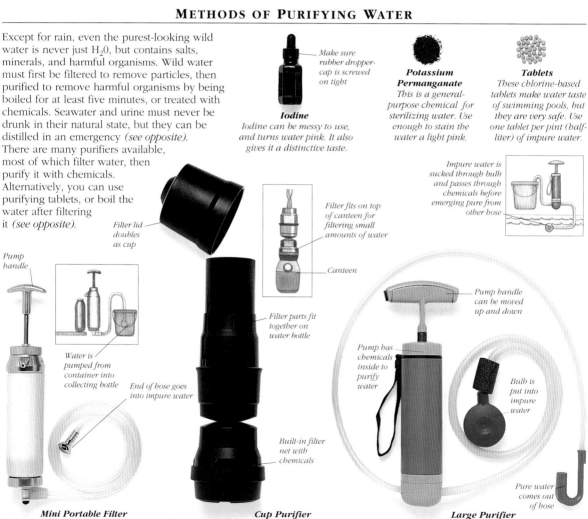

Iodine
Iodine can be messy to use, and turns water pink. It also gives it a distinctive taste.

Make sure rubber dropper-cap is screwed on tight

Potassium Permanganate
This is a general-purpose chemical for sterilizing water. Use enough to stain the water a light pink.

Tablets
These chlorine-based tablets make water taste of swimming pools, but they are very safe. Use one tablet per pint (half-liter) of impure water.

Impure water is sucked through bulb and passes through chemicals before emerging pure from other hose

Filter fits on top of canteen for filtering small amounts of water

Filter lid doubles as cup

Canteen

Pump handle

Water is pumped from container into collecting bottle

End of hose goes into impure water

Filter parts fit together on water bottle

Built-in filter net with chemicals

Pump handle can be moved up and down

Pump has chemicals inside to purify water

Bulb is put into impure water

Pure water comes out of hose

Mini Portable Filter
The end of the hose is put into a container of impure water. Purified water comes out of the spout as the handle is pumped up and down, and can be collected in a container.

Cup Purifier
This purifier can be stowed in a pocket when dismantled. Impure water is poured into the filter, which fits on top of a water bottle. Purified water drips through into the canteen.

Large Purifier
The bulb is put directly into a stream, and the end of the other hose is put into a bucket. Water from the stream is sucked through the purifier by moving the handle up and down.

IMPROVISED WATER TREATMENT

Tripod Filter

If you do not have a manufactured water filter-purifier, you can use a sock to filter wild water before purifying the water by boiling (see opposite). If you do use a sock, line it with a much finer one, fine sand, or a handkerchief, and after each filtering session, turn the whole thing inside out and rinse it well. Make a tripod to support your filter (see page 119).

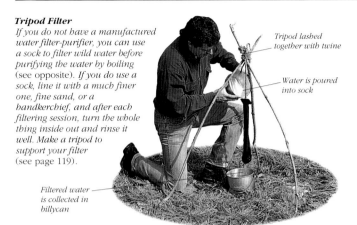

Tripod lashed together with twine

Water is poured into sock

Filtered water is collected in billycan

DISTILLING SALTY WATER

In an emergency, you can obtain pure, freshwater from impure water, such as seawater, by distilling. Boil the impure water and collect the steam on a cloth placed over the top. Use several cloths, one after the other. Lift them off the pot with a stick to avoid being scalded. When they have cooled, wring out the pure water in them.

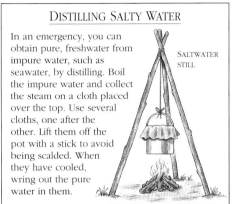

SALTWATER STILL

DANGERS OF NATURAL WATER

When animals drink, they transfer into the water a variety of microorganisms and intestinal parasites harmful to humans. Some of these can do a lot of damage over a long period of time, while others can make you ill immediately. Since urban dwellers have not acquired a tolerance to these contaminants, they are badly affected by them. Although mountain streams should be pure, the wide range of industrial chemicals used on the land, as well as possible soil seepage from human settlements, make it safest to assume that all water collected in the wild must be purified before being drunk.

Lurking Danger
Collecting water in the wild can be dangerous. If using waterholes where wild animals drink, take care to avoid predators.

SIGNS OF BAD WATER

Animal skulls and bones may not always be present to indicate bad water. If the water is polluted by chemicals, look for powdery deposits around the edges (or boil a small amount and examine the residue). The absence of vegetation, or a lot of green algae on the surface, also indicate that the water is unfit to drink.

Stagnant Pond
Cattails and rushes often indicate stagnant water, which should be avoided.

How to Prevent Waterborne Diseases
The only way to avoid contracting waterborne diseases is to purify your water. If a member of your party becomes ill from drinking the water, segregate him and his nurse. Feed the victim using separate cups, plates, and utensils. You should be particularly careful with the victim's excreta and soiled garments, which will contain large quantities of the organism that has affected him. Take extra care with camp hygiene so that no one else in the party becomes infected (see page 56).

WATERBORNE DISEASES

Disease	Causes	Symptoms
Leptospirosis (severe form = Weil's disease)	Transmitted to humans from animals infected with *Leptospira* bacterium (rats, cattle, mice, dogs, pigs). Caught through contact with infected animal urine or fetal fluids. Enters through skin abrasion or lining of mouth, nose, throat, or eyes.	Causes influenza-like symptoms (fever, chills, headache, muscle pain). More severe forms lead to meningitis, jaundice, kidney failure, hemorrhage, and heart damage.
Bilharzia (schistosomiasis)	Caused by parasitic flatworm in slow-moving, freshwater streams. Can enter skin directly, lodging in intestine. Also transmitted by parasites in freshwater snails.	Causes itching, hives, asthmatic attacks, enlargement of the liver, and irritation of the urinary tract.
Dysentery	Contracted by drinking water contaminated with infected sewage.	Causes diarrhea with blood and/or mucus, and infection of colon. Complications of infection include hepatitis, abscess of liver and lungs, and perforation of bowel.
Hookworms	Parasite larvae enter human body in drinking water or directly through the skin.	Adult worms lodge in the intestines, causing anemia and lethargy. Larvae in the bloodstream may cause pneumonia.
Giardiasis	Caused by parasite *Giardia* in water contaminated with infected urine or feces.	Causes diarrhea and abdominal cramps. Increasingly prevalent in North America, Africa, and Asia.

CARRYING AND STORING WATER

EVEN IF YOU are camped right beside a stream you will need vessels of some sort for containing water. For instance, you may want to keep water handy for use when cooking. You may also need a container for scooping water from a stream. In addition, because camping beside a water source is not always the most sensible

option, carrying water will almost certainly be a daily or twice-daily chore. As you forage for food, explore, and work, you will have to carry water with you because you may not be able to find it when you need it.

Conserving Water
Water is precious – you should never waste it. You may not be able to easily renew your supply.

WATER CONTAINERS

There are many different kinds of container for carrying both hot and cold liquids. They range from solid plastic or steel flasks or bottles, to collapsible fabric bags that can be folded up when they are empty. Make sure that you can tell the difference between your water containers and those in which you carry stove fuel.

Flask
A metal vacuum flask is almost unbreakable and holds hot or cold liquids.

Plastic Bottle
A light, tough plastic bottle is ideal, but it will melt if placed too close to a fire.

Steel Bottle
This is strong but it can be heavy when filled with water.

Belt Pouch
A belt pouch enables you to carry water within easy reach while traveling, but allows you to keep your hands free.

Bottle with Cup
This bottle has a handy plastic cup as a lid, much like a vacuum flask.

Small Water Bag
This can be folded up when not in use. Do not lay it on the ground, because it can easily be damaged.

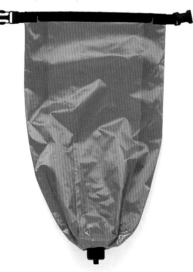

Collapsible Canteen
This is a traditional, popular water container. Take care that you do not break the tab linking the cap to the bottle, in case you lose the cap.

Large Water Bag
Useful for a large camp, this water bag can be suspended from a tree in a breeze, keeping the contents cool.

CARRYING WATER

With water-carrying a daily chore, and the likelihood in many areas of safe campsites being some distance from a water source, large water containers must be filled and transported back to camp. It is best to carry the water container on your back, leaving your hands free to negotiate obstacles. If you can, use a small bottle to fill the container to the very brim. This prevents water from sloshing around, and avoids wasting water.

Water Carrier
Make a frame (see page 135) to carry a large container.

BARK WATER CONTAINER

1 You can improvise a water container from flexible green bark, such as birch. Cut a piece into a rectangle.

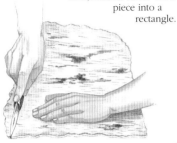

2 Soak the corners in water to soften the bark, then gently crease the sides.

Crease sides and corners to make box

Coat container with tree resin to waterproof it

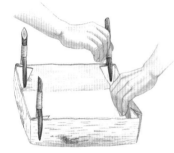

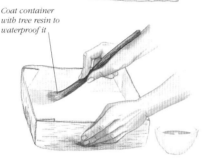

3 Make pegs from split twigs bound with grass. Glue the sides of the box together with pine resin, which can be scraped from tree bark. Peg them until they are dry.

4 When the container has dried in shape, remove the pegs and waterproof it with pine resin, using a chewed twig as a brush. Allow the box to dry before using it.

IMPROVISED CONTAINERS

Bamboo Segment

Bamboo stems consist of hollow segments divided by "walls," and make excellent water containers.

Cut a thick bamboo stem about 1 in (2.5 cm) below one segment ring, and the same amount below the next one. This will leave a hollow container with an open end.

Gourds

Gourds and squashes can be hollowed out and dried for use as water containers. Cut the top off the gourd to get at the flesh with a knife, or scrape the insides clean with a long, pointed stick.

WILD WATER RULES

- Always filter and purify water gathered in the wild *(see page 74)*.
- Try to collect enough water to cater for your needs, as well as a reserve supply for emergencies, when you cannot find fresh water.
- When it rains, put out as many containers as you can, in order to collect as much rainwater as possible – you never know when you might need it.
- Treat water with respect. Never waste any of it, even if you have a surplus, since you may one day be short of water.
- Never drink untreated urine or seawater. In an emergency, these can be distilled *(see page 75)*.
- Drink plenty in cold conditions, as well as in hot ones, since they can cause dehydration, and walking in snow or skiing can make you sweat.
- Do not eat food if you have an inadequate water supply, since water is needed for digestion.

STORING WATER

1 You may have to store water during the rainy season to last over the dry months, or because you need more water than you can carry from a water source. Choose a site into which groundwater will flow, for example a natural hollow, and dig down to clay or bedrock.

Hold groundsheet in place with large rocks, but take care not to damage it

2 Line the hole with a groundsheet, or plaster it with wet clay, smoothing the clay until it makes a watertight surface. Cover the hole during the day with a vinyl groundsheet or woven vegetation mat *(see page 49)* to minimize evaporation. Remove the cover at night and when it rains so that rain and dew will fall in the pond. Collect the water regularly, before it evaporates.

CHAPTER FIVE

FINDING AND PREPARING FOOD

AWAY FROM REFRIGERATORS, stoves, and all the equipment of a modern kitchen, a very different, simple approach is required to food gathering, storage, and cooking. Away from the familiar diet of home, it is essential to understand what foods your body needs, in what quantities *(see page 14)*, and where those foods may be found. A full range of vitamins and minerals is difficult to obtain in the wild. Meat and fish would provide virtually everything you need. However, although it may be relatively simple to gather plants, invertebrates, and even fish, it is far more difficult to hunt animals for meat, and the energy you expend in hunting makes it inadvisable in a survival situation, unless you are an experienced hunter. Most food items are best eaten immediately, before heat, insects, or bacteria can spoil them. If you have to spend a long time in one place, however, it is necessary to build up a surplus of food and preserve it for times when food is scarce.

NATURAL SUSTENANCE
We can take a variety of prepared foods with us into the wilderness, yet, if we are in a survival situation without these items, we need not starve. The wilderness is full of natural foods, ranging from plants to insects. Although they may be unfamiliar to your palate, one day they could save your life.

FOOD FOR TRAVELING

FOOD CAN BE TAKEN on backpacking trips in cans, dehydrated in foil bags, or in its natural state, in some sort of container. Canned foods are cooked and ready to eat (hot or cold), but heavy to carry. Dehydrated foods are much lighter, but require large amounts of water for rehydration, and in some regions you would have to carry water specially for this purpose. The temptation to eat dehydrated food without leaving it for a long enough period to soak up water must be resisted. It will absorb water from your body and may cause uncomfortable and even dangerous intestinal blockages.

High-calorie Foods
Sweet foods provide little nutritional value, but they are a welcome dietary variation to more useful items. Mountaineers and polar explorers often rely on hard candies to help provide the large amount of calories necessary for survival (see page 15).

CHOCOLATE
CUSTARD POWDER

DEHYDRATED
ICE CREAM

STRAWBERRY
PUDDING MIX

FRUIT-FLAVORED
HARD CANDIES

Breakfast Foods
Breakfast foods are vital for energy at the start of the day. Cereals such as oats and muesli can also provide roughage (fiber), which prevents the digestive tract from clogging up. Dried fruit contains fiber, and trail mix contains a wide range of nutritious morsels.

TRAIL MIX

MUESLI

DRIED FRUITS

OATS

Rice and Legumes
Rice provides necessary carbohydrates, but can be difficult to cook on a camp stove, and uses a lot of fuel. Legumes provide fiber and protein. They must be well soaked before cooking, particularly kidney beans. Follow the manufacturer's instructions.

RICE

LENTILS

KIDNEY BEANS

DRIED PEAS

Trail Snacks
To maintain energy, it is best to nibble constantly during the day to keep hunger pangs at bay, and to have a big meal at night, which you can digest thoroughly while sleeping. Trail snacks include candies, chocolate, cookies, and crackers, all of which provide energy and carbohydrates.

CUSTARD COOKIE

GRANOLA BAR

PLAIN CRACKERS

CHOCOLATE COOKIE

DIGESTIVE BISCUITS

CHOCOLATE BAR

Beverages

Beverages are luxuries with little nutritional value. However, they provide warmth and comfort. Dried milk can be a source of calcium, as well as making drinks tasty. Hot chocolate is a delicious drink on a cold evening.

COFFEE

TEA

HOT CHOCOLATE

DRIED MILK

Main Meals

Freeze-drying is a method of dehydration that leaves the structure and texture of foods, particularly fruits, intact. Dehydrated food is lightweight and easy to carry, but must be soaked in water before being cooked.

SOYA MEAL

FREEZE-DRIED MEAL

DEHYDRATED MEAL

VEGETARIAN DRIED MEAL

Mixers

Flour and salt are the basic staples, from which a wide variety of dishes can be prepared (see page 117). Suet can be invaluable if you cannot obtain necessary fats from your food. Sugar can help to make wild food pleasant.

FLOUR

SUET

BROWN SUGAR

SALT

Flavorings

Anything that enlivens camping food is worth carrying, especially if you are going to rely on wild food (see page 93). Curry powder adds a distinctive flavor to food, as do garlic cloves, onions, spices, ketchup, and sauces.

GRAVY CUBES

ONION SAUCE

SOUP

KETCHUP

MEAT AND FISH

Although red meat and fish provide necessary protein, all kinds of meat are difficult to keep fresh. It is therefore best to carry cans or preserved products. Once cans have been opened their contents must be consumed immediately, so always buy cans that are not too large to empty in one meal. Canned foods can, however, be heavy to carry in a backpack. Preserved meats, such as salami, are more lightweight, but their variety is often limited. You can preserve your own meat or fish in several ways *(see page 118)*. An alternative to canned or preserved meats is a selection of complete meals prepared with soya protein or tofu, as well as pasta and vegetables.

SARDINES

PASTA MEAL

FRANKFURTERS AND BEANS

SALAMI

EDIBLE PLANTS

UNLESS YOU ARE in the middle of an arid desert, there will always be plants, and many will be edible and nourishing. The problem is knowing which ones are nutritious, while avoiding the ones that are poisonous or could make you ill. Some otherwise nourishing plants have fine hairs and barbs, which irritate the mouth and throat, or poisonous seeds. Furthermore, at different times of the year, some plants become less edible – and even poisonous. Others are edible but only mildly nourishing – collecting and eating them uses more calories than they actually provide.

TEMPERATE PLANTS

Avoid old plants and shoots, which are fibrous and tough, and may taste unpleasant. Young shoots are more nourishing than old ones, and may be edible without cooking. You should also choose young leaves, rather than old ones, picking them whole from the stem. Below are a few examples of temperate edible plants.

Sea Kale (Crambe)
Sea kale grows on temperate seashores. Its thick leaves and underground stems can be boiled and eaten, and taste a bit like cabbage.

Wall Pepper (Sedum)
Wall pepper grows on rocks, walls, and gravel in temperate regions. It has a sharp, peppery taste. Its leaves can be eaten raw as a salad vegetable, or cooked and used as a tasty flavoring for soups.

OTHER TEMPERATE PLANTS

Seaweeds such as laver *(Porphyria)* can be boiled, baked, or dried. Carrageen seaweed produces a kind of gelatin that can be used to make a dessert *(see page 93).* Dandelion *(Taraxacum)* leaves and dock *(Rumex)* leaves can be used like spinach, while wild garlics such as ramps *(Allium)* can be used as flavorings.

Bistort (Polygonum)
This plant is found all over Europe, with related species in North America. It grows up to 2 ft (60 cm) tall, in grassy areas or woods in temperate areas, and can be recognized by its long, pink flower heads. The leaves and shoots can be boiled and eaten. The roots are also edible when roasted, but should be soaked in water first.

Wintercress (Barbarea)
This plant grows in Europe, North America, and New Zealand. The leaves can be eaten raw or boiled.

Goutweed (Aegopodium)
This herb is found in Europe and Asia. The young leaves and leaf stems taste best when the shoots are about 6 in (15 cm) high.

Summer Purslane (Portulaca)
Summer purslane grows in temperate salt marshes below the high-tide mark. The leaves can be picked at any time of the year. Simmer them in water, and flavor with lemon juice, if available. Eat summer purslane with other foods, since eating a lot of one thing can lead to malnutrition.

TROPICAL PLANTS

Many kinds of plants flourish in the warmth and humidity of the tropics. In the absence of seasons, they grow all year. There are a great many different varieties, with particularly nourishing fruits and vegetables. Test unfamiliar plants before you eat them. Below are just a few common varieties found in tropical areas.

Bamboo
(Pseudosasa)
Cut young bamboo stems from the base of the plant and split the husk with a knife. The tender flesh inside can be cooked in water like asparagus. You can also eat the seeds. There are many different kinds of bamboo, found in many parts of the world.

Amaranthus (Amaranthus)
This plant can grow up to 3 ft (1 m) high. Cut the leaves and stems into pieces and boil them in salted water like spinach. Young shoots can be eaten raw in salads.

OTHER TROPICAL PLANTS

Plant species vary from region to region, and there are hundreds that are edible. Many bear delicious fruit, although you will be unable to reach it if it grows high in the canopy of a tropical forest. Plants that can be reached include Ceylon spinach (*Basella*), whose stems and leaves are rich in vitamins, and sugarcane (*Saccharum*), the stems of which can be chewed raw.

TASTE TEST

First crush a leaf. If it smells bad, or like almonds, discard it. Rub the juice on the inside of your arm. If there is no irritation, place a small piece on your lips, then in the corner of your mouth, then on the tip of your tongue, then under your tongue, all for five seconds at a time. If there is no stinging, swallow a small amount and wait for five hours, consuming nothing else. If you have no unpleasant reactions, you can eat the plant.

Palms
The young shoots of palms such as the coconut palm (Cocos), the sugar palm (Arenga), and the sago palm (Metroxylon) are all edible. The sago palm also has starchy pith inside its trunk that can be boiled like rice into sago pudding. Not all palms are edible, however, so you should learn to identify safe ones.

Palm Heart
The growing tip, or heart, of some palms can be eaten, either raw or cooked. Do not eat palm fruit unless you can identify it.

TREES

Most trees produce fruit, berries, and nuts of some kind, all of which can be highly nutritious (*see page 88*). The tender buds, shoots, and inner bark of many trees are also edible, and some trees have sap that can be drunk. The needles of some evergreen trees are rich in vitamin C, and can be steeped in hot water to make tea (*see page 93*).

Spruce (Picea)
The inner bark of the spruce is rich in vitamin C. It is best taken from the bottom of the trunk, near the roots. Peel back the outer bark and boil the inner bark until it is soft before eating it. The needles can be used to make a refreshing drink (see page 93).

Maple (Acer)
The maple has sugary sap that can be collected from natural wounds, or tapped from a slit in the bark. The sap can then be boiled until it thickens into a high-energy syrup.

OTHER TREES

The young needles of the pine (*Pinus*) taste good and can be made into tea (*see page 93*). The inner bark of aspen (*Populus*) is very nutritious, while birch (*Betula*) has delicious sap. Collect sap by cutting a V in the bark, but do not damage more than a quarter of the tree's girth. Other edible trees include the carob (*Ceratonia*) and the tamarind (*Tamarindus*), both of which have pulpy pods.

POISONOUS PLANTS

THE NUMBER OF poisonous plants is very much less than the number of edible ones, particularly in temperate regions. Some are poisonous on contact, causing rashes and severe irritation *(see page 181)*. Others are toxic when eaten, and can cause vomiting, diarrhea, and sometimes death.

Some poisonous plants resemble edible ones, so the only way to avoid disaster is to learn what each poisonous plant looks like. Always exercise extreme caution when tasting plants *(see page 83)*, particularly in a survival situation, when medical help is not readily available.

TEMPERATE PLANTS

The leaves and stems of some plants are poisonous, as well as some flowers, roots, and sap. Even brushing against some of them can induce them to release their poison from stinging hairs or pores. There are far more edible plants in temperate regions than poisonous ones, but the toxic plants can sometimes be deadly.

Foxglove
(Digitalis)
All parts of the foxglove contain digitalis, a highly toxic heart stimulant. The plant grows to a height of 5 ft (1.5 m), and can have distinctive purple, pink, yellow, or white, bell-like flowers.

Lupine (Lupinus)
This plant grows in North America, Europe, and Asia. All parts can cause fatal inflammation of the stomach and intestines. The plant has purple, pink, white, or yellow flowers.

OTHER TEMPERATE PLANTS

One of the deadliest temperate plants is the purple-flowered monkshood *(Aconitum)*, which grows in damp woods. Deadly hemlock *(Conium)* and cowbane *(Cicuta)* can be recognized by their white flowers, which are carried like an umbrella. Avoid all umbelliferous plants, since most of them are poisonous. Poison oak and poison sumac *(Toxicodendron)* both cause irritation after contact.

Castor Bean Plant (Ricinus)
Although this plant is native to tropical regions, it has been introduced into temperate areas. It is often cultivated for the purgative oil released from its crushed seeds. In the wild, however, the seeds can be fatal if ingested.

Poison Ivy
(Toxicodendron)
Poison ivy is found in woods in North America. It can be trailing or upright, like ordinary ivy, but may be distinguished by its greenish flowers and white berries. It causes a burning rash after it touches skin.

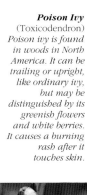

Buttercup
(Ranunculus)
All members of this genus cause severe and painful inflammation of the intestines if eaten. They are found almost worldwide, and all species have at least five glossy, yellow, overlapping petals.

WARNING

Many common poisonous plants in temperate regions resemble edible ones, so unless you are certain of correct identification, you should avoid eating them. Even a mouthful of some, such as the cowbane, can cause paralysis and death in minutes.

Death Camas (Zigadenus)
The lethal bulb of the death camas can be confused with a wild onion (see page 86). The plant has long leaves and white flowers, and grows up to 2 ft (60 cm) high. It is commonly found in wooded and grassy areas of North America.

TROPICAL PLANTS

Tropical plants are so varied and plentiful that, for your own safety, you should stick only to the ones you can identify. If you do need to consider eating unfamiliar species, always apply the taste test first *(see page 83)*, and only eat very small amounts. Below are a few examples of poisonous plants found in tropical areas.

Jatropha glandulosa
Several species of tropical plant in the Jatropha *genus have poisonous leaves, seeds, sap, or fruit. The seeds are violently purgative.*

Sapium insigne
The sap of this plant is milky and highly toxic. Do not get it on your skin, or it will cause blisters. Avoid all plants with milky sap, since they are likely to be poisonous.

Jatropha podagrica
This plant has a turniplike base, but all parts of it are highly poisonous. The only way to identify unfamiliar plants is to learn them from a reliable source, such as a local guidebook, or from the people who live in the area.

Jatropha integerrima
This plant is found in wooded areas throughout the tropics. All parts of it can cause inflammation of the intestines, along with diarrhea and vomiting. These conditions can lead to dehydration (see page 181), which could endanger your life in a survival situation if you are unable to find prompt medical help.

OTHER TROPICAL PLANTS

The nettle tree *(Laportea)* grows near water throughout the tropics. It causes burning rashes when touched, and has poisonous seeds. The beachapple *(Hippomane)* has toxic fruit and sap. The cowhage *(Mucuna)* grows in woodland and scrub, and its pods and flowers irritate the skin if touched. If they come into contact with the eyes, these parts can cause blindness.

TREES

There is no set rule for identifying which trees are poisonous and which are safe to eat. Parts of some trees can be eaten, while other parts may be poisonous. You should be particularly careful when dealing with tropical trees, since seeds and fruit from some can be lethal, while sap from others can blister skin and cause blindness.

Blinding Mangrove (Excoecaria)
This small tree is found in mangrove swamps and estuaries in Australasia, southeast Asia, and tropical Africa. You should avoid it whenever possible, since its sap can blister the skin and cause blindness if it gets into your eyes.

California Laurel (Umbellularia)
California laurel grows in North America. Its tough, oval, evergreen leaves smell strongly aromatic and are poisonous. It has yellow flowers and green or purple berries.

OTHER TREES

The seed pods of the laburnum tree *(Laburnum)* are deadly, as are the berries of the yew *(Taxus)*. The black locust *(Robinia)* of North America contains poisonous substances in its bark, flowers, and seedpods. The rhengas tree *(Gluta)* of southeast Asia has irritant sap, while the sap of the sandbox tree *(Hua)* of South America can cause blindness. Avoid eating parts of any tree unless you can positively identify it.

ROOTS, TUBERS, AND BULBS

THE ROOTS, TUBERS, or bulbs of some plants are rich in vitamins and high in starch, and can be eaten in a survival situation. Some are harmful if eaten raw, so it is best to always cook them before eating them. Scrub the roots first, then boil or parboil them before roasting them on a spit over a fire *(see page 116)*. The skins of many roots are rich in vitamins and minerals, so avoid peeling the roots if the skins are in good condition. Bear in mind, however, that some roots such as those of comfrey must be peeled to eliminate harmful substances. Learn a few edible roots and disregard the rest.

EDIBLE ROOTS

The only way to determine whether a root or bulb is edible and safe to eat is to learn to recognize the plant that grows from it. Plants in different regions often look alike, or have similar bulbs, so never just assume that because a root or bulb looks familiar, it is safe to eat – for example, the bulb of the deadly death camas resembles a harmless onion *(see page 84)*. Almost all bulbs and roots should be cooked thoroughly before being eaten.

Salsify (Tragopogon)
Salsify is 2–3 ft (60–90 cm) high and grows in dry waste areas. It has purple, dandelion-like flowers. Its long leaves and parsniplike tuber are edible, and it is often cultivated.

Water Chestnut (Trapa)
This plant lives in freshwater throughout Europe and Asia. Its hard seeds are also edible, either raw or roasted.

Water Lily
(Nymphaea)
The water lily has heart-shaped, floating leaves, and grows in tropical and temperate freshwater almost worldwide. Its seeds, tuber, and stem are all edible, although the seeds are somewhat bitter.

OTHER EDIBLE ROOTS

The roots of dandelion *(Taraxacum)*, galingale *(Cyperus)*, and some other plants can be roasted to make a coffee substitute. The rootstock of other plants, for example the wild calla, or bog arum *(Calla)*, can be ground to a powder and used as flour *(see page 92)*. The roots of sweet vetch *(Astralagus)* can be eaten raw or cooked, as can the tubers of the Jerusalem artichoke *(Helianthus)*, which grows wild in North America.

Arrowhead (Sagittaria)
Arrowhead can be found near freshwater. It grows up to 3 ft (1 m) high and has arrow-shaped, erect leaves and small, three-petaled flowers. Its tubers are edible raw, but are better cooked.

Sweet Flag
(Acorus)
The distinctive sweet flag can grow to a height of 4 ft (1.3 m), and is only found beside freshwater. Its rootstock is strongly aromatic and can be eaten. It should first be sliced, then boiled down to a syrup before being eaten.

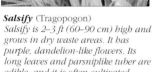

Peanut
(Arachis)
Despite its name, the peanut does not bear true nuts. Its "nuts" are really seedpods and grow underground, attached to stems. The peanut plant is small and bushy, with stubby, oval leaves and flat, yellow flowers.

POISONOUS ROOTS

Generally speaking, if a plant's roots are poisonous, its leaves, stem, flowers, and sap usually are, as well. The lesser celandine, or pilewort, is a good example of this – even handling the plant can result in blistered skin. However, there are exceptions to this rule. Some roots are only edible if cooked, and may be lethally poisonous if eaten raw. Always take great care. Unless you can be certain of correctly identifying a plant, do not eat it.

Manioc (Manihot)
The tubers of the manioc, or cassava, are lethal if eaten raw. They must be soaked for 48 hours, then cooked thoroughly before being eaten.

Daffodil (Narcissus)
It is easy to recognize the daffodil by its familiar flower. If there is no flower, leave the plant alone.

Bog Arum (Calla)
Also known as the wild calla, the bog arum has a very distinctive flower spike inside a hood. It grows beside freshwater. The roots can be eaten or ground up to make flour (see page 92), but they must be cooked first, since they are poisonous if eaten raw. All other parts of the plant are poisonous, and should be avoided.

WARNING

Since it is so difficult to distinguish poisonous roots from edible ones – unless the plant is very distinctive – it is best to avoid eating any roots. As long as you can positively identify a handful of species, just stick to those and ignore all the rest.

Wild Yam (Dioscorea)
Although some species of wild yam are cultivated for food in tropical areas, a few are poisonous unless they are peeled and cooked. Unless you can identify safe varieties, therefore, it is best always to peel and cook all wild yams. They have large leaves and often grow around tree trunks.

Taro (Colocasia)
Taro grows on wet ground throughout tropical regions. The plant reaches a height of 5 ft (1.5 m), and has long, green, wedge-shaped leaves, and a yellow-orange flower. Its tubers are poisonous if eaten raw, but they can be consumed after being cooked, and taste a bit like potatoes.

OTHER POISONOUS ROOTS

The tubers of the wild potato (*Solanum*) can be eaten, but must always be cooked first. Its tomato-like fruits, however, are poisonous. The wild tomato (*Lycopersicon*), which is edible, looks so similar to the potato plant that it is best to avoid both. The death camas (*Zigadenus*) has a bulb that looks like an onion, but it is lethal (see page 84). The tubers and roots of the lesser celandine (*Ranunculus*) and the cowbane (*Cicuta*) are also deadly.

Swallow-wort (Vincetoxicum)
This has sharply pointed, heart-shaped leaves and small, yellowish white flowers. If ingested, its roots and seed pods cause vomiting and water loss, and its milky sap is also toxic. It is common in temperate regions.

Starflower (Ornithogalum)
This temperate plant grows up to 1 ft (30 cm) tall. Its bulbs can be eaten as long as they are cooked first, but the rest of the plant should be avoided.

NUTS AND FRUIT

Both NUTS AND fruit provide possibly the most important source of survival food. In temperate regions, wild fruits appear from midsummer onward, with nuts coming later and in the autumn. Most wild fruits are hard to store, unless you make jelly or dry suitable species *(see page 118)*. Bear in mind that, in gathering fruit and nuts, you are competing with birds and animals, particularly when it comes to collecting nuts, which some animals gather as their prime source of winter nourishment. Do not bother with any fruit or nuts that are over-ripe or moldy, since they may make you ill.

EDIBLE NUTS

Nuts provide both protein and fat. With particularly oily nuts, such as beech, you can separate their oil and store it for use in cooking. Boil the nuts gently in water, then skim the oil from the surface. The nuts can then be ground into flour *(see page 92)*. Nuts are the easiest wild food to store, and are very good to eat while traveling.

Hazel (Corylus)
Hazelnuts grow on tall shrubs and trees in temperate areas, and have serrated, heart-shaped leaves and brownish yellow catkins. The nuts come in hairy husks.

Walnut (Juglans)
Walnut trees grow in temperate areas. They have distinctive gnarled bark. The nuts have a green, pulpy husk, which rots away after falling from the tree. The nuts are high in calories.

Pistachio (Pistacia)
Pistachios grow in Europe, Asia, and Australia. Their nuts can be eaten raw or roasted.

OTHER EDIBLE NUTS

Pecans *(Carya)* are fairly common in wet areas throughout North America. They contain more fat than any other nut, vegetable, or fruit. Macadamia nuts *(Macadamia)* from Australia are also good to eat. Pine nuts *(Pinus)* are edible, although they taste better roasted than raw.

Chestnut (Castanea)
Chestnut trees have long, serrated leaves and spiky husks, inside which the nuts develop. To eat the nuts, you must first peel them, then boil and mash them, or roast them over a fire.

POISONOUS NUTS

Nuts must be tasted carefully, using the taste test *(see page 83)*. Although there are few really poisonous nuts, some can be dangerous unless they are cooked, while others may make you ill if they are moldy. If any nut has an uncharacteristic sweet, almondlike smell, discard it, since it may contain irritating prussic acid.

Horse Chestnut (Aesculus)
The horse chestnut, which grows in temperate regions, has large, handlike leaves, pale flowers, and sticky buds. It can grow up to 100 ft (30 m) in some areas. Its poisonous seedcases are less heavily prickled than those of the chestnut, and the nuts inside the husks ("buckeyes") are much larger than those of the edible chestnut.

Cashew (Anacardium)
The nuts of the cashew are poisonous unless peeled and boiled. Take great care when they are cooking, since the fumes can cause blindness. The cashew grows in tropical areas.

OTHER POISONOUS NUTS

Although they are edible, almonds *(Prunus)* can contain prussic acid, and taste bitter as a result. Acorns, from oak trees *(Quercus)*, are also edible, but they must be boiled, or steeped in cold water for several hours, then roasted, to remove their bitter taste.

EDIBLE FRUIT

Edible fruits contain a great many essential nutrients, including sugars and vitamins A, B_2, and C. Birds and mammals use fruits as a major food source and will compete with you. Insects may also attack fruit, but you can benefit from this by eating any nutritious larvae you find inside. Do not eat too much of any fruit.

Cloudberry (Rubus)
The cloudberry grows in northern-temperate and arctic regions. The bramblelike plant grows to about 1 ft (30 cm) tall, and has white flowers and fruit that resemble raspberries.

Passionfruit
(Passiflora)
The passionfruit has long, vinelike stems, trilobed leaves, tendrils, and white and purple flowers. It grows in tropical areas, particularly in South America. The edible purple fruits are egg-shaped and juicy.

OTHER EDIBLE FRUIT

Wild grapes *(Vitis)* are common in warm parts of the world. Their leaves can be boiled and eaten, as well. Various species of the wild strawberry *(Fragaria)* hide away in woodland and dry, grassy areas. They are rich in vitamin C, very sweet, and delicious.

Cranberry (Vaccinium)
This grows in northern temperate moorlands, tundra, and woods.

Juniper (Juniperus)
Juniper grows in northern temperate mountains in the form of large shrubs or small, compact bushes. In some parts of North America, they are known as "Oregon grapes." The mature indigo berries can be eaten, but they are a little bitter.

POISONOUS FRUIT

Because fruits are designed to attract mammals and birds (which, having eaten, then spread the seeds in their feces), many poisonous berries resemble edible ones. This can be a hazard if you are trying to survive in the wilderness on natural foods. As with leaves and fungi, learn a few edible kinds and avoid the rest.

Sorbus
Although the fruit of some Sorbus *species is edible, in general, white berries are poisonous. Do not risk eating any berries of this color. Other plants with poisonous white berries include the baneberry and some kinds of nightshade.*

Duchesnea
The fruits of Duchesnea, *also known as "mock strawberries," can be fatal. The plant grows in parts of Asia and North America.*

Virginia Creeper (Parthenocissus)
The dark blue or purple berries of this temperate plant resemble grapes. No blue or purple berries of a vinelike plant with tendrils are edible.

OTHER POISONOUS FRUIT

There are many poisonous fruits, particularly in warm regions. Some of these are only mildly poisonous and can result in diarrhea or nausea if ingested in quantity. Others are highly toxic and only a small amount can be fatal if eaten. In a survival situation, the risks are greatly increased, especially if you are in a weakened state. Some common poisonous fruits include the purple berries of the deadly nightshade *(Atropha)*, which are lethal if ingested. The cuckoopint *(Arum)* has red berries that can cause severe digestive upset if eaten. The baneberry *(Actaea)* has white or black berries that can cause vomiting and internal irritation. The tropical strychnine tree *(Strychnos)* has orangelike fruits with deadly seeds. The fruits of the crabapple *(Malus)* can cause diarrhea if eaten in quantity.

FUNGI & LICHEN

FOR MANY PEOPLE around the world, gathering fungi and lichen is a regular activity. Apart from being absolutely delicious, dew-fresh fungi contain minerals and some protein, and provide the staple of many national dishes. However, great caution must be exercised when gathering and eating these foods. Some fungi are lethal, but may very closely resemble edible varieties. Even experienced fungi gatherers can make mistakes – sometimes what is safe to eat in one country looks almost the same as a poisonous variety of another country. Only eat fungi if you are certain of correct identification.

EDIBLE FUNGI

There is no logical way to identify edible fungi. Go gathering only with experts, and train yourself to identify just one or two edible varieties, with special reference to their habitats. Also learn poisonous varieties, particularly the deadly ones. Reject all but healthy, unmarked examples. Below are just a few examples of edible fungi.

Puffball (Calvatia utriformis)
Found in summer and autumn, among fields and meadows, the puffball is best if eaten when young and its flesh is white.

Morel (Morchella *spp.*)
This white mushroom is found in spring on sandy and sand-clay soils, under trees or in the open.

Cauliflower Fungus (Sparassis crispa)
This fungus is found in autumn in coniferous woodland, growing around the bases of trees and on their roots. Its flesh has the scent of anise and the flavor of walnut.

Orange Peel Fungus (Aleuria aurantia)
This fungus needs sunlight to grow, and is found in bare patches of woodland and in grassy areas in autumn. Despite being good to eat, its flesh has no striking flavor or scent.

OTHER EDIBLE FUNGI

The Boletus varieties have a traditional mushroom shape, but have pores underneath, rather than gills. They are generally delicious. A few species are moderately poisonous, but these can be distinguished from the edible ones because they taste unpleasant raw, and have reddish or orange pores and stems. Select only mushrooms with yellow- or cream-colored pores. Shelf fungi, which grow on the sides of trees, are generally safe to eat, but some varieties are tough and tasteless. All wild fungi must be cooked before eating, in order to help destroy mildly toxic compounds. Remember, however, that cooking will not make poisonous varieties safe to eat. Fungi differ slightly worldwide, and you should learn the ones in your area or in the place to which you are traveling.

Hen-of-the-woods (Grifola frondosa)
Found from spring to autumn, this bracket fungus grows on deciduous trees. It has a mushroom odor and a sweet flavor.

Beefsteak Fungus (Fistulina hepatica)
This fungus is found on oak trees in autumn. Its red flesh tastes bitter when raw, so it must be soaked, then stewed before being eaten.

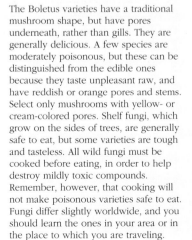

POISONOUS FUNGI

There are no features that characterize all poisonous fungi. Amanitas are among the most poisonous, and are perhaps the easiest to identify, but other kinds look completely different. Worse, some poisonous ones resemble edible mushrooms in other countries. The signs of fungus poisoning vary.

Unless you can positively identify a fungus as an edible variety, leave it alone. Below are a few of the most poisonous species of mushroom.

WARNING

Although the Amanita fungi contain the most deadly of all mushrooms, not all poisonous fungi look like them. You should always rely on making a positive identification of an edible variety, rejecting all others, unless you are certain that they are safe.

Death Cap (Amanita phalloides)
The most deadly poisonous of all, the death cap is found in woodlands, under beech or oak trees. It has an olive-green cap, a pale stem, white gills and flesh, and a large volva.

Panther Cap (Amanita pantherina)
This fungus is often deadly. Found in beech woods, it has a brown, white-flecked cap, white gills, and two or three rings around its stem.

Fly Agaric (Amanita muscaria muscaria)
This easily recognizable mushroom is found in autumn, particularly in beech and pine woods. It has a bright red cap flecked with white.

OTHER POISONOUS FUNGI

Some poisonous varieties of fungi often appear identical to edible ones in other areas. For example, while many of the Agaricus species can be eaten, the yellow-staining mushroom (*Agaricus xanthodermus*) is very poisonous. It can be recognized by its strong smell of iodine, and the yellow bruise that forms when it is touched. Other poisonous varieties of fungi include the fool's mushroom (*Amanita verna*), which is white and found in sandy soil under broad-leaved trees; and several Cortinarius species, some of which are deadly.

RECOGNIZING POISONOUS FUNGI

Poisonous Amanita mushrooms are fairly easy to identify. They all have a volva, or cup, at the base of the stem, white gills, and rings around the stalk.

Destroying Angel (Amanita virosa)
Deadly poisonous, this fungus is found during summer and autumn in woods. Its white flesh smells sweet and sickly. Young specimens can look like an edible Agaricus mushroom.

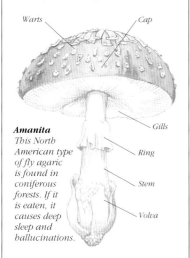

Warts   Cap

Gills

Ring

Stem

Volva

Amanita
This North American type of fly agaric is found in coniferous forests. If it is eaten, it causes deep sleep and hallucinations.

EDIBLE LICHEN

Lichen are usually found growing on rocks, often in northern or arctic regions. There are no poisonous kinds, but they must all be soaked in water overnight and boiled well to remove irritating acid, before being eaten.

Reindeer Moss (Cladonia rangiferina)
This hardy plant grows in arctic regions, and is named for its resemblance to reindeer antlers. Before being eaten, reindeer moss must be soaked in water for several hours, then boiled well to make it digestible.

Rock Tripe (Umbillicaria spp.)
This nutritious lichen grows in northern temperate and arctic regions. It must first be soaked, then boiled before being eaten.

PLANTS AS FOOD

GATHERING PLANT FOODS is not just a matter of foraging for anything that seems edible. You must collect enough of one or more species to make a meal, or part of a meal. Restricting yourself to gathering only a few species lessens the chances of including something inedible or poisonous *(see page 84)*. When gathering plants, make sure you leave enough of each species to allow regeneration, thereby providing another meal. Crushed plants spoil very quickly, so carry them in a box or bag.

DIGGING FOR ROOTS

Some plants store starch in their roots for use in the following growing season. In the spring this turns to sugar, which feeds the new shoots. Roots are thus most nutritious in autumn, and sweetest in spring. Take care when gathering roots in spring, however, since some plants may be hard to identify at this time.

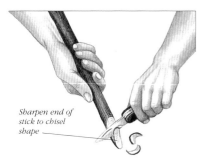

Sharpen end of stick to chisel shape

1 Cut a strong stick from a hardwood such as hickory, and sharpen one end to a chisel shape. The end can be hardened in a fire for even more strength.

Dig to one side of plant, loosening earth around the root

2 Dig deeply to the side of the plant. Loosen the earth around the root until it can be removed in one piece.

PREPARING ROOTS

You should prepare and cook roots as soon as possible after gathering them, to prevent them from spoiling. Roots should be carefully cleaned but not peeled, since the skin often contains valuable vitamins. Cut the roots into chunks and boil them in water. This removes the bitter chemicals present in some roots. The chunks are cooked when they are soft enough for you to be able to insert a fork into them.

MAKING FLOUR

Most seeds cannot be properly digested unless they are first ground into flour. You can add the flour to stews or mix it with a little water to make dough, which can then be baked into pastry or damper bread *(see page 117)*. You can also make flour from many nuts *(see page 88)*, as well as from roots and flower heads.

Toss seeds to separate them from the husks

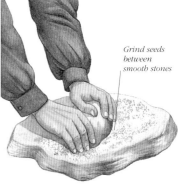

Grind seeds between smooth stones

1 To make flour from seeds, begin by bending the plant's seed head into a bag. Either shake the head to dislodge the seeds, or pull off the seeds with your hand. Lay the seeds in the sun to dry.

2 Thresh the seeds by rubbing them to loosen the husks. Then winnow by tossing and shaking in a container. Being lighter, the husks (chaff) will separate from the seeds, and be blown out of the container.

3 Grind the seeds by rubbing them between a large stone with a depression in the center, and a smooth stone. Use a steady, circular motion. Take care that the resulting flour does not blow away.

USING SEAWEED

Carrageen seaweed *(Chondrus)* can be eaten fresh, dried, or cooked into a gelatin-like pudding. It is rich in iodine, minerals, and vitamins A and B. It is found on lower-shore rocks in spring and early summer. You can also boil and eat the leaves of laver *(Porphyria)*, sea lettuce *(Ulva)*, and various kelps *(Alaria)*.

Dry seaweed on a rock in the sun

1 Gather the seaweed by cutting it from the rocks with your knife. Lay it in the sun to dry. As they dry, the strands will grow paler and become leathery.

2 After rinsing the seaweed to remove grit, cut it into pieces.

3 Add the seaweed to water or milk, and simmer it over a fire until the mixture begins to thicken.

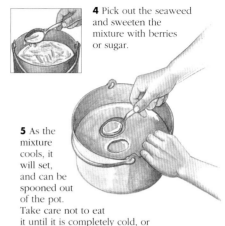

4 Pick out the seaweed and sweeten the mixture with berries or sugar.

5 As the mixture cools, it will set, and can be spooned out of the pot. Take care not to eat it until it is completely cold, or you may burn your mouth.

MAKING DRINKS

Needles from evergreen trees such as pine *(Pinus)* and spruce *(Picea)* are rich in vitamins A and C and can be used to make tea. You should collect only fresh green needles with no discoloration. A substitute for coffee can be made from chicory leaves *(Chicorium)* or acorns *(Quercus)*.

1 To make tea from evergreen needles, gather two teaspoons per cup of water. Bruise them by rubbing them with a large stone.

2 Drop the needles into boiling water. Keep the pot hot but not simmering, and let the needles infuse for between 5 and 10 minutes, stirring them occasionally.

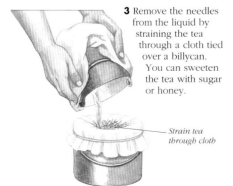

3 Remove the needles from the liquid by straining the tea through a cloth tied over a billycan. You can sweeten the tea with sugar or honey.

Strain tea through cloth

OTHER DRINKS

In Australia, leaves from the eucalyptus tree *(Eucalyptus)* impart a refreshing menthol-type flavor to ordinary tea. This brew is known as "billy tea." The dried flower heads of clover *(Trifolium)* and the leaves of nettle *(Urtica)* and ground ivy *(Glechoma)* can also be used to make tea. Sap from maple trees *(Acer)* can be mixed with water and drunk.

NATURAL FLAVORINGS

Wild plant foods are often rather bland in taste, and you may want to liven them up a bit with spices and seasonings. Prepared spices such as curry powder, cinnamon, and cloves, carried in your backpack, can be added to dishes as required. Alternatively, you can collect spices and flavorings in their wild state and dry them for use later on. An example of a spice that you may find growing wild is nutmeg, the kernel of a fruit from an evergreen *(Myristica)* native to the east Indonesian islands. After being dried, the kernel can be grated or chopped to flavor baked foods, puddings *(see above)*, or dishes made from vegetables such as spinach or squash. Savory flavors can be obtained from herbs such as basil and thyme.

CINNAMON

CURRY POWDER

CHILI POWDER

PEPPERS

NUTMEG

GARLIC

INVERTEBRATES

THE IDEA OF eating slugs, snails, or grasshoppers makes most people feel that they would rather go hungry or wait until something more appetizing comes along. In a survival situation, however, an acceptable meal is unlikely simply to drop into your lap, and while you wait, you will get weaker and less able to investigate other sources of food. Experimentation is vital, and to survive, no potential source of food should be rejected – regardless of how squeamish you might feel. Some invertebrates, such as insect grubs, contain more protein than vegetables, so it is worth your while to collect them.

EDIBLE INVERTEBRATES

Although many kinds of invertebrate are edible, you do not simply pop slugs or grasshoppers into your mouth, chew well, and swallow. Only parts of these creatures are edible, and they must all be well cooked before being eaten. Some must even be specially prepared *(see page 96)*. Below are a few examples of edible invertebrates.

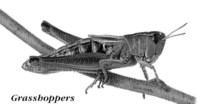

Grasshoppers
All hopping insects have large leg muscles, which can be eaten. Roasting kills parasites and gives the meat, by wilderness gourmet standards, a good flavor.

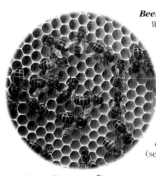

Bees
Wild bees and their pupae and larvae are all edible. In addition, bees produce honey, which provides instant energy. Take care when dealing with bees, since their stings can cause anaphylactic shock (see page 180).

Snails
Worms, slugs, and snails provide excellent eating, but avoid all sea snails and any bright land snails, which may be poisonous.

Ants
All ants can sting or bite, but they can be eaten if gathered carefully (see page 96). Some honey ants store nectar and water in their distended abdomens.

Butterflies and Moths
Butterflies and moths can be eaten, but they do not provide much nutrition unless caught in large numbers. Caterpillars are much easier to catch and make more of a meal.

OTHER EDIBLE INVERTEBRATES

Insects have a higher dietary value than vegetables, and are plentiful everywhere, although you do have to gather a great many to obtain sufficient nutritional value from them. Beetle grubs are particularly juicy. Some indigenous peoples rely heavily on grubs to supplement their diets, and spend many hours collecting them. Do not forget aquatic insects, such as the whirligig beetle (Gyrinidae), although they can be difficult to catch unless you use a fine mesh net. Other edible invertebrates include termites, sowbugs, and shellfish. It is not advisable to eat spiders, since many have irritating hairs or toxins in their mouthparts to kill their prey, and these can be harmful to humans.

Starfish
Starfish can often be found on driftwood. Crabs and shrimps are also edible, and may be found in rock pools at low tide.

Sea Urchins
Some echinoderms, such as the the cake urchin (Echinocyamus), can be dug up on a sandy beach and eaten. Take care when collecting them, since some have long spines.

POISONOUS INVERTEBRATES

The rules of common sense apply to collecting invertebrates for food. Avoid brightly colored insects, those eating carrion, sickly or dead individuals, or any that have a potent smell, since they may be poisonous. Invertebrates eaten by other animals may still be harmful to humans. Take care when collecting invertebrates *(see page 96).*

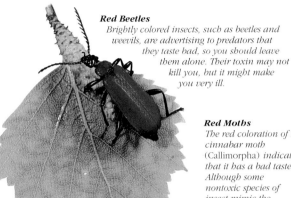

Red Beetles
Brightly colored insects, such as beetles and weevils, are advertising to predators that they taste bad, so you should leave them alone. Their toxin may not kill you, but it might make you very ill.

Cone Shells
All the hundreds of types of cone shell shoot a harpoon barb that injects poisons. In some varieties this is lethal. Cone shells bury themselves in sand, and you may step on one accidentally.

Red Moths
The red coloration of the cinnabar moth (Callimorpha) *indicates that it has a bad taste. Although some nontoxic species of insect mimic the colors of poisonous varieties, it is best to avoid all those with bright colors.*

WARNING

As with all wild food, it is best to learn to identify a few edible invertebrates and avoid the rest. If you are in a survival situation, you may be weak and susceptible to smaller amounts of poison than you would be normally.

OTHER POISONOUS INVERTEBRATES

Hairy caterpillars and bristleworms have irritating substances in their spines that can cause a rash if you touch them. Centipedes, especially the large, tropical species, often have poisonous substances in their skins. Some species of yellow ladybird (Coccinellidae) are also poisonous. Although most octopus species are edible, the blue-ringed octopus of Australia *(Hapalochlaena)* has a lethal sting, so it is best to avoid all species unless you can positively identify them. You should also avoid pupae buried in the soil, and formica ants *(Formica),* which can squirt formic acid at attackers. If you cannot identify invertebrates, leave them alone.

Marine Hydrozoans
Stinging hydrozoans such as hydra (Hydra) *are found in warm currents. The Portuguese man o' war* (Physalia) *can have stinging tentacles up to 42 ft (12 m) long. Avoid these creatures if possible. You should also avoid jellyfish, some of which can deliver a poisonous sting* (see page 180).

Wasps
Wasps are very aggressive, and their stings work even after they die. Never try to catch wasps to eat. If you are stung on the face, the swelling may impede breathing, sometimes resulting in death.

Shellfish
Shellfish are generally edible when cooked, but they are also potentially dangerous. To feed, they sieve large quantities of water, and may thus concentrate pollutants and poisons within their bodies. All mollusks must be collected live and prepared and eaten as soon as possible.

Sea Anemones
Anemones can sometimes be found clinging to rocks in tidal pools. Most have tentacles that produce an irritating sting, and they should therefore be avoided. Most creatures that kill their prey with stings can be harmful to humans, and they should be avoided if possible.

INVERTEBRATES AS FOOD

INVERTEBRATES are far more plentiful than other animals, and are often the only creatures living in the most extreme conditions and environments. It is easier to gather invertebrates such as insects than to catch fish, and doing so also expends less energy.

However, invertebrates may appear less palatable than other creatures. In order to overcome this, you may want to chop them up or grind them finely, then add them to other, highly flavored dishes, rather than eating them whole.

FLYING INSECTS

Most flying insects, such as moths, can be eaten, but the honey bee provides the best food. Adult bees and larvae can be eaten, and they provide honey. However, since bees can be dangerous, only collect them if there is no other option.

Bees and Honey
To gather bees and honey, hold smoking grass to the nest entrance until the nest is full of smoke. Seal up the hole and leave it overnight. In the morning, cautiously dig into the entrance with a stick and scrape out the dead bees and honeycomb.

Night Fliers
At night, stretch a light-colored sheet between two branches and peg its bottom edge taut. Place a flashlight behind the sheet, and put a bowl of water on the ground in front. Moths will be attracted to the light, hit the sheet, and fall into the water.

PREPARING INSECTS

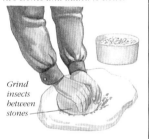

Remove stings from bees. Cut off the wings and legs of all insects. Insects provide the best nutrition if eaten raw, but they can be made more palatable by being boiled or roasted.

Grinding
Insects may be ground between two stones and added to stews.

Grind insects between stones

CRAWLING INSECTS

Beetle grubs are very nutritious, and can be found in rotting tree stumps or under bark. Probe rotten wood with a stick to see if there are any grubs under the surface. Caterpillars are found on their food plants, often in large colonies, but bear in mind that many have irritating hairs that may sting when touched.

1 To collect termites or ants, first cut a long, straight stick and peel it so it is smooth. Then push it slowly into a termite or ant nest. Have a container at hand so that you can collect the insects without dropping any on the ground.

2 Withdraw the stick slowly and gently. Termites will have attacked the stick and will still be attached to it by their jaws. Scrape them off into a container. You can then prepare them as above.

TRAPPING INSECTS

You can collect insects in a trap. Dig a hole the depth of your billycan and sit the can in it. Lay a slab of wood over the hole, balanced on two stones. This will leave a shallow space between the wood and the ground around the hole. Insects will crawl under it seeking shade, and will fall into the trap. Adding a drop of water to the billycan will provide a further attraction.

PITFALL TRAP

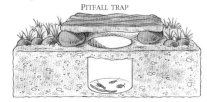

SHELLFISH

Shellfish are easy to collect on most beaches, and can be very nutritious. However, you must make sure that they are still alive when you collect them, since their flesh deteriorates quickly after death. Always cook and eat shellfish immediately after collection. Do not collect them near any source of pollution.

Digging for Razor Clams
Razor clams burrow vertically into sand, leaving breathing holes at the tops of their tunnels. You can hook them through these holes with a piece of wire or a thin stick. Alternatively, sprinkle salt around the burrow entrances and pull up the shells as they surface.

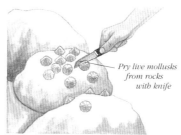

Pry live mollusks from rocks with knife

Periwinkles and Limpets
Pry small mollusks such as limpets from rocks at low tide. Only take those that are alive – they will be clinging tightly.

WARNING

Caution when dealing with shellfish cannot be overstated. They must never be eaten raw, and should be boiled or steamed for at least five minutes, as soon after collection as possible.

COOKING SHELLFISH

Boil shellfish in their shells for at least five minutes before eating them. Discard mussels that fail to open in boiling water, since this means that they are rotten. After boiling, limpets and periwinkles can be extracted from their shells with a fork.

Billycan hangs from forked twig (see page 116)

Shellfish Stew
Boil shellfish to eliminate harmful substances.

OTHER INVERTEBRATE DELICACIES

Many snails, slugs, and worms are edible, and can be gathered at dawn. Keep snails and slugs alive on a diet of green leaves for 24 hours before killing them by dropping them into boiling water. You can boil snails, but slugs are better roasted. Soak worms in salty water for 24 hours, then squeeze out their guts before adding them to stews or drying them.

Honey Ants
Honey ants feed on nectar and water, and individuals become living storage jars, hanging up in the nest.

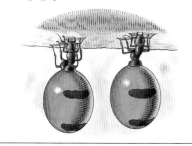

DRESSING A CRAB

When collecting crabs, avoid being pinched by their claws. With large species, you may have to tie up their claws to prevent them from fighting and damaging each other. Kill by plunging them into vigorously boiling water.

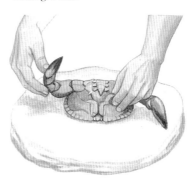

1 A crab must be dressed carefully so that all the poisonous organs are removed. To prepare a crab for eating, first twist off the legs, then the large claws. All contain edible meat.

2 Open the crab's shell by inserting the tip of your knife between the two halves and twisting it.

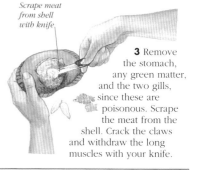

Scrape meat from shell with knife

3 Remove the stomach, any green matter, and the two gills, since these are poisonous. Scrape the meat from the shell. Crack the claws and withdraw the long muscles with your knife.

FRESHWATER FISH

FRESHWATER FISH LIVE in rivers, streams, and lakes, and in the estuaries of rivers above where the freshwater becomes salty and enters the sea. A handful of species travel the length of rivers, while some saltwater fish, notably salmon, migrate inland to spawn in the relative safety of inland streams.

The condition and size of freshwater fish vary according to the amount and variety of food they eat, as well as to the seasons. Although lakes and some rivers may have deep stretches well away from the banks, most freshwater fish live in the relatively shallow and narrow waters at the edges.

EDIBLE FISH

Most fish found in freshwater can be safely eaten, although some species are more pleasant to eat or easier to prepare than others. Some fish have a lot of tiny bones that make their preparation difficult, and the bones can be dangerous if they get caught in your throat. Below are a few examples of edible freshwater fish.

Bream (Abramis, Pagellus)
The bream belongs to the same family (Carp) as the goldfish and the minnow, or "tiddler." It feeds quietly on the bottoms of deep, slow-flowing rivers throughout Europe and Asia. Some individuals can grow to a very large size.

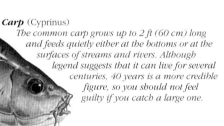

Tench (Tinca)
The tench lives in the still water of the lower reaches of rivers before they merge with the sea. It is found in Europe, North America, and Australia.

Carp (Cyprinus)
The common carp grows up to 2 ft (60 cm) long and feeds quietly either at the bottoms or at the surfaces of streams and rivers. Although legend suggests that it can live for several centuries, 40 years is a more credible figure, so you should not feel guilty if you catch a large one.

Trout (Oncorhynchus)
The trout is closely related and very similar to the salmon (see page 100). The rainbow trout lives in cool, clear streams and lakes in Scandinavia, North America, Australasia, Africa, and India.

Rudd (Scardinus)
The rudd lives in still water where there is a lot of vegetation, behind which it can hide. It is found in North America, Europe, and Scandinavia. The rudd is a surface feeder, although some old, large individuals often lie on the bottom.

OTHER EDIBLE FISH

There are a great many other species of edible freshwater fish, especially in tropical rivers and lakes. Common species around the world include the dace and chub (*Leuciscus*), and the roach (*Rutilus*). Observation will determine which species are surface or bottom feeders, and experimentation will tell you which are the best for eating. Be careful, however, when handling an unknown species. If in doubt, grill it, remove the skin and bones, then boil the flesh.

DANGEROUS FISH

Predatory fish are more aggressive than their prey, and also eat smaller members of their own species. Many of these fish have sharp barbs, which may be connected to poison sacs. Their skin mucus may also be toxic, causing a rash on human skin when touched. The mucus may make the fish poisonous to eat unless skinned.

Pickerel (Esox)
This is a North American member of the pike family, and can grow up to 3 ft (1 m) long. It prefers still, clear water with vegetation, and lives in rivers and streams that drain into the Atlantic. It has sharp teeth.

Tandan (Tandanus)
A member of the catfish family, the tandan lives in still water in Australasia and the Indo-Pacific region. Other catfish are found worldwide. The catfish's dorsal or pectoral fin can have a strong spine, sometimes attached to a poison sac. Catfish are also covered in poisonous mucus.

OTHER DANGEROUS FISH

Many edible freshwater fish can cause injuries with their sharp teeth or spines, or have skins coated with poisonous mucus. The infamous piranha *(Serrasalmus)* of tropical South America is an example of a voracious, dangerous fish, while the electric eel *(Electrophorus)*, also of South America, can injure a swimmer or wader with a powerful electric shock.

Bullhead (Ictalurus)
The bullhead has poisonous spines and is covered in toxic mucus. It must be handled carefully, and should be skinned before being eaten (see page 110). The bullhead eats plants and insects, feeding mostly on the bottoms of slow, still streams, particularly in North America and Europe. It is a type of catfish, and has the characteristic whiskers of this family.

Perch (Perca)
The perch is a voracious feeder, moving mainly in schools, which can considerably reduce fish stocks, especially of smaller fish. It is found in still or slow-flowing rivers and streams in Europe, Asia, North America, and Australia. It is good to eat, but be careful of its sharp dorsal fin.

WARNING

Once dead, unless they are preserved by being dried, smoked, or pickled (see page 118), all fish rapidly become dangerous to eat because of the growth of bacteria. Unless you have killed it yourself, therefore, it is best not to eat any dead fish, regardless of how fresh you believe it to be.

Pike (Esox)
The pike is solitary and aggressive, with razor-sharp teeth. In some areas it is known as the "river wolf" because of its greed and destructiveness, and it will fight and eat fish of its own size. It does, however, make good eating. It is found in Europe and North America, in most types of water.

Walleye (Stizostedion)
Sometimes known as a "pikeperch" because of its similarity to its close relatives, the pike and the perch, the walleye is named for its large, glassy eyes, which glow in the dark when light is shone on them. It is found chiefly in North America, and belongs to the perch family, so it is good to eat. However, it has a sharp dorsal fin, so be careful when handling it.

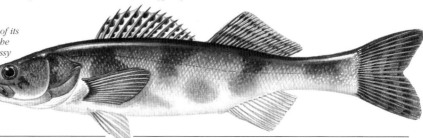

SALTWATER FISH

As a GENERAL rule, the biggest saltwater fish live in deep seas, while large schools of smaller fish live in shallow waters just offshore, where sunlight can penetrate to the bottom, enabling vegetation to grow. Fish may migrate long distances for food and to breed, assailed by a host of predators. Large fish will sometimes come close enough to the shore to be caught by a net or a hook and line, but are more likely to be caught from a boat offshore. In a survival situation, if you have no boat, you can wade in sea shallows or estuaries to catch saltwater fish, or walk out to deep channels at low tide.

EDIBLE FISH

There are only a few fish that cannot be eaten. The most sensible and healthy way of consuming fish is raw, which preserves all their natural oils and fragile food values. To cook fish, steam, grill, or bake them *(see page 117)*. Do not, however, eat the skin, which may be coated with toxic mucus or have dangerous spines.

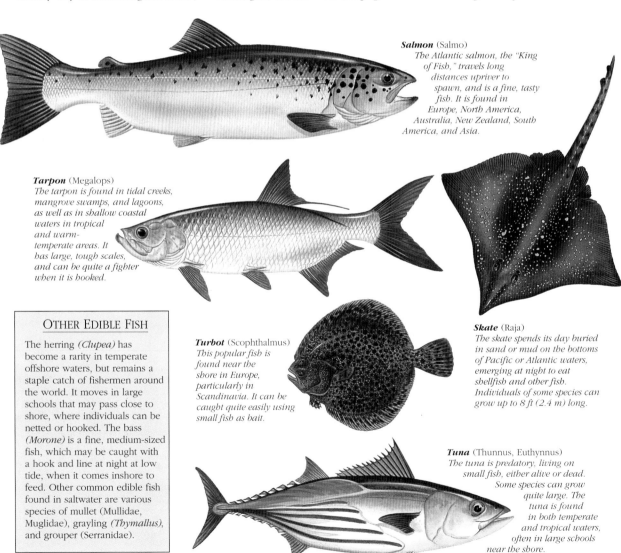

Salmon (Salmo)
The Atlantic salmon, the "King of Fish," travels long distances upriver to spawn, and is a fine, tasty fish. It is found in Europe, North America, Australia, New Zealand, South America, and Asia.

Tarpon (Megalops)
The tarpon is found in tidal creeks, mangrove swamps, and lagoons, as well as in shallow coastal waters in tropical and warm-temperate areas. It has large, tough scales, and can be quite a fighter when it is hooked.

OTHER EDIBLE FISH

The herring *(Clupea)* has become a rarity in temperate offshore waters, but remains a staple catch of fishermen around the world. It moves in large schools that may pass close to shore, where individuals can be netted or hooked. The bass *(Morone)* is a fine, medium-sized fish, which may be caught with a hook and line at night at low tide, when it comes inshore to feed. Other common edible fish found in saltwater are various species of mullet (Mullidae, Muglidae), grayling *(Thymallus)*, and grouper (Serranidae).

Turbot (Scophthalmus)
This popular fish is found near the shore in Europe, particularly in Scandinavia. It can be caught quite easily using small fish as bait.

Skate (Raja)
The skate spends its day buried in sand or mud on the bottoms of Pacific or Atlantic waters, emerging at night to eat shellfish and other fish. Individuals of some species can grow up to 8 ft (2.4 m) long.

Tuna (Thunnus, Euthynnus)
The tuna is predatory, living on small fish, either alive or dead. Some species can grow quite large. The tuna is found in both temperate and tropical waters, often in large schools near the shore.

DANGEROUS FISH

Even though the biggest fish tend to inhabit deep waters, large and dangerous species do patrol shallow waters looking for an easy meal.

Hungry sharks have been known to come up to beaches to seize animals and bathers. They can sense blood and the sound of distressed animals or fish in water over long distances. Some fish have spines or stings that can cause excruciating pain if hooked on human flesh. Others have sharp teeth.

Stingray (Urolophus, Dasyatis)
The stingray has venomous spines and a whiplike tail. Its sting can be fatal if not treated promptly. It lives in the North Pacific and in tropical waters.

Barracuda
(Sphyraena)
The barracuda has razor-sharp teeth and may attack swimmers. Small species are edible, and can be found in shallow water, but they too can bite. They also leap when hooked, and can therefore be difficult to catch. The barracuda is found in warm- temperate and tropical waters worldwide.

OTHER FISH TO AVOID

Triggerfish (Balistidae), which live in shallow, tropical seas, each have a single spine protruding from the abdomen like a trigger. Their flesh is poisonous if eaten. The tropical stonefish *(Synanceia)*, toadfish (Batrachoididae), and scorpionfish (Scorpaenidae) all have venomous spines. Weever fish (Trachinidae), found off Europe and West Africa, lie buried in sand, and their spines can cause excruciating pain.

Mackerel (Scomberomorus)
The mackerel makes excellent, if oily, eating. In spring it moves in huge schools offshore, where it can be netted. However, it swims fast, and has sharp teeth, fighting hard when caught. It is found worldwide.

WARNING

When spear fishing, get out of the water as soon as you spear a fish. The smell of blood and the sound of its struggling will travel a long way, attracting predators. Avoid splashing, since predators perceive this as a fish in trouble.

Marlin (Makaira, Tetrapturus)
The marlin is found in warm-temperate and tropical waters. Although it is very good to eat, catching it can be difficult, since it swims fast and fights hard when caught. It also has a tough, sharp, swordlike bill. The marlin is best caught by trolling at the surface or in mid-water.

Wahoo (Acanthocybium)
The wahoo leaps from the water when hooked, making it hard to catch. It also has razor-sharp teeth, so it can be dangerous when landed. It is found worldwide in warm and temperate waters.

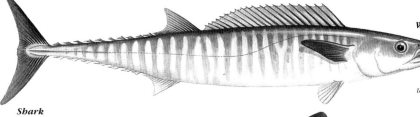

Shark
There are hundreds of species of shark worldwide, many of which are aggressive and will fight when hooked. These species sometimes "play dead" when landed, catching fishermen off guard. The leopard shark (Triakis) lives in shallow, inshore waters along the Pacific coast of North America. Shark liver is poisonous if eaten.

ANGLING EQUIPMENT

CATCHING FISH IS very much a question of trial, error, and a lot of patience. Without strong, ready-made equipment, fish may be caught and then get away. Fish can be hooked, trapped, netted, snagged, speared, or even picked up in your hands *(see page 100)*. Hooks, lures, and floats can be made of all kinds of material, both natural and manmade. Line can be made from natural grasses *(see page 34)*, or you can use the fishing line in your survival kit *(see page 28)*. You can improvise a rod from a stick. Take great care not to break your improvised equipment when fish bite, and make sure you have ready alternate methods of snagging or netting to ensure that nothing gets away.

THORN HOOK

Cut notch around stem

Tie line around notch

Finished Hook
Use this hook for fish that swallow bait whole, such as eels and catfish. The hook may also catch in the gills or mouths of other fish.

1 Cut a section of bramble stem about 1 in (2.5 cm) long, with a large, strong thorn.

2 Using a pocketknife, cut a notch in the end of the stem so that the line does not slip when it is tied around it.

3 Tie the fishing line around the stem notch, making several turns over the top.

NAIL HOOK AND FEATHER LURE

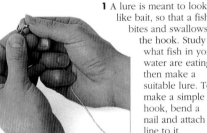

1 A lure is meant to look like bait, so that a fish bites and swallows the hook. Study what fish in your water are eating, then make a suitable lure. To make a simple hook, bend a nail and attach a line to it.

2 Tie a feather above the hook to act as a lure. It may resemble an insect and attract a fish.

Finished Lure
Make sure that the hook is tied securely to the line, so that you do not lose the hook when a fish bites.

ROSE-HIP FLOAT AND PIN HOOK

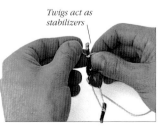

Thread line through rose hip

Twigs act as stabilizers

1 You can use natural materials to make a float. To use a rose hip, make a hole in it with a knife, a sharp stick, or a thorn.

2 Thread fishing line or string through the rose hip. A float keeps a baited hook at the best depth for the fish being sought.

3 Tie small twigs above and below the float to act as stabilizers and to prevent the float from slipping up and down the line.

4 Attach your hook (in this case a safety pin) at the desired depth below the float.

BAIT

Bait may be spread on the surface of the water, attached firmly to hooks, or placed inside traps. Insects, small fruits, worms, bread, raw meat, and pieces of fish all work well as bait. Live bait attracts fish by its movement, indicating injury and an easy meal. The secret of successful baiting is to tempt fish with their normal diet.

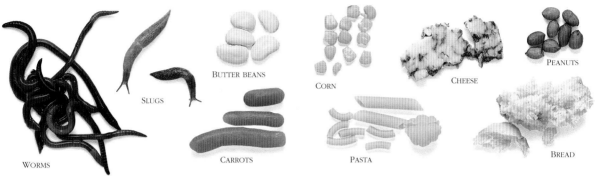

WORMS

SLUGS

BUTTER BEANS

CARROTS

CORN

PASTA

CHEESE

PEANUTS

BREAD

TRAP HARPOON

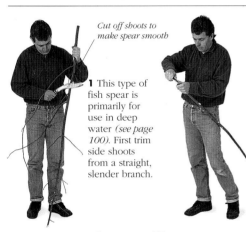

Cut off shoots to make spear smooth

1 This type of fish spear is primarily for use in deep water *(see page 100)*. First trim side shoots from a straight, slender branch.

Sharpen spear to a long point

2 Sharpen the thick end of the shaft to a good, long point. This point may be hardened by carefully dipping it in the flames of a fire. Carve opposite sides of the point to a flat surface, to which the trap will be lashed with cord.

3 Bind two sharp sticks to either side of the spear shaft so that they close over and beyond the point, making it hard for an impaled fish to wriggle off. The trap sticks are then wedged apart with a straight stick, which will fly off if pushed, allowing the trap sticks to close.

Spikes on sides of point prevent fish from escaping

SPIKED HARPOON

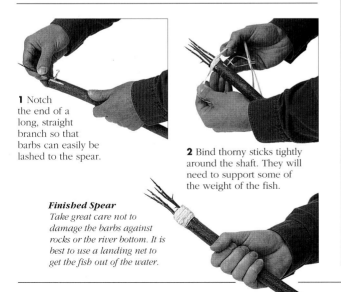

1 Notch the end of a long, straight branch so that barbs can easily be lashed to the spear.

2 Bind thorny sticks tightly around the shaft. They will need to support some of the weight of the fish.

Finished Spear
Take great care not to damage the barbs against rocks or the river bottom. It is best to use a landing net to get the fish out of the water.

TAKING CARE WHEN FISHING

Take great care when using improvised fishing gear, since it may break easily, causing you to lose either your catch or your balance. If you fall into the water, apart from the danger of drowning, you could contract pneumonia or infection from waterborne diseases *(see page 75)*. Do not enter muddy water without a stick for support and to feel the ground in front of you. Be aware that other animals – such as predators – may be fishing or drinking nearby.

Hunting the Fisherman
Look out for animal trails to watering points, and ensure that you are not offering yourself as bait for a predator.

ANGLING TECHNIQUES

To A MODERN sport fisherman, these traditional techniques will seem very crude. However, both his success, and yours with these methods, depend not upon equipment, but upon knowledge of the prey. Spend time observing where the fish go at different times of the day, when and where they feed, and what they eat. Then determine strategies for catching them. When using improvised fishing gear, take care not to break or lose it, and always think first of your own safety. The techniques described here can be used in freshwater rivers and streams or in saltwater creeks. Some of these techniques are illegal in many parts of the world, and should only be used in a matter of life or death.

USING HOOKS AND LINES

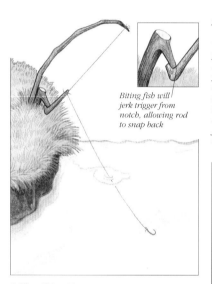

Biting fish will jerk trigger from notch, allowing rod to snap back

Running Line
The more hooks you have in the water, the greater your chances of a catch. But with this method your bait will be nibbled away faster than with a single hook. Only use this method in a survival situation, either in freshwater or across a saltwater creek.

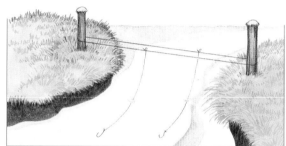

Self-striking Line
A self-striking line will operate by itself. When a fish bites, the line will be jerked out of the notch and the rod will fly back, embedding the hook in the fish's mouth.

ICE FISHING

Using an ice saw or knife, cut a small hole in the ice near the bank to check that it is at least 2 in (5 cm) thick, and will bear your weight. Cut a fishing hole about 1 ft (30 cm) across. Do not smash the ice, since this may weaken it, causing you to fall in. Tie your hooked and baited line to a flagged stick across the hole.

Baited Hook
Tie your line to a flag so that you do not have to keep checking your hook.

Fish Caught
When a fish is hooked, the flag is pulled upright, and you can collect the catch.

SPEAR FISHING

Trap Harpoon
This type of spear grabs the fish and keeps it from wriggling off the point.

TICKLING A FISH

1 This primitive method is illegal in most countries. It is most successful in sheltered water. Feel along the bank with your palms upward and your hands flat.

2 Slide your hands under a resting fish very slowly, thumbs uppermost. Then grab the fish and throw it well onto the bank.

Using a Harpoon
Spear fishing takes time and great patience. Be careful not to break your spears against rocks or the river bottom. Keeping the point of your spear in the water avoids splash. Strike very quickly once you see a potential catch.

LANDING A FISH

Pull upward to set hook

1 When a fish bites, "strike" sharply by pulling up the rod. Take great care not to break your gear, particularly when drawing fish toward the bank.

2 Take your time pulling in the fish. Use the net as early as you can to take the weight of the fish, entering the water yourself, if necesssary. Do not get carried away, however, either by your enthusiasm or by fast water. Your safety is more important than anything else.

USING A GAFF

Gaffing
As an emergency alternative to netting, grab the fish with a gaff. Do not lift the fish high in the air.

Gaff made from bent fork hooks fish

WHERE TO LOOK FOR FISH

Hidden Bounty
Fish are to be found where they can eat without feeling insecure, which varies according to species, the environment, and the time of day. Slack water (when a river is in flood), overhanging banks, large logs, and rocks all offer shelter, and in hot weather with bright sunshine, fish will seek shaded water or deep pools. In cold weather, look for fish in shallow water, for example at the edge of a lake, in an area warmed by the sun.

In fast or flood water, check downstream of boulders, or on the insides of bends, where the river flows more slowly than on the outsides

Overhanging trees create patches of shade where fish can rest on hot days

Check undercut banks quietly, without upsetting the fish

Fallen tree offers cool shelter

Check floating weed patches

Bubbles or rings on water's surface indicate feeding fish

Fish may rest in still water downstream of gravel bars, where fast water swirls back on itself to make a pool

FISHING NETS AND TRAPS

IN A SURVIVAL situation, fishing nets and traps are more convenient than hooks and lines, simply because they can be left for a couple of hours, or overnight, allowing you to get on with other things. Nets can be made from string, rope, or natural cord *(see page 34)*, with saplings as handles. You can also make a net from discarded clothing. Traps can be made from sticks and cord, woven from rushes or tough grasses, or improvised from manmade materials such as bottles. Improvised gear can be very effective, and should only be used in an emergency *(see page 104)*.

MAKING A LANDING NET

USING AN UNDERSHIRT

1 Thread the forks of a thin sapling into the hem of an undershirt, through two small nicks in the seam.

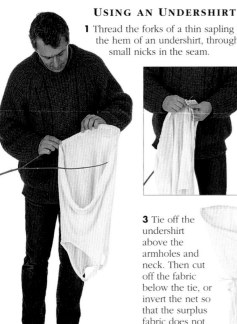

2 Cut a nick in the hem at the point where the forks meet and pull the ends of the stick through. Tie the sapling ends together with cord, and push them inside the hem.

3 Tie off the undershirt above the armholes and neck. Then cut off the fabric below the tie, or invert the net so that the surplus fabric does not drag in the water when you use it.

USING CORD

1 Tie the ends of a forked sapling together to form a circle.

2 Tie one end of pieces of cord to the circle. Tie the other ends of the cord to the opposite side of the circle to form loops.

3 Weave more cord in and out of the loops hanging from the sapling circle to create a net.

MAKING A GILLNET

Rope holds top of net steady

String is knotted around each hanging cord

Gillnets can be any size. Suspend a rope between two trees and tie one end of several pieces of cord at regular intervals along it. Pull the cords tight by tying their bottom ends to a narrow branch. Weave more cord in and out of the hanging strings, tying a knot around each one to secure the mesh. You can adjust the mesh to the size of fish you want to catch. The finished net can be cut from the rope and branch.

MAKING A BASKET TRAP

Hoop braces bars of trap and holds them apart

2 Make a hoop by tying together the ends of a sapling.

1 This trap can be used in a river or tidal creek. Bind together a bunch of saplings at their thick ends.

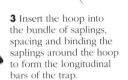

3 Insert the hoop into the bundle of saplings, spacing and binding the saplings around the hoop to form the longitudinal bars of the trap.

4 Tie in a second hoop at the opposite end to create the chamber of the trap. You can make it as long and as wide as you require.

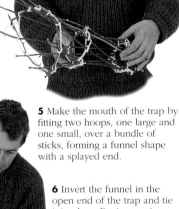

5 Make the mouth of the trap by fitting two hoops, one large and one small, over a bundle of sticks, forming a funnel shape with a splayed end.

6 Invert the funnel in the open end of the trap and tie it in place. Begin weaving cord around the bars to make the sides of the trap.

Tie cord to each bar to form mesh

7 Fill in the sides of the trap with cord. Fish can push their way in, but will not be able to get out *(see page 105).*

(see page 105)

OTHER TRAPS

Crab Cage
This trap is simple to make. Lash sticks together to form a box. You can adjust the size of the box to the type of creature you wish to catch. The door of the trap only opens inward, preventing the prey from leaving. Bait the trap and weight it with a rock to keep it on the bottom of the river or sea. Place the trap in shallow seawater to catch crabs and lobsters, or in a freshwater stream to catch crayfish.

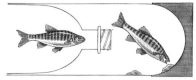

Bottle Trap
Cut the neck and shoulders off a plastic bottle, invert the top, and insert it into the base. Fish swim in through the neck to reach bait at the end, but cannot find their way out. Place the trap in a stream and check it regularly.

USING FISHING NETS AND TRAPS

YOU CAN LEAVE a hooked line overnight, but unless you check it at first light the next day, any fish caught is likely to be taken by larger fish, or to wriggle off, usually taking your hook with it. Unlike hooks, traps can be left for a few days at a time. Nets must not be used in the same way – they should only be set for short periods of time, or used for trawling. Fish of all sizes can be entangled or damaged in a gillnet, and if such a net is left across a flowing river, it can rapidly take or injure every fish in a stretch of water, irrespective of whether it is edible or not. For this reason, gillnets are illegal in many parts of the world. A gillnet should only be used in an emergency survival situation.

USING A GILLNET

1 In a desperate, long-term survival situation, you may have to dam a stream to catch fish to preserve for the oncoming winter. Build a rock wall in the center of a stream, choosing a bend where the water slows as the bed widens.

Set wall at angle across stream

2 Hammer three stout posts into the stream bed about 3 ft (1 m) apart. Set them diagonally across the stream so that the water does not knock over the finished log wall. Lay a couple of logs against the posts on the upstream side. Hammer in three retaining posts. Then add more logs to build up the wall.

Fish are forced down open channel and are caught in gill net

3 Hammer two posts on either side of the channel next to the wall, and tie your gill net between them *(see page 102)*. Fish will be diverted by the dam down the channel and will get caught in the net. When not fishing, remove the net and the horizontal logs in the wall to avoid catching fish unnecessarily and straining the posts.

PURSE SEINING

As the name indicates, a purse seine gathers fish as if in a drawstring purse. One person takes the end of the net over the shoulder and enters the water, while the other remains on the shore. The first person walks out to the limit of the net, then curves back to the shore, creating a purse with the net. As the person reaches the shore, any fish caught within the net are encircled and trapped. The net can then be dragged onto the beach and the fish killed.

Fishing on the Shore
Schools of fish can be caught in shallow water by two people using a large net.

ROCK WALL TRAPS

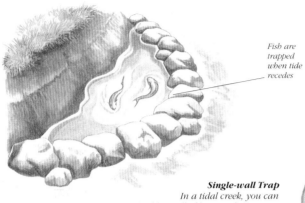

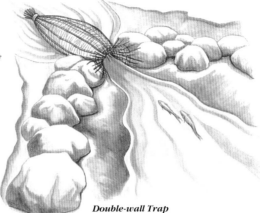

Fish are trapped when tide recedes

Single-wall Trap
In a tidal creek, you can build a wall of large rocks in a curve from the bank. When the tide recedes, fish may be trapped in the little pool created between the wall and the bank. On a seashore, if there is no turf bank or cliff, you can use the same principle, but you should build your wall in a complete circle. Any gaps between the large rocks can be plugged with small stones to prevent fish from escaping.

Double-wall Trap
Build two rock walls in a funnel shape, with the opening of the funnel facing downstream. Fish swimming downstream will be guided by the walls into a bottleneck. You can place your trap or net at this narrow opening to catch them (see page 102).

USING A DIP NET

1 Many fish dislike muddy water, since they find it hard to breathe with the reduced level of oxygen. Stir up the mud on the bottom of a pool with your feet. The fish should come to the surface in order to breathe.

Have net ready to catch fish

Stir up mud on bottom with feet

2 Use the net slowly and carefully, but when fish are inside, lift it quickly from the water, gathering the top of the net together like a bag to prevent the fish from jumping out.

Fish coming to surface can be caught in net

USING A BAITED NET

Some fish can be caught using a baited net. Use an undershirt net *(see page 106)*, or make one from a sock. Push a forked stick through the sock's hem as a handle. Bait the net with dung or fish offal, and trawl it slowly through the water.

Baiting Eels
Eels are often attracted to a net baited with offal or animal dung.

POINTS TO CONSIDER WHEN FISHING

■ Water is always dangerous, whether it is fast-flowing, still, shallow, or deep. Even a fall on wet rocks can be fatal.
■ Think through every aspect of how you intend to catch fish, trying to imagine the hazards before accidents occur – and take precautions against them.
■ Fish are adept at slithering back into the water. Think particularly about how you are going to land fish safely once you have caught them.
■ Underwater hazards vary from entangling weeds and dangerous creatures such as crocodiles, to deep potholes and strong currents. Do not enter a river or stream if you can avoid it, even if you can see the bottom.
■ Never jump or dive into water. Do not swim or bathe until you have taken cautious reconnaissance.
■ Take great care when using improvised fishing equipment, such as a spear, since it may break and cause you to fall in.

PREPARING FISH FOR COOKING

IMMEDIATELY AFTER LANDING a fish, kill it with a stick or stone, using a firm blow to the back of the head. You must gut a fish as soon as possible after catching it, then either cook and eat it, or preserve it for later use *(see page 118)*. In hot climates, only a short time in the sun can cause fish to spoil, since their moist skin is an ideal breeding ground for bacteria and flies. Once a fish has been scaled, skinned, and filleted, it is less likely to go bad. In cold climates you can afford to leave filleting for six to twelve hours after killing, which allows time for the nerve endings to die. This makes butchering easier than if you do it when the fish is freshly caught. The bones, skin, and head of the fish may be boiled in water to create stock – provided that you do this immediately. The stock must be treated in the same way as unpreserved flesh – kept cool and eaten as soon as possible.

FILLETING A FISH

Filleting removes the parts of a fish that are likely to spoil, while leaving as much of the flesh as possible. In addition, the fish may pick up contaminants from the environment, which can lodge in its internal organs. For example, metals such as mercury, present in small quantities in the sea, concentrate in the liver and can be fatal to humans if eaten, particularly in quantity. Harmful substances do not usually collect in the muscles of a fish.

Do not bear down on your knife – use only its point

Take care not to cut into the tail muscles

1 Most fish do not need to be skinned before being cooked. However, their scales must be removed. Scrape off the scales from the tail to the head with your knife, moving the blade away from you.

2 Insert the point of a sharp knife into the anal opening. Taking care to cut only through the outer belly, slit the fish open to just behind the gills. Do not cut the tail muscles or puncture the internal organs.

3 Carefully pull out the internal organs. Spread the fish open to check that everything has been removed. Save the roe (eggs in a female, or milt in a male) to eat, then wash the fish thoroughly, inside and out.

Cut off head and use to make stock

Pull out spines and ribs

4 Trim off the head, tail, and fins. Open up the body and separate the ribs from the flesh, using the point of your knife blade. You may find it easier to remove the bones after the fish has been cooked.

5 Separate the top of the spine from the flesh with the tip of your knife. Then, slowly and firmly, pull the spine and ribs away from the flesh in one piece. If the ribs do not come out cleanly, you may have to scrape the flesh from them with your knife.

SKINNING FISH

Not all species of fish must be skinned before being cooked, particularly the small ones. However, some fish secrete irritating or poisonous mucus on their skins. Others, such as catfish and sharks, have very tough skins. It is therefore best to remove and discard the skin before the fish is eaten.

Skinning a Fillet
Separate the skin and flesh. Hold the skin taut with one hand and cut the flesh from the skin in a sawing motion.

SKEWERING FISH FOR COOKING

Fish are best if eaten immediately after being caught and killed. The simplest, quickest cooking methods result in the tastiest flesh. Fish do not require much cooking. Grill them at an angle over an ember fire or impale them on a spit *(see page 116)*. Single fish can be fried whole in a pan, steamed, or baked in mud *(see page 117)*.

1 Open out the fillet, then insert two thin, supporting sticks across the top and bottom. Green sticks will char the least. Do not use wood with a lot of sap, since it may spit.

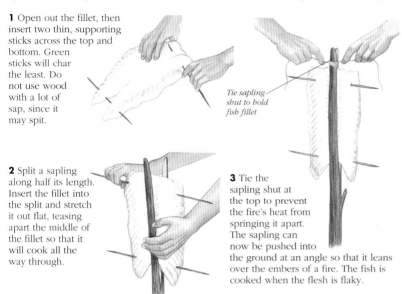

Tie sapling shut to hold fish fillet

2 Split a sapling along half its length. Insert the fillet into the split and stretch it out flat, teasing apart the middle of the fillet so that it will cook all the way through.

3 Tie the sapling shut at the top to prevent the fire's heat from springing it apart. The sapling can now be pushed into the ground at an angle so that it leans over the embers of a fire. The fish is cooked when the flesh is flaky.

COOKING SMALL FISH

Fry, grill, or roast small fish whole, without filleting them – there is no point in filleting anything that is less than 6 in (15 cm) long. After gutting, impale them on a green stick and grill over the embers of a fire, or in a pan. Do not remove the heads and tails, since they keep the flesh together.

Skewering
Gut small fish but leave the heads and tails on. Skewer the fish on a stake. You can then hold them over a fire.

SKINNING AN EEL

Eels make very good eating, but must first be gutted, skinned, and filleted before being cooked. Their length and slipperiness make skinning very difficult, unless you do it immediately after they are killed. Gut an eel using the method shown opposite, then skin it as shown below. You can also skin whole fish using this method.

1 Push a strong stick through the eel's gills just behind the skull. Hang the stick between two forked, upright sticks.

2 Grasp the eel with a cloth and cut through the skin all around the head. (Although it is dead, the eel may still twitch.)

3 Separate the top of the skin from the flesh. Then, using a firm, steady action, peel the skin down toward the tail. You will probably need to use both hands to get a good grip.

Using both hands, pull skin downward

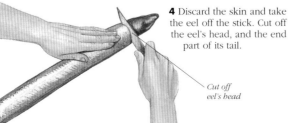

4 Discard the skin and take the eel off the stick. Cut off the eel's head, and the end part of its tail.

Cut off eel's head

Take care not to cut through the ribs

5 Holding the eel in place with a rough cloth, run a sharp knife steadily along the backbone, parallel to the surface on which the eel is lying. Do not cut too close to the backbone.

COOKING UTENSILS

THE BASIC COOKING utensils for camping are a pot, a stove or fire upon which to cook, and a wooden spoon. To conserve fuel when cooking, both pot and stove or fire must be sheltered from the wind, and a secure lid should be placed on the pot. Hygiene and tidiness when cooking are vital. Wash your hands first, then take from your backpack only what is needed to make your meal. Most backpacking food is best cooked and eaten as an all-in-one stew made with a lot of water in one pot. Experienced backpackers tend to mix together fruit, dessert, and main meals. This helps to conserve fuel and also saves on washing up.

Outdoor Cooking
Keep stoves sheltered from the wind, and make sure they do not fall over. Take care not to touch a hot pot with your bare hands.

POTS AND PANS

Eating straight from a pot, especially when cooking over an open fire, can result in burned fingers, lips, mouth, and tongue. The use of plastic plates and cups prevents this. Carrying a variety of cooking vessels is unnecessary, unless you are traveling with a large group of people or are in a vehicle. Choose one kind of pot that you are likely to use the most, and take good care of it.

Mug
A tough, plastic mug is invaluable. It should have a strong handle.

Plate
A plate holds a portion of food, leaving the rest to stay warm in the pot.

Bowl
A bowl can be used for breakfast cereal, soups, or stews.

UTENSILS

Retain your lightweight camping utensils for your own use only and, since they will go into your mouth, keep them scrupulously clean. Dirty utensils can cause mouth ulcers and other infections. To clean utensils, simmer them in boiling water whenever possible. If you lose or break your knife, fork, or spoon, you can carve new ones from wood *(see opposite)*. You can improvise utensils and dishes from sticks, bark, shelf fungi, bones, and clay.

Shallow Nonstick Pan
A nonstick pan is a help when camping, but take care not to damage the coated surface, since food can then stick to it quite badly.

Deep Nonstick Pan
A deep pan is useful when cooking for more than one or two people.

Kettle
A lightweight kettle allows you to use other pans for cooking food, rather than for heating water for hot drinks.

FORK   KNIFE   TEASPOON

UTENSIL HOLDER

Billycan Set
A high-quality billycan set is light and contains a variety of pans, and sometimes a kettle.

Frying Pan
Special, lightweight frying pans are available for camping. Take care not to burn them.

Aluminum Pot
Aluminum pots heat up quickly, but can burn food if not watched constantly.

MAKING A CLAY POT

Make rolls of clay between your hands

Keep walls vertical

Blend wet clay into gaps between coils

1 You can find clay in steep stream banks. Make a thick, circular base to give the pot strength and stability.

2 Keeping the sides straight, build up the walls of the pot with the rolls of clay.

3 Smooth off the lip of the top coil with your thumb once the desired pot height is achieved.

4 Smooth the pot with water. When the pot is dry, stand it in a fire to harden.

MAKING A WOODEN SPOON

Begin carving a spoon shape at one end of the wood

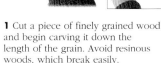

The bowl must be narrow enough to fit into your mouth

Use a knife to smooth away any splinters

1 Cut a piece of finely grained wood and begin carving it down the length of the grain. Avoid resinous woods, which break easily.

2 Always cut away from you in case the knife slips. The spoon should be small enough to fit comfortably into your mouth, although a narrow handle is not important.

3 Carving the bowl is the most difficult and time-consuming part. Take care not to make the wood so thin that it breaks. Smooth away any splinters.

MAKING A WOODEN BOWL

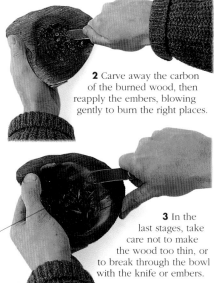

2 Carve away the carbon of the burned wood, then reapply the embers, blowing gently to burn the right places.

1 Carve a bowl from a block of wood or a burl. Wood burls can be extremely hard, so carving takes a long time. The careful use of embers from a fire can speed things up.

Keep burning and cutting to hollow out the bowl

3 In the last stages, take care not to make the wood too thin, or to break through the bowl with the knife or embers.

IMPROVISED POTS AND PANS

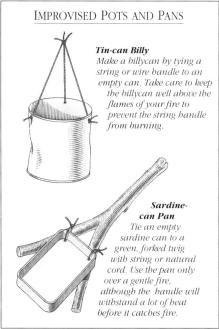

Tin-can Billy
Make a billycan by tying a string or wire handle to an empty can. Take care to keep the billycan well above the flames of your fire to prevent the string handle from burning.

Sardine-can Pan
Tie an empty sardine can to a green, forked twig with string or natural cord. Use the pan only over a gentle fire, although the handle will withstand a lot of heat before it catches fire.

STOVES AND OVENS

THE SIMPLEST FORM of cooking device is an open fire, or solid fuel blocks that burn with a regular flame for long enough to make a hot drink. If you cannot build a fire easily or safely, however, you will need a stove with a controllable flame that lights easily and burns fuel efficiently. For more elaborate cooking you can build an oven or a steam pit. Keep your stove, preheating tablets, matches, and cooking pot and lid in a side pouch of your backpack where you can easily reach them whenever you stop.

Filling a Stove
Choose a stove according to your cooking needs and whether you can get replacement gas cylinders or fuel. Before filling a stove with fuel, make sure that the flame is really out.

CAMPING STOVES

Small pan supports

Mini Stove
This ultra-lightweight stove burns a butane/propane fuel mixture. It is not suitable for supporting large pans.

Foldaway supports

General-purpose Stove
This fast-burning stove is for all-around use, and has foldaway supports for cooking with large pans.

Unleaded Fuel Stove
Burning unleaded gasoline, this stove has a purge control so that the generator can be blown clean.

Multifuel Stove
One of the most popular stoves around the world, this model will burn unleaded gasoline, kerosene, or aviation fuel.

WARNING

All stoves must be treated with great care. The danger of an explosion must always be kept in mind. Cooking areas must be well ventilated, since stoves use up oxygen and give off lethal carbon monoxide. When a pressurized gas stove goes out, vapor builds up, and any flame or spark will create a fireball explosion.

Nonpressurized Stove
This popular stove burns methyl alcohol and has a built-in windshield, as well as pans that pack away together. There are no mechanical parts to break down, and it is very stable, although it does not burn very fast.

FUEL

Fuel bottles must be easily distinguishable from water bottles so that you do not mix them up. They must be absolutely free from leaks, since leaking fuel could pollute food and rot clothes and equipment. Availability of fuel must be considered before travel, as well as safe disposal of cylinders.

SOLID FUEL

GASOLINE BOTTLE   KEROSENE BOTTLE   BUTANE/PROPANE CYLINDER

MUD OVEN

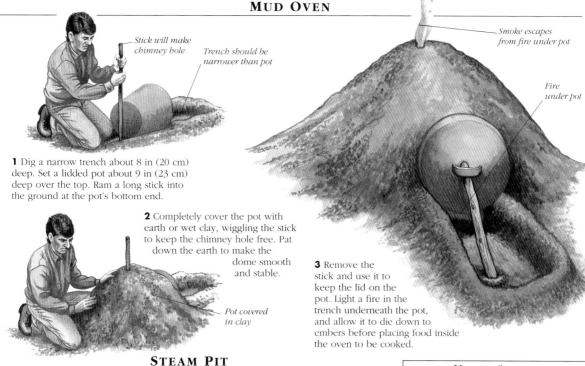

Stick will make chimney hole

Trench should be narrower than pot

Smoke escapes from fire under pot

Fire under pot

1 Dig a narrow trench about 8 in (20 cm) deep. Set a lidded pot about 9 in (23 cm) deep over the top. Ram a long stick into the ground at the pot's bottom end.

2 Completely cover the pot with earth or wet clay, wiggling the stick to keep the chimney hole free. Pat down the earth to make the dome smooth and stable.

Pot covered in clay

3 Remove the stick and use it to keep the lid on the pot. Light a fire in the trench underneath the pot, and allow it to die down to embers before placing food inside the oven to be cooked.

STEAM PIT

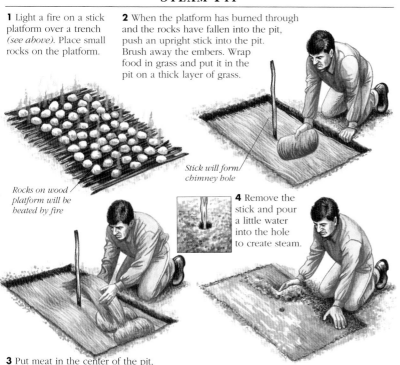

1 Light a fire on a stick platform over a trench (see above). Place small rocks on the platform.

2 When the platform has burned through and the rocks have fallen into the pit, push an upright stick into the pit. Brush away the embers. Wrap food in grass and put it in the pit on a thick layer of grass.

Stick will form chimney hole

Rocks on wood platform will be heated by fire

4 Remove the stick and pour a little water into the hole to create steam.

3 Put meat in the center of the pit, where there is the most heat. Put a thick layer of grass over the food. Cover the pit with earth.

5 Seal the the pit with earth, patting it smooth. Leave the pit for about four hours, during which the food will cook.

YUKON STOVE

Essentially a chimney above a fire, a Yukon stove will burn even damp wood, and cook very effectively at its top end. First build a tepee fire (see page 60) but do not light it. Erect a wall of stones around the tepee, using clay for mortar, and seal the outsides with clay. The cone shape of the structure increases the airflow around the fire, so creating more heat. Light the end of a long stick and push it into the fire from above. Use plenty of dry wood to get the fire going. When it is going well, you can dry wet wood on top of the stove.

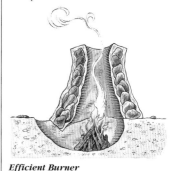

Efficient Burner
The Yukon stove burns fuel efficiently and with great heat.

COOKING METHODS

T HE MOST BASIC form of cooking is roasting, usually using a spit over the flames or the embers of a fire. In a survival situation, it is important to cook everything you are not sure about in order to kill harmful bacteria, parasites, and chemicals. Cooking also helps make many wild foods more palatable and

digestible than they would be if eaten raw. In addition, a hot meal cheers you up immensely.

Cooking Over an Open Fire
You can cook stews in a billycan suspended over your fire, or you can wait until the flames have died down, then use the embers for other forms of cooking (see opposite). If you have plenty of water, always keep some boiling for making hot drinks.

PAN RESTS

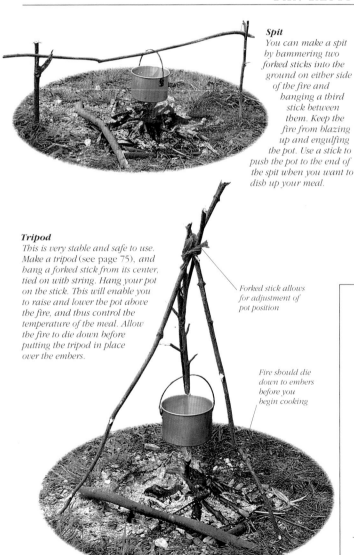

Spit
You can make a spit by hammering two forked sticks into the ground on either side of the fire and hanging a third stick between them. Keep the fire from blazing up and engulfing the pot. Use a stick to push the pot to the end of the spit when you want to dish up your meal.

Dingle Stick
This is useful when you are cooking stews, which may need to be moved off the fire to adjust the temperature. Hammer a forked stick into the ground and balance a long stick in the fork so that one end hangs over the fire to hold the pot. Tie the other end loosely to the upright. The pot can easily be pushed off the fire with a stick.

Tripod
This is very stable and safe to use. Make a tripod (see page 75), and hang a forked stick from its center, tied on with string. Hang your pot on the stick. This will enable you to raise and lower the pot above the fire, and thus control the temperature of the meal. Allow the fire to die down before putting the tripod in place over the embers.

Forked stick allows for adjustment of pot position

Fire should die down to embers before you begin cooking

USING BAMBOO

Being tough and hollow, bamboo makes an excellent cooking pot. Using a pointed stick, make a hole in each of the walls between the hollow compartments, leaving the bottom end intact. Pour water into the stem so that it does not quite reach the first stem ring. Lean the stem over a fire with the top end resting in a forked stick. Heat the stem to boil the water, and this will steam food placed in the top.

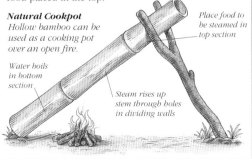

Natural Cookpot
Hollow bamboo can be used as a cooking pot over an open fire.

Place food to be steamed in top section

Water boils in bottom section

Steam rises up stem through holes in dividing walls

COOKING ON HOT ROCKS

1 Make a closely laid bed of large, flat rocks. Do not use slate or other types of layered rock, since they may shatter when they are heated under the cooking fire.

2 Place tinder on the rocks and cover it with dry sticks. Then light the tinder. The fire can be left to burn down to ashes while you prepare your food *(see page 110)*.

3 Using a bunch of green twigs, brush the ash and embers from the surface of the rocks. Take care not to touch them with your hands because they will be extremely hot.

Food cooks directly on top of hot rocks

4 Place food on top of the rocks. Items that need long, slow cooking should be placed towards the edges, where the rocks are cooler than in the center. Keep putting on more food, until the rocks have cooled. Unpeeled potatoes can be buried under the hot rocks and left to bake.

BAKING IN MUD

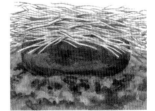

1 You can bake food such as fish in a casing of mud in the fire. First gather a large bundle of long grass and leaves.

2 Wrap the food in the leaves and bind it up with twisted grass strands to make a neat, secure package.

3 Encase the entire package in mud. Make sure the food is completely and evenly covered, and well sealed.

4 Place the package on a bed of hot embers and build a fire up over the top. A fish should be cooked in about an hour.

COOKING TIPS

■ Herbs and spices are invaluable for making food (especially wild food) palatable. Also useful are fresh garlic, onions, and stock cubes.
■ Boiling water and using it to create an "all-in-one" stew is usually the easiest form of outdoor cooking. Mixing together everything from canned fish and cookies to dried fruit sounds dreadful, but with the addition of curry powder and lots of fresh air, such a meal will taste delicious.
■ If cooking by boiling, it is important to drink all the water, as well, in order to obtain the maximum nutritional value from the food (unless you are boiling away harmful substances).

DAMPER BREAD

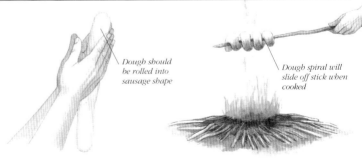

Dough should be rolled into sausage shape

Dough spiral will slide off stick when cooked

1 This Australian camp delicacy is easy and quick to make. First make a pliable dough from flour and water, then roll it into a long, thick sausage shape.

2 Wind the dough in a spiral around a stick, and hold it over the embers of a fire until it is cooked. The bread should easily come off the stick when it is done.

PRESERVING FOOD

ONCE GATHERED, ALL food starts to deteriorate. Without refrigeration, fresh meat and fish are questionable a day after being killed in all but the very coldest regions, while without proper storage, vegetables and other plants quickly lose their nutritional value. For mid- to long-term survival in the wild, food must be gathered at a time of plenty and preserved for times when wild food is scarce. A balanced diet is hard to gather daily. Scouring the landscape for enough food for even a day uses up a lot of calories. In all but short-term survival situations, you should begin preserving and storing food immediately, keeping your bought supplies, such as canned food, for real emergency rations.

DRYING FOOD

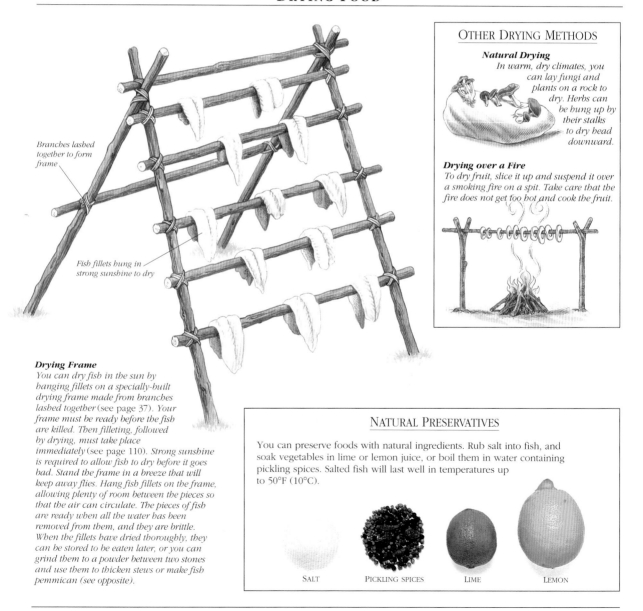

Branches lashed together to form frame

Fish fillets hung in strong sunshine to dry

OTHER DRYING METHODS

Natural Drying
In warm, dry climates, you can lay fungi and plants on a rock to dry. Herbs can be hung up by their stalks to dry head downward.

Drying over a Fire
To dry fruit, slice it up and suspend it over a smoking fire on a spit. Take care that the fire does not get too hot and cook the fruit.

Drying Frame
You can dry fish in the sun by hanging fillets on a specially-built drying frame made from branches lashed together (see page 37). Your frame must be ready before the fish are killed. Then filleting, followed by drying, must take place immediately (see page 110). Strong sunshine is required to allow fish to dry before it goes bad. Stand the frame in a breeze that will keep away flies. Hang fish fillets on the frame, allowing plenty of room between the pieces so that the air can circulate. The pieces of fish are ready when all the water has been removed from them, and they are brittle. When the fillets have dried thoroughly, they can be stored to be eaten later, or you can grind them to a powder between two stones and use them to thicken stews or make fish pemmican (see opposite).

NATURAL PRESERVATIVES

You can preserve foods with natural ingredients. Rub salt into fish, and soak vegetables in lime or lemon juice, or boil them in water containing pickling spices. Salted fish will last well in temperatures up to 50°F (10°C).

SALT   PICKLING SPICES   LIME   LEMON

BUILDING A TEPEE SMOKER

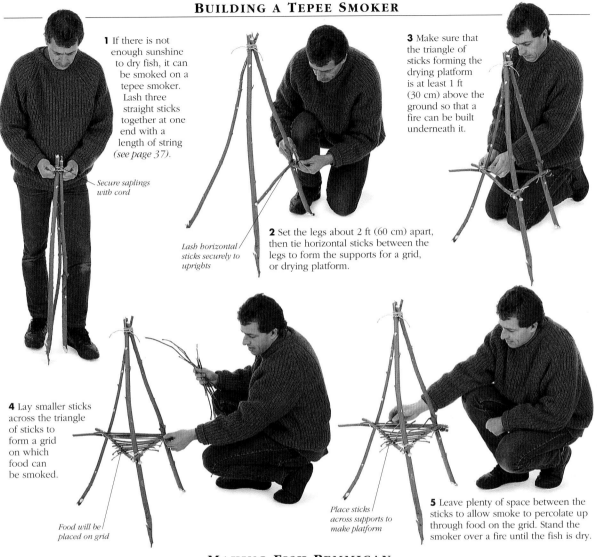

1 If there is not enough sunshine to dry fish, it can be smoked on a tepee smoker. Lash three straight sticks together at one end with a length of string *(see page 37)*.

Secure saplings with cord

Lash horizontal sticks securely to uprights

2 Set the legs about 2 ft (60 cm) apart, then tie horizontal sticks between the legs to form the supports for a grid, or drying platform.

3 Make sure that the triangle of sticks forming the drying platform is at least 1 ft (30 cm) above the ground so that a fire can be built underneath it.

4 Lay smaller sticks across the triangle of sticks to form a grid on which food can be smoked.

Food will be placed on grid

Place sticks across supports to make platform

5 Leave plenty of space between the sticks to allow smoke to percolate up through food on the grid. Stand the smoker over a fire until the fish is dry.

MAKING FISH PEMMICAN

Mix powdered fish with fat

1 You can preserve cooked fish by making pemmican. First soften congealed fat from the fish in your hands.

2 Cut or grate the cooked fish into powdery pieces and mix it with the fat. You can add seasonings if you wish.

3 Add berries to taste, and separate the mixture into small clumps, each about the size of a golf ball.

4 Roll each clump into a sausage shape and leave it in the sun to set hard. Pemmican will remain edible and nutritious for years.

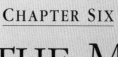

CHAPTER SIX

ON THE MOVE

FOR MOST PEOPLE, enjoying the great outdoors means moving through it, perhaps camping overnight and then moving on again. Traveling on foot, in a vehicle, or by boat, is integral to a wilderness vacation. It is important to have all the right equipment, and to make a comprehensive plan, with your safety always in mind. In survival situations, you are uprooted from your normal existence, and need to carry all your food and equipment across possibly unfamiliar terrain, perhaps to an unknown destination. Traveling under such circumstances is potentially dangerous. You may not know where the next water will be found, or how far you are from civilization. In addition, rescuers are more likely to find you if you stay in one place. When in a survival situation, therefore, unless there is a very good reason for traveling, it is best to stay put. If you do have to travel, for example because flooding or forest fires threaten your campsite *(see page 122)*, make sure you have all the proper equipment for the particular terrain you will cross, and plan your route carefully.

CROSS-COUNTRY TRAVEL
Travel in wild areas is vastly different from moving in urban ones. There are different considerations, ranging from terrain to mode of transportation. Walking across country requires sturdy boots, while the use of animals involves specialized equipment and extra food supplies.

TRAVEL PLANNING

EVEN IF YOU are on a well-planned expedition, traveling may expose you and your party to many unpredictable risks. In a survival situation, these risks become more pronounced. It is important to be properly prepared and to have a sound plan. If you are waiting to be rescued you should stay where you are. You may have to move camp, however, for various reasons.

Animals may move in on your food supplies, or a natural disaster, such as a flood or forest fire, may destroy the vegetation around you. Before you start your journey, you should carefully assess the terrain you will have to cross.

Floods
Floods destroy vegetation and leave a thick layer of mud everywhere. This may make it difficult to find plants to eat and dry wood with which to construct shelters and fires.

ASSESSING THE TERRAIN

Mountains
Treeless mountains provide little shelter, and there is a danger of rock falls, snow, ice, and changeable weather. You may need special equipment and mountaineering skills to negotiate dangerous slopes (see page 146).

Temperate Forests
In a forest there is often the danger of dead trees falling on you. Dangerous animals, such as wild pigs, may inhabit forested areas (see page 166). Although shelter materials and food may be easy to find, movement may be difficult.

Deserts
Water is the key consideration in the desert (see page 142). With no clouds to retain heat, temperatures can soar during the day and drop severely at night. If you have to cross a desert, you should travel only at night, from one waterhole to the next.

ASSESSING YOUR COMPANIONS

A group of survivors must elect a leader, who should assess the capabilities of each individual before making a plan to travel. Each person's strengths and weaknesses must be carefully and privately considered by the leader, whose plan of action will be determined by what the group as a whole is capable of doing. Leadership is very difficult, especially under the pressure of a life-or-death situation, and particularly if some people are unwilling to be led.

Mothers and children are quite resilient, but need careful consideration

Injured people may hold back the others and expose them to danger

Individuals may be inappropriately dressed for walking

Working Together
The group will have the best chance of survival if it stays together, its integrity maintained through good, caring leadership.

Watch out for signs of depression, and involve everyone in the activity of the group

Older people may be vulnerable to heart attacks – or they may be the fittest ones in your party

Being Prepared
Before moving anywhere, you must find out as much as possible about the land that you intend to cross. Do not always assume that maps are accurate (see page 126), particularly when planning where to get water. A series of short, lightly equipped reconnaissance expeditions is well worth the effort before you travel anywhere.

Rivers
Rivers are dangerous, and you should approach them with care. To cross a river, you may have to search for fallen logs to use as bridges, or shallow, narrow parts that you can wade (see page 150). There may also be dangerous animals such as crocodiles living there (see page 75).

Jungles
The heat and moisture of jungles are unpleasant and unhealthy for humans, but allow insects and bacteria to flourish. Small cuts get infected, food goes bad, and clothing is permanently soaked with either rain or sweat, or both. Travel is particularly difficult in secondary jungle (see page 145).

Savannah
Water is an important factor to consider in tropical grassland. You may have trouble finding shelter (see page 53). Bear in mind that you may also be exposed to danger from the predators that hunt the large herds of herbivores usually grazing these enormous areas.

USING BINOCULARS

Binoculars save a lot of legwork. Adjust their width and focus until you can see one sharp image, then look through them into the terrain. Survey the area from different vantage points, trying to understand where streams and rivers flow, and the lie of the hills.

Scanning
Scan very slowly, looking hard into, rather than at, the landscape.

Beach and Sea
The sea must never be underestimated. It is always dangerous. In tidal areas, walking along flat sand at low tide is much easier than negotiating inland dunes or cliffs. You must, however, watch constantly to ensure that you know which way the tide is going. There may be dangerous creatures on the beach or in shallow water (see page 109).

FINDING DIRECTION

DIRECTION-FINDING IS the most important aspect of navigation, so a reliable compass is your most important tool while you are on the move. A watch or clock comes a close second, since it can indicate both direction and elapsed time, by which you can estimate the distance you have traveled;

that other essential part of navigation (see opposite). There are many different types of compass, all of which work because they are attracted to the poles of the Earth's magnetic field. If you do not have a compass, you can find basic directions by using the sun and stars, and by watching animals and plants.

COMPASSES

Compass needles indicate magnetic north and magnetic south, the poles of the Earth's natural magnetic field. If you imagine the Earth as containing a large, vertical bar magnet, the poles are at the top and bottom of the magnet, where the magnetic charge flows out. There are many different types of compass. Walkers should keep a simple compass for emergencies (see page 28), but use a protractor-type compass (such as a Silva compass) for basic navigation and orientation (see below). Prismatic compasses contain built-in prisms, through which their bearings are read, and are sturdy and accurate. Some of these compasses incorporate mirrors, as well as, or instead of, prisms. However, they are quite expensive. A simple Silva compass is all you really need for accurate navigation, in order to avoid complications and errors.

Pointer shows direction you should follow after setting your map

Distance measurements for different map scales

Bearings are read on dial

Parallel lines for orientating compass to north-south grid lines on your map

Silva Compass
A protractor compass allows you to measure bearings on a map without having to move the compass from its position (see page 130). This saves carrying a separate protractor and using mental arithmetic to calculate your route.

MAKING A COMPASS

If a piece of magnetized ferrous metal (containing iron) is freely suspended, it will swing around until it hangs in a north-south axis. This is because it is attracted by the Earth's magnetic field. You can take advantage of this to make your own compass, by magnetizing a piece of metal.

Instead of using a piece of silk to magnetize a needle, a magnet will do the job faster

1 Magnetize a needle by stroking it repeatedly in one direction with a piece of silk, such as your scarf (see page 142). This generates a charge of static electricity.

Allow needle to move freely by floating it in bowl of water

2 Float a blade of grass in a bowl of water, and place the needle on it. The needle will orient itself so that it points in a north-south direction.

3 When the needle has settled, check the position of north using other guides (see opposite), and mark the north end of the needle. You can now use the needle as a compass.

USING A RAZOR BLADE

In an emergency, you can make a compass from a razor blade, if you have one, instead of a needle. However, you should blunt the blade first on a stone, and be extremely careful when magnetizing it as above.

Razor Compass
Magnetize a blunt razor blade and suspend it on a piece of string so that it can swing freely and point north-south.

USING THE SUN

Since the sun always rises in the east and sets in the west, it can be used as a simple indicator of direction. So as long as you can see the sun and know the approximate time of day, you can orient yourself in relation to the sun. You can also make a sundial, or use a watch or clock as a protractor to find north and south.

SOUTH — DIRECTION OF SUN

Northern Hemisphere
Point the hour hand at the sun. Imagine a line halfway between the hour hand and 12 o'clock. South will be at the head of that line.

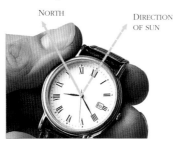

NORTH — DIRECTION OF SUN

Southern Hemisphere
In the southern hemisphere, point the 12 o'clock mark on the watch at the sun. North lies halfway between 12 o'clock and the hour hand.

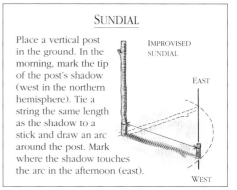

SUNDIAL

Place a vertical post in the ground. In the morning, mark the tip of the post's shadow (west in the northern hemisphere). Tie a string the same length as the shadow to a stick and draw an arc around the post. Mark where the shadow touches the arc in the afternoon (east).

IMPROVISED SUNDIAL

EAST

WEST

USING THE STARS

Stars never move relative to each other. They only appear to move across the sky because of the movement of the Earth. Only one star appears not to move – the North, or Pole, Star. This star can be used in the northern hemisphere to find north. In the southern hemisphere, you must use the Southern Cross to find south.

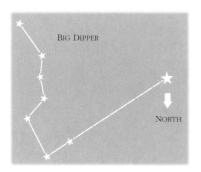

BIG DIPPER

NORTH

Northern Hemisphere
Looking at the Big Dipper, draw an imaginary line between the two stars that form the front of the dipper, and continue it about four times the distance between those stars to find the North Star. This star lies over north on the horizon.

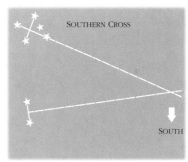

SOUTHERN CROSS

SOUTH

Southern Hemisphere
Use the Southern Cross to find approximate south. Draw an imaginary line from the cross-piece, about 4 1/2 times its length. South should be on the horizon below this point. Two bright stars below the cross help you to find the right point.

NATURAL DIRECTION INDICATORS

The natural world is far better attuned to the Earth's magnetic field and to direction than humans. Plants always grow toward the sun – facing south in the northern hemisphere and north in the southern hemisphere. Sunflowers follow the movement of the sun across the sky. The North Pole plant of South Africa leans towards the north. Tree rings are often wider on the side facing the sun.

Termite Mounds
Some termite nests are built along a north-south axis. They thus receive maximum warmth in the mornings and evenings, yet are shaded at noon.

Weaverbirds
Some birds can be used as basic direction finders. For example, some species of weaver build their nests only on the west sides of trees. If you are in an area where these birds live – for example, South Africa – they are reliable guides to direction.

USING MAPS

MANY TYPES OF map exist, each designed for different purposes. Choosing the right map is vital if you are entering unfamiliar territory. You will need large-scale maps of the whole area you intend to visit, as well as for the parts you intend to walk over. Maps on a scale of 1:50,000 are ideal for walkers (this scale means that, for every measurement on the map, the real distance over the ground is 50,000 times greater). They have evenly spaced grid lines, which may correspond to units of latitude and longitude. The lines divide the map into squares, each of which is identified by the coordinates of the vertical and horizontal grids. Learn to allow for inaccuracies on some maps.

UNDERSTANDING A CONTOUR MAP

The landscape is shaped by water, which runs across it in streams and rivers, creating ridges, hills, and valleys. Manmade features, such as roads, can change very quickly. To understand the lay of the land using a map, first identify the rivers, then the valleys and ridges in between, which change very little during the life of a map.

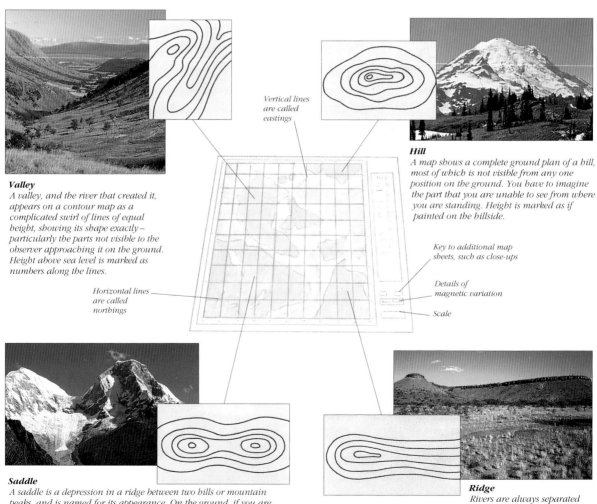

Vertical lines are called eastings

Valley
A valley, and the river that created it, appears on a contour map as a complicated swirl of lines of equal height, showing its shape exactly – particularly the parts not visible to the observer approaching it on the ground. Height above sea level is marked as numbers along the lines.

Hill
A map shows a complete ground plan of a hill, most of which is not visible from any one position on the ground. You have to imagine the part that you are unable to see from where you are standing. Height is marked as if painted on the hillside.

Key to additional map sheets, such as close-ups

Details of magnetic variation

Scale

Horizontal lines are called northings

Saddle
A saddle is a depression in a ridge between two hills or mountain peaks, and is named for its appearance. On the ground, if you are looking from one end, you can see only one hill. A saddle is generally shown on a map as two circles, joined with curved contour lines.

Ridge
Rivers are always separated by ridges. These are drawn on a map like the fingers of a hand, coming down on either side of a hill. It is often easier to walk along the top of a ridge than in a valley, particularly in a dense jungle.

GRADIENTS

Map contour lines join together areas of the same height. The heights of some contour lines are also marked. They are usually written facing down the slope, as if painted on the side of the hill.

Cliff
It is important to know the heights of the steps between contour lines. Large contour intervals may conceal cliffs.

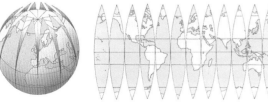

Steep Slope
Lines very close together indicate very steep slopes.

Convex Slope
You cannot see the top of a convex slope while you are standing at the bottom. The contour lines are close together at the foot of the slope, and spread out toward the top.

Concave Slope
You can see the summit of a concave slope from the bottom, and it has a gentle gradient at the bottom. On a map, its contour lines bunch up together toward the top.

GRID REFERENCES

A grid allows you to find a position on a map exactly. The vertical lines are called eastings, while the horizontal lines are known as northings. Eastings are always quoted first when a grid reference is given. Reference letters may also be given for the section of the map in which the position lies. When determining a grid reference, follow the vertical line just left of the position to the foot of the map to find its coordinate, or eastings – for example, 04. Estimate the number of tenths from the grid line to the position – in this case, 5. Repeat with the horizontal grid line just below the position (410). Add the reference letters, if necessary.

Position lies on northing

Position lies in between two eastings

Accurate Position
The above method provides a six-figure grid reference (045410). If your map includes grid reference letters, you can insert the ones relevant to your position before the reference numbers.

MAP PROJECTIONS

A map tries to show with a very high degree of accuracy the surface details of the ground, an irregular sphere. Projecting the world onto the surface of a cylinder or cone creates many inaccuracies and distortions, so these have to be adjusted when a map is printed. Because of this, most maps are not completely accurate, particularly in higher latitudes. The best-known map projection is the Mercator, which is universally used at sea.

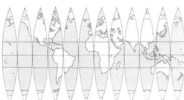

Peeling the Earth
When the Earth is "peeled" like an orange, its skin will lie flat, but there are large gaps between the segments at high latitudes. Filling these in to draw a flat map creates distortion.

Cylindrical Projection
The Mercator projection shows the whole world as if it has been projected onto a cylinder of paper. When this cylinder is unrolled, the world can be shown in a flat plane. Although conveniently rectangular, with lines of latitude and longitude crossing at right angles like they do on the globe, the Mercator Projection makes countries in the polar latitudes too large.

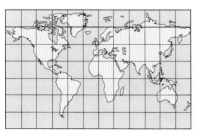

Conical Projection
There are many types of projections, with different properties. The above map is formed by projecting the world onto a cone, and then unrolling it. The conical projection is often used in atlases for regional maps. Although there are still distortions, particularly toward the bottom of the cone, they are not as great as with some other projections.

FINDING YOUR LOCATION

IT IS IMPOSSIBLE to be totally lost. Even air-crash victims know the country or area in which they have come down. Finding your location is a process of narrowing down the options until you can determine a point on a map. Being able to give an accurate grid reference by radio ensures your early rescue. If you know that your location is on a particular map sheet, then you are hardly lost. By determining the lay of the land and finding prominent features, then relating them to your map, the narrowing-down process will not take long. You may need to make your own map for a variety of reasons – for example, you may not have a map, or the one you have is inaccurate. Making your own map ensures that your campsite, and water and food locations can be found again.

POSITION FINDING

To find out where you are using a map and compass, you must relate your position to the features you can see and can identify on the map. A back bearing gives the direction from a feature to your observation point. Taking back bearings from one or more features will give you a fairly accurate idea of your position.

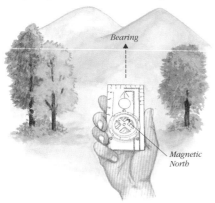

1 Take a bearing to a prominent feature, such as a saddle, to your right-hand side. Turn the compass dial until the north arrow on the dial points in the same direction as the magnetic needle.

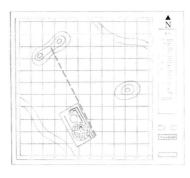

2 Place the compass on the saddle symbol on the map. Move the compass until the arrow points to north on the map. Draw a line from the saddle along that bearing (the back bearing).

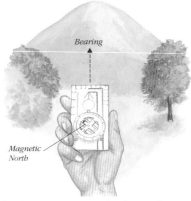

3 Take a bearing to another feature that you can see clearly. This should be roughly at a 90-degree angle from the first, and at least ⅝ mile (1 km) away from yourself. The summits of well-defined hills are best.

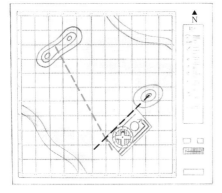

4 Draw a back bearing from the second feature on your map, following the method described above. Your position is where these lines intersect. If you like, you can take a third bearing for greater accuracy.

USING GPS

The Global Positioning System has radically altered navigation, both at sea and on land. This system uses a constellation of 24 satellites, which transmit radio signals to Earth. Using a receiver, you can intercept these signals to determine your position very accurately. Fixed transmitters calculate the satellites' position in orbit. The readings give a very accurate record of your progress wherever you go. Navigation in a featureless desert, or at sea, was previously a combination of taking compass bearings, then confirming your location using a sextant and chronometer. Traditional methods are a backup to GPS.

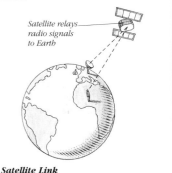

Satellite relays radio signals to Earth

Satellite Link
Ground terminals bounce signals to and from satellites in orbit around the Earth. These signals can be picked up by special receivers to aid in navigation.

MAKING YOUR OWN MAP

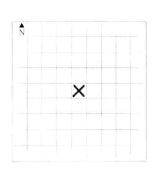

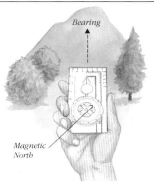

Bearing

Magnetic North

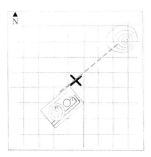

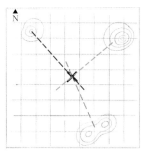

1 Draw a grid of squares, each one representing ¼ sq. mile (0.6 sq. km). Place an X in the centre to represent yourself.

2 Move to a good vantage point. Take a bearing to a feature and estimate its distance *(see below)*.

3 Draw that bearing on your map, lining up the grid in a north-south direction. Add the hill at the estimated distance.

4 Take bearings to two other features and mark them on the map. The point at which they intersect is your position.

MEASURING THE DISTANCE

To position a feature on your map, you must first determine its distance from you. You can use back bearings to do this, but you must first move from "X" to another position, which can be marked exactly on your map. The bearing from your new position to the feature gives you an intersection with the first bearing – and the feature can then be marked on your map. Its distance away from you can then be calculated fairly accurately.

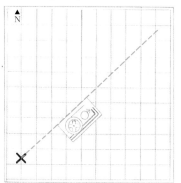

1 You can measure the distance to a feature from your position either on a printed map or on a map that you have made yourself. If you have drawn a grid, the squares must all be accurate. First take a bearing to a feature, such as a hill. Draw the bearing on your grid from the cross (your position) in the direction of the feature.

2 Walk on a bearing of 90 degrees from north for a known distance *(see page 131)* until your next bearing to the hill is at least 30 degrees different to the first one. Plot your new position, and the new bearing. Where the two bearings intersect is the position of the hill. You can work out the distance to the hill by counting grid squares.

MAGNETIC VARIATION

Direction-finding is confused by there being three slightly different norths. In most parts of the Earth, this magnetic variation is small enough that most walkers do not to have to worry about it. However, in other areas, such as the high northern latitudes, magnetic variation increases significantly, and may, in some areas, make compasses useless. It is therefore vital to know the magnetic variation for your area when you are navigating. This must then be subtracted from or added on to your bearing, depending on your location. Magnetic variation for the area covered is marked at the foot of most maps, using three arrows.

MAGNETIC NORTH

GRID NORTH

TRUE NORTH

Three Norths
Magnetic north is where a compass points; grid north is the north marked on maps; and true north is the actual geographic pole. Magnetic variation is the difference between grid north and magnetic north.

TIPS OF LOCATION FINDING

■ The golden rule is "Trust Your Compass." Most people get lost through believing their own confused senses instead of their compasses.

■ Always measure your own bearings and distances.

■ Make sure you understand how the terrain works, and where the valleys, hills, and ridges run.

■ Set your map using your compass *(see page 130)*, then spot the main features by eye and identify where you are going on the ground before setting off on a bearing.

NAVIGATION BASICS

OVERLAND NAVIGATION consists of a combination of map and compass work, with the aim of moving across varied terrain in the safest and easiest fashion. It is nowhere near as precise as navigation at sea, where the only variations offshore are tides and wind. Speed of movement is greatly affected by terrain, rock and soil type, weather, climate, and vegetation. Navigation across land requires a constant reassessment of route, not only to avoid danger, but also to avoid getting lost.

Migration
Many birds have built-in navigational abilities, which enable them to return to the same breeding grounds every year from the other side of the globe.

SETTING YOUR MAP

Before you begin a journey, you should set your map with your compass, so that you know where you and your destination are on the map.

Apart from the bearing of your destination, you will also need to know its distance from you, which you can measure using either the scale along the edge of your compass, or the scale at the bottom of your map. While walking on a bearing, check your map against the terrain you are crossing.

1 To find the bearing from point A to point B, lay the compass on the map between A and B, with the direction arrow at the compass end pointing the way you wish to go. Read the distance between A and B on the scale on the compass edge and compare it with the map scale.

2 Without moving the compass, turn the central dial until the parallel north-south lines align with the grid lines on the map. The north (red) arrow on the dial should point to grid north *(see page 129)*. This sets the bearing (the angle between the line A–B and magnetic north) into the compass.

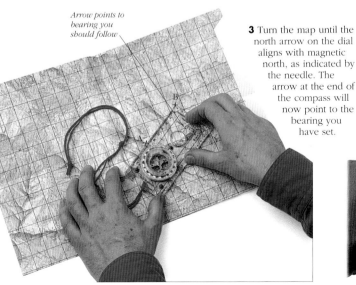

Arrow points to bearing you should follow

3 Turn the map until the north arrow on the dial aligns with magnetic north, as indicated by the needle. The arrow at the end of the compass will now point to the bearing you have set.

4 You can now hold the compass in your hand and follow the direction arrow. Make sure you keep the north arrow on the dial and the magnetic needle aligned. When following a bearing, always keep the compass level.

Keep dial aligned with magnetic needle

NAVIGATIONAL TECHNIQUES

On land, it is not always possible or sensible to walk in a straight line along a compass bearing. The following "tricks of the trade" show you how to use a compass bearing to negotiate difficult terrain by the easiest route, without wasting time checking your location or getting lost. It is important to emphasize that you must always have a bearing set on your compass *(see opposite)*, even if you only use it as a reference.

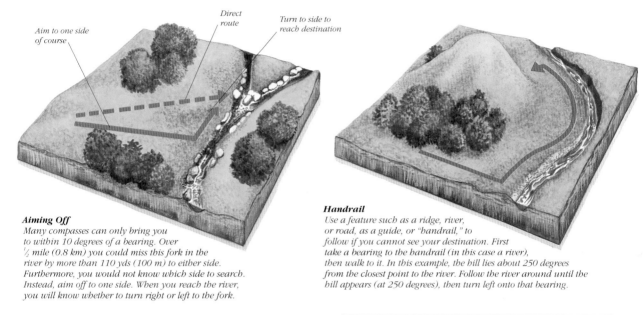

Aim to one side of course

Direct route

Turn to side to reach destination

Aiming Off
Many compasses can only bring you to within 10 degrees of a bearing. Over ½ mile (0.8 km) you could miss this fork in the river by more than 110 yds (100 m) to either side. Furthermore, you would not know which side to search. Instead, aim off to one side. When you reach the river, you will know whether to turn right or left to the fork.

Handrail
Use a feature such as a ridge, river, or road, as a guide, or "handrail," to follow if you cannot see your destination. First take a bearing to the handrail (in this case a river), then walk to it. In this example, the hill lies about 250 degrees from the closest point to the river. Follow the river around until the hill appears (at 250 degrees), then turn left onto that bearing.

Follow contours of hill to keep to the same height

Contouring
By keeping to the same height, you are following a contour line on the map – an invaluable method of direction finding, particularly in jungles, where contouring may be more accurate than using bearings. Contouring will also help you to save energy by not losing and gaining height.

ESTIMATING DISTANCE TRAVELED

Moving on foot, you can either count your paces (on every left foot) or use your watch. Pacing varies according to terrain and rate of travel. Time is a better way of measuring distance covered. Stop after the first 10 minutes to determine from the map the distance you have walked, and then, once you know your walking pace, you can stop once every hour to check your map and equipment. You will learn to assess your rate of travel with surprising accuracy. In rough country, carrying heavy equipment, 2.5 mph (4 km/h) is a good pace.

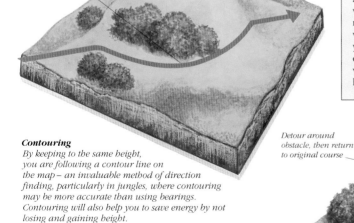

Detour around obstacle, then return to original course

Detouring
Large obstacles such as bogs are not always accurately marked on maps. When detouring, as when contouring, keep the straight-line bearing on your compass, and as you skirt around the obstacle, measure the distance. When you return to your bearing, you will know how far to walk back in order to return to the original line.

ASSESSING THE WEATHER

WEATHER IS THE day-to-day action of climate. Local changes are caused by differences in air pressure and temperature. As they pass over different types of terrain, localized air movements create winds and rain. Coastal areas usually have onshore winds by day and offshore winds at night. Some places, such as the interiors of continents, have quite stable weather, while others have complicated and changeable weather. True equatorial climates have no distinct seasons, but a daily routine of rain and sunshine.

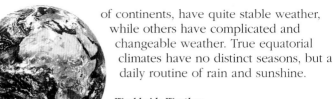

Worldwide Weather
Weather can either be localized in specific areas, or it can move right around the world, affecting places that are many miles apart – as in the case of a hurricane.

READING THE CLOUDS

Clouds are large masses of condensing water vapor. Their presence, type, and size indicate the temperature and pressure of air masses, enabling the prediction of approaching weather. The higher the clouds are, the better and more stable the weather is likely to be. Storm clouds are generally black, low, and massed in large clusters, while fair-weather clouds are high and white. Very low clouds may cover high ground with mist.

Cumulonimbus
Cumulonimbus clouds bring hail, winds, and thunderstorms. These dark, heavy clouds may grow very large, towering up into anvil shapes. They may sometimes contain thunderstorms, along with lightning (see page 171).

Cumulus
Fluffy cumulus clouds usually indicate good weather, but if they are clustered together and are dark in color, they can indicate rain. When they are floating over the open ocean, they can indicate that land is nearby (see page 165).

Stratocumulus
Stratocumulus clouds sometimes form on top of cumulus clouds, spreading out into a thick sheet. Stratocumulus clouds may produce light showers that disperse in the evening.

HOW LANDSCAPE AFFECTS WEATHER

When forced by mountain ranges or hills to rise, moisture-laden winds, particularly from over the sea, form clouds and lose their moisture as rain. This rain runs back down the forward edge of the mountains into the sea, causing the coastal strip to have very high rainfall. On the other side of the mountains, the now-dry winds descend and move inland. Because they contain no more rain, this creates a "rain shadow" that leaves the interior very dry (as on the east coast of Australia).

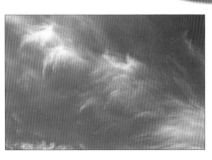

Cirrus
Cirrus clouds, also known as "mares' tails," are very white and wispy. They tend to form at very high altitudes in good weather. Because the atmosphere is so cold at that height, these small clouds are formed entirely of crystals of ice.

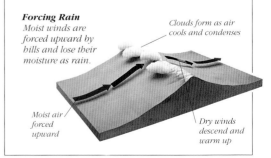

Forcing Rain
Moist winds are forced upward by hills and lose their moisture as rain.

Clouds form as air cools and condenses

Moist air forced upward

Dry winds descend and warm up

NATURAL WEATHER FORECASTERS

Many so-called "old wives' tales" are based soundly upon observation. For example, the ancient rhyme, "Red sky at night – sailor's delight; red sky at morning – sailor's warning" can often be an accurate prediction of weather.

Animal behavior can also indicate weather changes, as can a natural phenomenon such as a rainbow.

Rainbow
A rainbow results from sunlight shining through droplets of water vapor in the air following rain. The drops act as a prism, splitting the light of the sun into its component colors. A rainbow usually indicates good weather, particularly if it is seen in the afternoon.

Migrating Animals
Animals sense the movements in air pressure that precede all weather changes. As a storm or snow approaches, many herd animals that usually live at high altitudes will gather together and move to lower, safer ground.

Red Sunrise
A red sky at dawn often means that there is a lot of moisture in the air, since the sun is reflecting off clouds. This sign usually means that a storm is approaching, and is reflected in an old rhyme (see above).

USING EVERY NATURAL SIGN

A change in the weather can be indicated by a shift in the wind's direction or strength, or by changes in cloud formation. Prevailing winds usually bring particular weather from the same quarter each time. A dry, steady wind changing direction or slacking usually precedes rain. Morning mist or fog indicates stable weather, but wind – especially with low hill fog – may cause rain. A clear sky at nightfall indicates a cold, possibly frosty night, with no clouds to retain heat. Before rain, increased atmospheric pressure makes people's rheumatism more painful, causes plants to open their pores (and thus smell stronger), and makes wooden objects swell. Sounds seem to travel farther, and there is an awareness that something is about to happen.

Pine Cones
Pine cones react to humidity. If the air is dry, the scales shrivel and the cone opens up. Just before wet weather, the scales absorb moisture and the cone regains its natural shape.

WET WEATHER   DRY WEATHER

BEAUFORT WIND-SPEED SCALE			
Force	**Description**	**Velocity (mph)**	**Effects**
0	Calm	Less than 1	Smoke rises vertically
1	Light Air	1–3	Direction shown by smoke, but not by wind
2	Light Breeze	4–6	Wind felt on face; leaves flutter
3	Gentle Breeze	7–10	Leaves and small twigs in constant motion; wind extends flags
4	Moderate Breeze	11–16	Dust and loose paper raised; small branches are moved
5	Fresh Breeze	17–21	Small trees in leaf begin to sway
6	Strong Breeze	22–27	Large branches in motion; umbrellas used with difficulty
7	Near Gale	28–33	Whole trees in motion; difficulty felt when walking
8	Gale	34–40	Twigs broken off trees; progress generally impeded
9	Strong Gale	41–47	Slight structural damage; chimneypots and roof slates removed
10	Storm	48–55	Trees uprooted; considerable structural damage
11	Violent Storm	56–63	Widespread damage
12	Hurricane	64+	Countryside is devastated

Beaufort Wind-speed Scale
Changes in the weather are always heralded by variations in wind speed. Using the Beaufort Scale, the speed of the wind can be gauged by its effects on certain objects, as well as on the landscape and the sea. In this scale, wind speed is divided into 12 strengths, from flat calm to hurricane.

PREPARING TO MOVE

ONCE YOU HAVE decided to travel, it is vital to get everything prepared well in advance. Get your kit washed, repaired, and packed. Assess the terrain you will have to cross *(see page 122)*, and plan your route as accurately as you can. Build up reserves of food and water, and pack everything that might be useful to you on the trail or in your next camp, such as shelter materials. In a survival situation, if you move camp, make sure that you and your companions are fit enough to undertake a journey. It may be necessary to make equipment before traveling *(see opposite)*.

USING A BACKPACK

Your backpack should be packed to supply you with food and clothing while on the move, and also to carry the rest of your camping gear in comfort. Do not strap items on the outside – they will get damaged or lost. Put everything you will need to get at quickly in the outside pouches. Inside, within a large, strong, waterproof bag, you should pack the lightest, bulkiest items at the bottom, and the heaviest ones at the top, to keep the backpack's center of gravity as high as possible. Within your backpack, clothing, food, washing gear, a first-aid kit, and other batches of equipment must be secured inside separate waterproof bags. While in camp, keep the things you do not immediately need in your backpack to minimize clutter, and in case you need to leave your camp quickly.

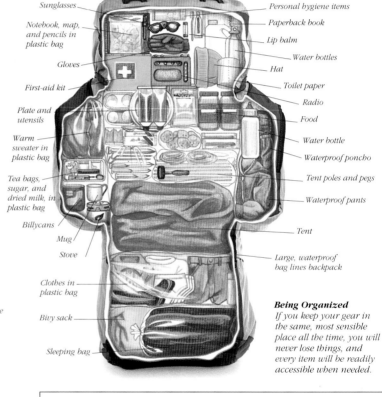

Sunglasses

Notebook, map, and pencils in plastic bag

Gloves

First-aid kit

Plate and utensils

Warm sweater in plastic bag

Tea bags, sugar, and dried milk, in plastic bag

Billycans

Mug

Stove

Clothes in plastic bag

Bivy sack

Sleeping bag

Personal hygiene items

Paperback book

Lip balm

Water bottles

Hat

Toilet paper

Radio

Food

Water bottle

Waterproof poncho

Tent poles and pegs

Waterproof pants

Tent

Large, waterproof bag lines backpack

Being Organized
If you keep your gear in the same, most sensible place all the time, you will never lose things, and every item will be readily accessible when needed.

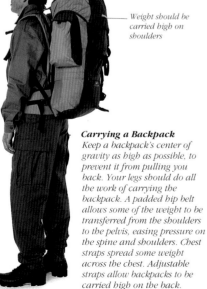

Weight should be carried high on shoulders

Carrying a Backpack
Keep a backpack's center of gravity as high as possible, to prevent it from pulling you back. Your legs should do all the work of carrying the backpack. A padded hip belt allows some of the weight to be transferred from the shoulders to the pelvis, easing pressure on the spine and shoulders. Chest straps spread some weight across the chest. Adjustable straps allow backpacks to be carried high on the back.

BAGS AND DAY PACKS

For short trips, a small pack containing food, clothing, and emergency supplies for 24 hours is much easier to carry than a large backpack. Personal hygiene items can be kept in a wash kit, while travel documents, wallets, and travelers' checks can be kept in waterproof document cases.

WASH KIT

DAY PACK

DOCUMENT CASE

MAKING A SIMPLE PACK FRAME

1 Cut a light bough about 1 ft (30 cm) below where it branches, leaving about 3 ft (1 m) above the fork. Trim off any knobs.

2 Cut notches on all three arms of the bough. Tie rope or double-thickness cord around the notches to serve as straps to go over your shoulders.

Gear tied securely onto frame

Straps held away from shoulders to prevent chafing

3 Tie the other ends of the cords around the notch on the central post. Make sure that the straps will fit over your shoulders snugly, but will not be too tight.

4 Wrap your gear in a groundsheet or waterproof poncho and tie it as high as possible onto the frame on the side opposite the straps.

5 Do not overload your improvised backpack – although this one will carry a good weight. Tie the two shoulder straps together in front to prevent the thin cords from cutting into your shoulders.

MAKING A TRAVOIS

2 Lash sticks between the two main poles about 4 in (10 cm) apart as struts.

Leave enough pole to allow for it to wear down

3 Do not lash the last strut too close to the ends of the poles, since the poles will wear down with use. Leave about 2 in (5 cm) of pole below the last strut.

Trim branches to make flat surfaces

Lash struts securely to poles

Poles should be as straight as possible

4 Make sure you tie all your gear securely to the travois. You can drag the travois yourself, or hitch it to an animal such as a horse or dog. Ensure that the load does not catch your heels or those of your animal, or get jolted off.

1 Cut two strong, straight poles at least 6 ft (2 m) long. Smooth the insides of the poles with a knife so that the load-bearing struts will fit securely when lashed to them.

WALKING

WALKING AS A means of transportation, particularly when carrying equipment, is very different to everyday urban walking. Walking as a group must be at the pace of the slowest member, and requires detailed planning, organization, and foresight. At the beginning of a journey, stop after 10 minutes to adjust your socks, boots, clothing, and equipment, checking that you are maintaining the right direction. Thereafter, go steadily, slowing down as you go uphill and downhill.

WALKING TECHNIQUES

Walk slowly and evenly, swinging your arms to maintain momentum and balance, and allowing your legs to swing forward naturally. Try to keep an even, steady pace – one that you can maintain for long periods of time without getting out of breath or hurting yourself. Try to stop at regular intervals to rest and check your gear.

Walking Uphill
Shorten the length of your stride when going uphill, keeping the same rhythm. Leaning forward, place your feet flat on the ground.

Walking Downhill
When walking downhill, open your stride and lean back slightly. Do not try to go fast. Descending can be hard on your knees, especially when carrying a backpack.

Walking on Sand
On soft sand, slow down and place each foot deliberately, putting weight on it gradually. Walking sideways prevents the toes from digging in.

WALKING IN A GROUP

When walking in a group of people, send an advance party of fit members ahead to check the route, find a path, and look for ways around obstacles. At the end of the day, these members can also find a campsite, erect tents or shelters, collect water, and light a fire. A sufficient number of fully fit people should stay with the main group to keep an eye on those who cannot walk as fast as the others, and to help any sick and injured people.

Keeping together
It is important for a group to stay together – except for the fit individuals who are scouting ahead – particularly in a survival situation. Do not let children or injured people fall behind. Maintain a pace that everyone can match.

The overall speed of the group must be determined by its slowest members

Each unfit or frail person must have a fit escort, the two walking in the middle of the group so that they are not left behind

Some people may need encouragement and extra consideration

Children must not be allowed to run ahead, frolic, or fall behind

The lead person must go steadily, waiting for the others after negotiating each obstacle to make sure that no one falls behind

PLANNING YOUR ROUTE

The best way to plan your route is to walk it first – although this is generally impractical, especially in a survival situation. Before setting out, find a high point, such as a hill, or a tree you can climb safely, and use binoculars and a map, and anything else available, to enable you to determine the easiest route (see page 122). In the jungle, ridgelines often have less vegetation than valley bottoms and so are easier to follow. There may, however, be easy footpaths alongside watercourses, created by local people. Always try to travel by the easiest route, particularly if you are in a survival situation.

Rest Stop
Regular rest stops are essential, particularly if you are walking with a group. Try to stick to 10 minutes for each stop, but do not start the clock until everyone has arrived and sat down. While everyone else is resting, scouts can check the route ahead.

WALKING AT NIGHT

Walk slowly at night, testing the ground with your foot at each step before putting any weight on it. Make the best use of the light of the moon and stars by keeping to open country, away from trees. Crouch down and look upward, silhouetting the way ahead against the sky. Look to the sides of objects, rather than directly at them. Stop regularly, remaining completely still, to listen ahead. Use your map and compass at all times.

Retaining Night Vision
Night vision takes 30 minutes or more to establish and must be carefully guarded. In order to look at your map or compass using your flashlight, close one eye. You will regain your night vision quickly.

HAZARDS OF WALKING

There are many hazards of walking in the wilderness, ranging from injuries to insect and snake bites. For example, various species of biting blackfly plague the northern woods and wetlands of North America. Other hazards include ticks, which you may accidentally brush off bushes onto your clothing (see page 180). You will have to adapt your walking style to the type of terrain you are crossing in order to avoid injuries (see page 145). Another hazard is heat exhaustion. Make sure you can vent your clothing to allow yourself to cool down without getting cold (see page 23).

Hornet
Various species of hornet (Vespa) can be a threat to walkers in temperate areas, causing painful stings.

MAKING A HUDSON BAY PACK

1 If you do not have a backpack, you can carry your gear in this improvised pack. First wrap a stone in each corner of a groundsheet or poncho to give a secure tying point.

Tie corner of sheet around stone

2 Spread your gear inside the poncho in a line to form a sausage. Wrap the poncho around the bundle of clothing, tucking in the ends.

3 Tie up the bundle securely with string, making sure that all your gear is tucked up inside and cannot fall out. Attach a length of cord from one end to the other as a strap.

Bundle lies across back like backpack

4 Sling the pack across your back, with the strap across your chest. You can pad your shoulder with vegetation to prevent the strap from cutting into your skin.

WALKING IN SNOW AND ICE

THE DANGERS OF walking in snow and ice stem from both the nature of the terrain and the effect of cold on the human body. Keeping warm is less of a problem in polar regions than overheating, following by sweating, while working or traveling.

You must be very fit to negotiate polar terrain, and have the right equipment – without it you would not survive very long. Traveling in snow and ice can even be dangerous in temperate areas, and should not be attempted without proper planning.

DRESSING FOR POLAR REGIONS

The intense cold of polar regions requires special clothing. To walk in such areas you need aids such as snowshoes, crampons, or skis, while dangerous areas of ice, such as glaciers, require ice axes for safe crossing. To prevent overheating, you must be able to vent your clothing, either by undoing zippers, or by removing layers. It is vital to adhere to the layering system *(see page 22)*, and to wear windproof clothing on the outside. Very low temperatures and chilling winds make it essential to be able to cover even the smallest area of exposed skin in order to prevent frostbite *(see page 141)*. Goggles are vital to prevent snow blindess.

VITAL EQUIPMENT

Some items are essential in polar regions. Goggles can prevent snow blindness. Crampons can prevent you from sliding on ice, while snowshoes help you to walk on the surface of deep snow. An ice ax is essential for support on icy slopes, while ski poles help you to keep your balance.

GOGGLES

SNOWSHOE

ICE AX

CRAMPON

SKI POLE

Hood
A hood should extend well forward to cover the face. A warm hat should be worn underneath.

Jacket
A jacket should be windproof and easy to vent, with plenty of room for several layers of clothing underneath. It should also have a layer of lightweight insulation inside.

Gloves
Three layers should be worn – thin contact gloves to prevent skin from sticking to metal, woolen inners, and outer mittens that are both windproof and waterproof. Gloves must be secured to the body and each other by lengths of cord going up the arms and over the shoulders so that you do not lose them.

Ice Spike
An ice spike can be used as a braking device if you slip and fall.

Pants
Mountain bibs (high-waisted pants with braces) should have a windproof outer layer, with insulation underneath. Pants should have rear zippers to permit natural functions without removing the jacket or exposing too much skin to the open air.

Ice Hammer
This is used for hammering ice screws into solid ice when climbing (see page 146).

Boots
These should consist of plastic insulated outer shells and thick inner boots soled for use in tents and around camp. They should be worn over several layers of thin and thick socks.

Keeping Warm
Clothing for cold regions should consist of several layers that trap warm air between them and so insulate the body (see page 23).

IMPROVISED SNOWSHOES

1 Bend a green sapling over your knee and flex it gradually along its length until it is pliable.

2 Using your knife, carefully scrape away the inside of the curve. This will further aid the bending of the wood.

3 Cut one side of both ends of the branch until they will rest flush against each other.

4 Fit the ends of the finished hoop neatly together. Bind the ends together with string.

5 Bind two short sticks together at their centers with string. Repeat with two more pairs of sticks.

6 Lash the three pairs of sticks across the hoop. These will support the foot.

Lash each pair of sticks across hoop

7 Weave string in and around the supporting sticks to form the base of the snowshoe.

8 Tie the finished snowshoes to your walking boots with string. Snowshoes spread the weight of the body over a larger area of snow than do the feet alone.

TECHNIQUES FOR CROSSING SNOW AND ICE

Deep Snow
For crossing large expanses of snowy ground in a group, it is best to walk in single file, within touching distance of each other. This prevents anyone from getting lost in a blizzard, and if you fall, the others can quickly help you up. An ice crust above deep snow will often bear your weight, but take great care. Use your ice ax as a walking aid.

CROSS-COUNTRY SKIING

Cross-country skis are long and thin. They are waxed to enable them to both glide and grip, allowing forward movement without sliding backward. Propulsion comes from the rear leg pushing backward, while the other leg glides forward. Cross-country skis are most efficient on deep powder snow where walking is not possible.

Silent Gliding
Cross-country skis allow efficient, yet almost silent, travel in wilderness areas where a walker may not be able to venture.

Negotiating Slopes
Crossing icy slopes or frozen lakes requires the greatest of care. You should rope yourself to your companions and use your ice ax to probe your path for hidden crevasses, as well as to support you if you slip. If the ice cracks, spread your weight over the largest possible surface area, and use your ice ax to pull yourself out. Never walk across a frozen reservoir. If water is being drained off, there will be an air gap of perhaps several yards beneath the ice and, if the ice breaks, you will not be able to pull yourself out. If you slip over on an icy slope, stab the pointed end of your ice ax into the ground and lean your weight on it. It may act as a brake to stop you from sliding down the slope.

TRAVELING OVER SNOW

USING SPECIAL RUNNERS or skis, fast and efficient movement can easily be accomplished across ice and deep snow. However, ice and even the shallowest of snow can be totally exhausting to cross. Only very fit, experienced people with the right equipment should attempt journeys in polar regions, where cold temperatures can dull all thought, almost endless winter nights make even the most cheerful person depressed, and even moderate winds can drastically increase the risk of frostbite.

Snow Vehicles
Snowmobiles have largely replaced dog sleds for both sport and everyday arctic living.

USING HUMAN POWER

On ice and crusted snow, pulks (sleds pulled by humans) are very efficient, especially if you are wearing skis. In soft snow, skiing requires more effort, and snowshoes are the easier option, but even those are hard work. Care must be taken not to overheat and perspire, since your sweat will get your clothing wet. Make sure you can vent your clothing to release excess heat.

Pulling a Pulk
Pulks save actually having to carry weight, and slide well across ice and crusted snow. They do, however, pick up momentum when going downhill, and can be difficult to slow down and impossible to turn. Ensure that you can get quickly out of the harness, but always keep your pulk under control, stopping at the end of each downhill traverse – although this is not always easy.

WARNING
Watch carefully for signs of frostbite. Fingers, nose, feet, ears, and face are affected first, since they have the least blood circulation. As skin begins to freeze it feels prickly. Then numb, waxy-looking patches appear. If not re-warmed, these patches become lumpy, then redden, blister, and die, before eventually dropping off.

Gear is lashed to pulk underneath waterproof cover

USING MAN'S BEST FRIEND

Sled runners are coated with hard plastic to provide friction

Steering is achieved by the driver shifting his weight from one side to the other

The sled is lashed together for flexibility and strength

Traditional Transport
Sled dogs were traditionally used for winter transport, and are still considered by explorers to be the best method of pulling supplies across snow and ice. Incredibly hardy, able to sleep out in blizzards and move quickly over all but very icy ground (which cuts their feet), dogs are much easier to maintain and far better company than the snowmobiles that have largely taken over in day-to-day polar living.

Working in Unison
The team works together as a pack, with the lead dog acting as the pack leader. He regards the driver as his own pack leader.

THE COOLING EFFECT OF WIND															
Speed	**Temperature (°F)**														
Calm	25	20	15	10	5	0	–5	–10	–15	–20	–25	–30	–35	–40	–45
Equivalent Chill Temperature (°F)															
5mph	22	16	11	6	0	–5	–10	–15	–21	–26	–31	–36	–42	–47	–52
10mph	10	3	–3	–9	–15	–22	–27	–34	–40	–46	–52	–58	–64	–71	–77
15mph	2	–5	–11	–18	–25	–31	–38	–45	–51	–58	–65	–72	–78	–85	–92
20mph	–3	–10	–17	–24	–31	–39	–46	–53	–60	–67	–74	–81	–88	–95	–103
25mph	–7	–15	–22	–29	–36	–44	–51	–59	–66	–74	–81	–88	–96	–103	–110
30mph	–10	–18	–25	–33	–41	–49	–56	–64	–71	–79	–86	–93	–101	–109	–116
35mph	–12	–20	–27	–35	–43	–52	–58	–67	–74	–82	–89	–97	–105	–113	–120
40mph	–13	–21	–29	–37	–45	–53	–60	–69	–76	–84	–92	–100	–107	–115	–123

☐ Conditions fairly comfortable with normal precautions

☐ Conditions very unpleasant; thermal outer clothing necessary

☐ Skin begins to freeze if exposed to open air for a prolonged period

☐ Outdoor travel can be dangerous; exposed skin can freeze in one minute

☐ Extremely dangerous conditions; exposed skin can freeze in 30 seconds

Windchill
The wind can be a killer in northern regions, where it can make the air several times colder than the actual temperature. As the wind increases, its effect on the temperature is multiplied.

MAKING A SLED

1 A sled or pulk can be made from a forked tree bough. Tie the ends of the branches to the bough to add tension to their curves.

2 Any cord touching the ground will rapidly wear through, so lash bracing pieces along the runners to make a support for a platform.

Make a handle from a branch and cord

Loaded Sled
Wrap equipment in a poncho and lash it securely to the sled.

3 Lash sticks between the bracing pieces in order to form the main carrying platform of the sled.

Sticks are lashed to braces to support load

4 Lash as many crosspieces as possible to the braces to form a secure platform on which to attach your gear.

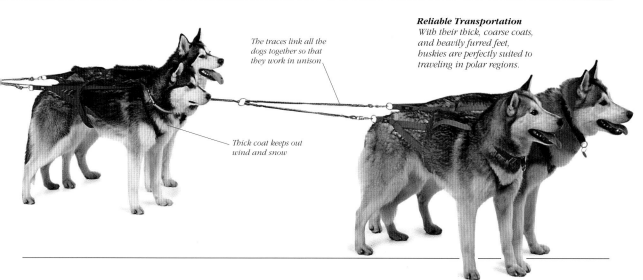

The traces link all the dogs together so that they work in unison

Reliable Transportation
With their thick, coarse coats, and heavily furred feet, huskies are perfectly suited to traveling in polar regions.

Thick coat keeps out wind and snow

CROSSING DESERTS

DESERTS ARE USUALLY unpeopled because they have neither enough water nor sufficient vegetation to sustain permanent communities. They are places of extreme climate; often very hot by day and, where there is no cloud cover to retain the heat, extremely cold by night. Conditions can also change rapidly, due to violent sandstorms and torrential downpours. The desert is a very alien environment, in which water is a vital commodity and only the toughest creatures survive.

DRESSING FOR THE DESERT

The main objective of desert clothing is to keep body heat constant. Clothes must protect the body from the heat of the sun during the day, and retain body heat at night when temperatures suddenly drop. All body parts must be covered as a protection both from the sun, and from the severe discomfort of sandstorms. Deserts have virtually no humidity, which makes their extreme heat more bearable than that of other hot regions. Because desert clothing does not have to protect you from rain, it can be comfortably porous, allowing for ventilation between the layers, and providing insulation at night *(see page 23)*.

Sunglasses
High-filter sunglasses prevent sun blindness.

Hat
A light-colored, brimmed hat reflects hot sunlight and insulates the head from the cold at night.

Cotton Shirt
A light, cotton shirt should have long sleeves to protect the arms from the sun. A T-shirt worn underneath controls sweat evaporation and helps keep you cool.

Jacket
A windproof jacket protects from thorny vegetation, sun, wind, and nighttime cold.

Belt
A woven or canvas belt not only prevents sand from getting beneath your clothes, but can also be used as a first-aid sling (see page 179).

Hands
Protect your hands from sunburn by covering them with sunscreen.

Cotton Pants
Tightly woven cotton pants are windproof and protect the legs from sun, sand, and thorny scrub.

Desert Clothing
Clothing for the desert must be lightweight and made of a porous but strong material. It should protect you from the strong, ultraviolet rays and heat of the sun during the day, and also from the cold at night.

Boots
Desert boots have thick, insulated soles, and porous suede uppers that allow the feet to breathe.

IMPROVISED EQUIPMENT

Because the desert can be such a dangerous place, it is important to have all the right equipment, especially clothes to protect yourself from the heat and from the ultraviolet rays of the sun. You can improvise sunglasses from film, a scarf from a towel or bandanna to protect your neck, and boots from cloth.

Goggles
Eyes must be protected from the sun at all times. Improvise goggles by cutting pinholes or slits in a strip of camera film tied around your head with string.

TYPES OF DESERT

An area of land is usually classified as a desert if it receives less than 10 in (250 mm) of rain a year. Deserts vary immensely around the world, depending on their location and climate *(see page 16)*. They can be stony wastes, large areas of shifting sand dunes, rocky hills and scrub, or desolate land that can nevertheless support specialized plants and animals.

Erg
Large, hot, sandy wastelands with dunes are known as ergs. They are found in Australia, North Africa, and Asia.

Stony Desert
Many stony wastelands are ancient sea beds. These deserts, found worldwide, are very inhospitable because of a lack of shelter and constant winds.

Cactus Desert
Some deserts can support specialized plants, such as cacti, which retain water in their tissues. These deserts are found in North and South America, Australia, and Asia.

Temperate Semi-Desert
Although woody shrubs grow here, it is too dry to support grassland. Temperate semi-deserts are found in North and South America, central Asia, and Australia.

PROTECTING YOURSELF IN A SANDSTORM

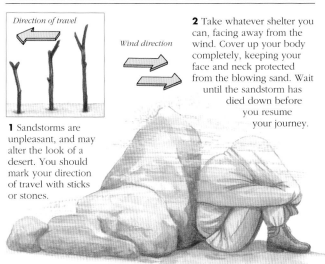

Direction of travel

Wind direction

2 Take whatever shelter you can, facing away from the wind. Cover up your body completely, keeping your face and neck protected from the blowing sand. Wait until the sandstorm has died down before you resume your journey.

1 Sandstorms are unpleasant, and may alter the look of a desert. You should mark your direction of travel with sticks or stones.

DESERT TRAVEL

In a desert survival situation, you should not move unless you have to. If you must travel, for example to find water, or if there is no hope of rescue where you are, you should move only by night when it is cool, if possible under a good moon. Since it is very difficult to determine exactly where you are in a featureless desert, finding oases (even assuming you know where they are) is far from easy.

Improvised Shade
You can make a patch of shade by hanging a space blanket or sleeping bag over a length of string tied between rock piles or stakes. Scoop a depression in the sand so that you have room to move under the roof.

Surviving Without Water
Humans need a minimum of 7–8 pts (4–5 liters) of water per day to be able to travel on foot with any degree of safety. In the desert, water conservation in your body is imperative, so you must work only at night, minimize exertion, and try to avoid perspiring. In temperatures of 122°F (50°C), without drinking water, you will only last up to five days if you do nothing but rest in the shade. This time is halved if you walk, even at night. In a survival situation, therefore, you should seriously question the need for any sort of movement, unless you have plenty of water.

DESERT SURVIVAL TIME WITH LIMITED WATER

°F	NO WATER	3 QUARTS	8 QUARTS	°C
Resting in the Shade				
122	2–5 days	2–5 days	3–5 days	50
86	7 days	5–8 days	14 days	30
68	12 days	14 days	23–25 days	20
Walking at Night				
122	1 day	2 days	3–5 days	50
86	4 days	5 days	5–7 days	30
68	9 days	10–15 days	5–15 days	20

TRAVELING THROUGH JUNGLES

DESPITE BEING HOT, sticky, and full of insects, the jungle is in many ways a garden of Eden. Food is plentiful, with no seasons to create shortages, and fresh water falls from the sky in large quantities. However, for those unfamiliar with the jungle, it is humid, dark, and noisy – an intimidating and uncomfortable place. The humidity and the intense labor of jungle travel make heat exhaustion a constant danger, so you must carry large quantities of water to help prevent this.

PREPARING FOR THE JUNGLE

You must cover up completely when traveling through jungle, wearing lightweight, strong clothing that will dry quickly. You are likely to be wet all the time, and must wash your clothing in fresh water daily to keep it from rotting. There is no point in having waterproof clothing, since it will make you sweat. A light pullover is useful for cold nights. Keep one set of clothes clean and dry for sleeping in. Pack all your kit away unless you are using it. Loosely attached items can be torn away by vegetation, so keep your most valuable items on strong cords around your neck.

JUNGLE MEDICAL KIT

You must not allow small cuts to become infected. Pushing through spiky or razor-sharp undergrowth inevitably cuts hands. Antibiotic powder is very good for preventing infection. When hacking through thick jungle, take great care to avoid machete injuries, which can disable you and are very difficult to keep from becoming infected. You will need lots of adhesive bandages for keeping small punctures and cuts covered.

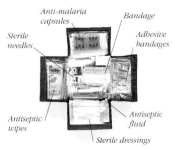

Anti-malaria capsules

Bandage

Sterile needles

Adhesive bandages

Antiseptic wipes

Antiseptic fluid

Sterile dressings

Tropical Medication
Special medical kits are available for tropical areas. They contain common first-aid items, as well as medication for countering jungle ailments.

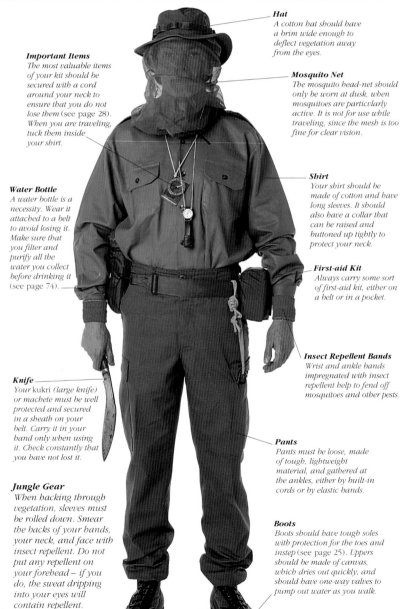

Important Items
The most valuable items of your kit should be secured with a cord around your neck to ensure that you do not lose them (see page 28). When you are traveling, tuck them inside your shirt.

Water Bottle
A water bottle is a necessity. Wear it attached to a belt to avoid losing it. Make sure that you filter and purify all the water you collect before drinking it (see page 74).

Knife
Your kukri (large knife) or machete must be well protected and secured in a sheath on your belt. Carry it in your hand only when using it. Check constantly that you have not lost it.

Jungle Gear
When hacking through vegetation, sleeves must be rolled down. Smear the backs of your hands, your neck, and face with insect repellent. Do not put any repellent on your forehead – if you do, the sweat dripping into your eyes will contain repellent.

Hat
A cotton hat should have a brim wide enough to deflect vegetation away from the eyes.

Mosquito Net
The mosquito head-net should only be worn at dusk, when mosquitoes are particularly active. It is not for use while traveling, since the mesh is too fine for clear vision.

Shirt
Your shirt should be made of cotton and have long sleeves. It should also have a collar that can be raised and buttoned up tightly to protect your neck.

First-aid Kit
Always carry some sort of first-aid kit, either on a belt or in a pocket.

Insect Repellent Bands
Wrist and ankle bands impregnated with insect repellent help to fend off mosquitoes and other pests.

Pants
Pants must be loose, made of tough, lightweight material, and gathered at the ankles, either by built-in cords or by elastic bands.

Boots
Boots should have tough soles with protection for the toes and instep (see page 25). Uppers should be made of canvas, which dries out quickly, and should have one-way valves to pump out water as you walk.

FEATURES OF THE JUNGLE

Green Canopy
In primary jungle, trees can grow up to 200 ft (61 m) high, creating a dense canopy that blots out the sun. The canopy follows the shape of the underlying ground, but from the air, all that can be seen is the dense vegetative roof. Most of the animals that live here inhabit the canopy.

Lush Vegetation
Secondary jungle grows where humans have burned the trees to make fields. After the harvest, they abandon these clearings, allowing sunshine to get down to ground level, where it stimulates tremendous growth. This kind of jungle is very difficult to negotiate. A path must be cut through the vegetation, and this is very exhausting work.

Shady Forest
Underneath the canopy, the jungle floor remains relatively free of vegetation. Giant lianas grow downward, and a host of flora and fauna inhabits different levels of the humid, shaded environment.

MOVING THROUGH THE JUNGLE

Although primary jungle is easy to move through, secondary jungle is dense, choked, and unpleasant to negotiate. Cutting the vegetation is hard work, making progress very slow. Biting insects and sharp, cutting vines abound, many of which have dangerous spikes. If you get entangled, the best way of freeing yourself is to move backward, reversing the process by which you became caught.

Wait-a-while
Some species of rattan, known as "wait-a-while vine," can rip clothing to shreds. If caught, you should wait patiently while a companion untangles you.

RAINFOREST ROUTINE

The closer you get to the equator, the more regular the days become. In equatorial areas, dawn and nightfall are at the same time each day, and it often rains at exactly the same times – usually just as it gets dark. There is no gradual dusk, as in higher latitudes, but sudden and complete darkness. The daily routine is to get up at dawn; work until noon, and take a break during the heat of the day. If you are on the move, you should start looking for a campsite no later than 3 p.m.

Removing Leeches
Do not just pull leeches off, since the mouthparts may remain and cause infection. Dab them with a burning stick or insect repellent to make them relax their grip, then remove them.

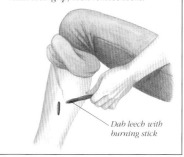

Dab leech with burning stick

THE HAZARDS OF JUNGLE TRAVEL

The jungle has many hazards, ranging from wild animals to diseases such as malaria. The constant dampness may cause fungal infections of your feet, so you should powder them regularly *(see page 24)*. Always shake out clothing and boots before putting them on, in case they have become refuges for poisonous snakes and spiders. Make sure you get an antimalaria vaccination, and take the appropriate medication before entering jungle areas. Use plenty of insect repellent and hang up a mosquito net at night to avoid being bitten.

Deadly Enemy
The female Anopheles *mosquito can carry the deadly malaria virus.*

SAFE CLIMBING

YOU SHOULD CLIMB only if there is no other way of getting around an obstacle – and never climb on your own. If you fall or get stuck, no one will know to summon help. The golden rule of all climbing is to maintain three points of contact with the rock, emulating the stability of the tripod. Think through every move, trying to keep three parts of your body (the toes, fingers, feet, or hands – never the knees) in contact with the rock at all times. Take great care to assess the condition of the rock and the stability of handholds and footholds. You should always use a rope, if you have one.

HANDHOLDS AND FOOTHOLDS

Handholds and footholds are the basis of rock climbing. Before relying on handholds or footholds, test them with a kick, or with a blow from the hand. Do not reach too far for holds, or stand on tiptoe to reach upward. Use your legs, rather than your arms, to support your weight, and push yourself upward.

Side Pull
There may be holds to the side that you can use for balance. Side pulls are best if you can also use your thumb to push inward.

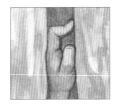

Hand Jam
You can often jam your hand or fist into a small crack, pulling yourself up on a hand jam when there is no actual hold.

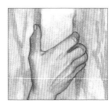

Large Pinch Grip
When you are unable to get a good grip on a protrusion, clasp it like a brick. Try to pinch through the rock.

Edging
Use a crack by placing the inside of your foot in it. Run your sole along the crack, with your ankle at 90 degrees to the rockface.

Large Pocket
Holes, or "pockets," make good footholds. Balance yourself so that your arms and legs take your weight evenly.

Medium Block
Try to place your entire sole on a block foothold. If the protrusion will only take the ball of your foot, however, keep your heels low.

BASIC CLIMBING

If you are a novice, you should not climb without the support of a rope belayed by an experienced climber. However, in a survival situation, you may have no choice. Before climbing, look for the easiest, safest route, and continue to look as you feel for holds. If you are in any doubt about your route, retreat and start again.

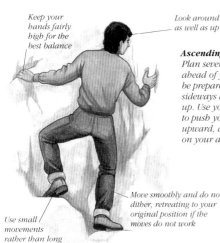

Keep your hands fairly high for the best balance

Look around as well as up

Ascending
Plan several moves ahead of your steps, and be prepared to traverse sideways as well as to go up. Use your leg muscles to push yourself upward, and do not rely on your arms.

Use small movements rather than long ones that risk overstretching

Move smoothly and do not dither, retreating to your original position if the moves do not work

Lower yourself carefully into footholds – if they do not support your weight, you must be able to come back up

Descending
Going down feels unnatural, and holds can be difficult to see. Start off on a gentle slope facing outward. Then turn sideways as it steepens, until you are facing the rock. Look for holds – do not scrabble with your feet.

Always look for handholds and footholds above and to your sides, in case you get stuck going down

After finding a foothold, do not stand on tiptoe, but keep your heels low

BELAYING

Belaying is a method of supporting someone with a rope to prevent him from hitting the ground if he falls. You should secure yourself to the rockface ("belay point") before you begin. To support someone who is descending, or if your partner needs more rope to ascend, pay out the rope to him in the reverse of pulling it in.

Pulling In
Pass the "live" rope (L) from your partner through your right hand and around your back, and twist it around your left wrist. As your partner ascends, take up the slack in the rope and pass it around your body, through the forearm twist, and into your right hand again. Let the slack end of the rope (S) form a pile at your feet.

Paying Out
To belay someone who is descending, reverse the process. Keep the rope twisted around your left arm, but do not allow a twist to form in the live end (L), since this could break your arm if your partner falls. Grip the rope correctly with both hands at all times.

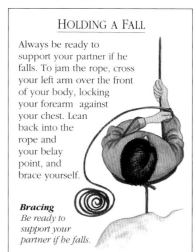

HOLDING A FALL

Always be ready to support your partner if he falls. To jam the rope, cross your left arm over the front of your body, locking your forearm against your chest. Lean back into the rope and your belay point, and brace yourself.

Bracing
Be ready to support your partner if he falls.

RAPPELING

Rappeling is a quick and easy method of descent using a rope. Pass your rope around a secure anchor point, then throw the rope over the edge. Stand astride the rope and reach behind with your right hand to pull both sides of the rope around your hip, over your left shoulder, and across your back. Grip the downside of the rope with your right hand, and the upside of the rope with your left. Keeping upright, walk backward down the cliff, letting the rope slip through your hands and around your body.

Rappeling
Control your speed with your right hand.

MULTIPITCH ASCENTS

In order to climb rockfaces higher than the length of your rope, you must use multipitch techniques, stopping at suitable ledges to belay the other members of your team before continuing up the rockface.

1 The lead climber ascends, finding the easiest and safest route up the rockface. If the first segment of the rockface is very steep and dangerous, the leader may insert pegs into the rock as he climbs, into which he loops safety slings to take the rope. The second climber pays out the rope while being securely attached to the rockface.

2 Upon reaching a ledge, the lead climber secures himself to the rockface, then belays the second climber, who ascends to join him. If the leader has used safety slings, the second climber removes them as he ascends the rockface.

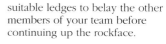

Second climber is belayed by the leader

EMERGENCY CLIMBING

THE EASIEST CLIMBS can turn difficult. Even experienced climbers get stuck, falling or having to be rescued. These more advanced techniques are used by experts to get out of trouble. They are dangerous and not nearly as easy as they might appear from these drawings. In a survival situation, you must overcome serious problems using the resources available. You should therefore understand these techniques in case you ever have to use them. If, however, you intend to try out some of these techniques, consult a climbing manual and take an experienced climber with you.

CHIMNEYING

Chimneying is a method of climbing inside rock clefts wide enough for the whole body. You must, however, look ahead and work out exactly how you will extricate yourself at the top. You could get stuck at this point.

1 Check for other routes before entering a rock cleft. Keep near the outside of the cleft on dry rock. Brace yourself with both legs and hands pushing outward.

2 Press one foot against the back wall and the hand on that same side against the front wall. Move your buttocks and back up the wall, pushing with your legs.

TAKING A REST

Chimneying puts strain on muscles and must be taken steadily. Rest regularly, leaning back against the wall with your legs and arms straight.

RESTING

MANTELING

From below, bulges in the rock face may seem daunting, particularly when you cannot see beyond to look for holds. The technique that is used to overcome such an overhang is known as manteling. You should attempt this only if there is no way around an obstacle. It is a difficult technique, which requires you to be very fit.

1 Pull yourself up to the overhang until you are able to get both elbows onto it, supporting your weight on your feet.

Lift ankle onto overhang while leaning on elbows

2 Lean on one elbow, keeping your chest and head as close to the rock as possible. Hook one ankle onto the overhang.

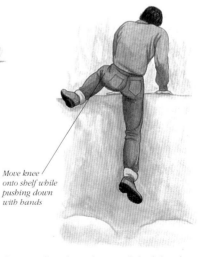

Move knee onto shelf while pushing down with hands

3 Pushing down with both hands, move your knee onto the shelf. Push yourself smoothly upward and onto the overhang.

TYING A PRUSSIK LOOP

A prussik loop is a type of slip knot that tightens under load, but can easily be loosened. Prussik loops are a safe way to attach yourself to a rope, and can be used for climbing up a rope, perhaps after a fall, or up over an overhang.

1 Make a loop in your hand with one rope (here, colored gold) and bend it over the other rope (colored red). Feed the ends of the gold rope back through the gold loop.

2 Loosely wrap the gold rope around the red rope again as in Step 1, to make four loops.

3 Pull on the gold rope and slide up the loops to tighten them around the red rope so that they are all even. Take care not to cross any of them.

4 For extra friction, repeat steps 2 and 3 until you have made four tight loops around the red rope. Adjust the knot until the turns are level and tight.

CARABINER

A carabiner is a clip that is useful for joining ropes or equipment (*see page 152*). Carabiners with a spring-clip opening are quicker and easier to connect than those with a screw-in gate, but screwgate ones are the safest for belaying, rappeling, and other perilous situations (*see page 147*).

Screwgate Carabiner
Always use this for techniques that rely on very secure connections, such as when belaying or rappeling.

PRUSSIKING

With two short ropes and a climbing harness, you can climb a fixed rope and escape from serious trouble. In an emergency, if you do not have a proper climbing harness, one may be improvised from a rope. Make a loop to sit in, and secure it to a rope around your waist with a figure-eight knot (*see page 35*).

The upper knot must never be out of reach

1 Secure your harness rope (here, colored green) to a fixed line with a prussik knot (A). Attach a second short rope (here, colored blue) to the fixed line with a prussik knot (B). Make a loop in the lower end of the second rope and put your foot through it.

Twist the knot before pushing it up

2 To climb, push upward with your leg muscles until you are standing upright, with your leg straight. To move the upper knot (A), pull on the fixed rope below the knot. Then twist the knot to loosen it, and slide it up as far as you can reach.

Your weight is supported by a loop of rope

Brace yourself against the rockface to keep your balance

3 Slowly move to a sitting position and let the figure-eight knot on your harness take your weight. By tightening the fixed rope under the lower knot (B), you can move that knot upward, ready for standing upright and ascending further.

CROSSING WATER

RIVERS AND STREAMS are always dangerous – from their headwaters, or source, where they are fast flowing, narrow, and shallow, to the slow-moving deeps of their lower reaches. Even if water appears to be calm and slow moving, shallow and safe, assume there are hidden dangers. In even the clearest waters you can never see everything below the surface. Headwaters are easier to cross than deep water, but take care when crossing fast water. Slower waters are generally deeper than fast ones, and may contain treacherous weeds, mud banks, and dangerous hidden obstacles. Never wade or swim across water if there are safer options available – do you actually need to cross?

WHERE TO CROSS

The best place to cross any kind of water is where there is a bridge, pontoon, or ferry. Therefore, before getting wet, scout upstream and downstream. You may find a bridge or a wide, even section where the river bed is firm, and where a wet crossing can be made in safety. Check that the far bank is not too steep.

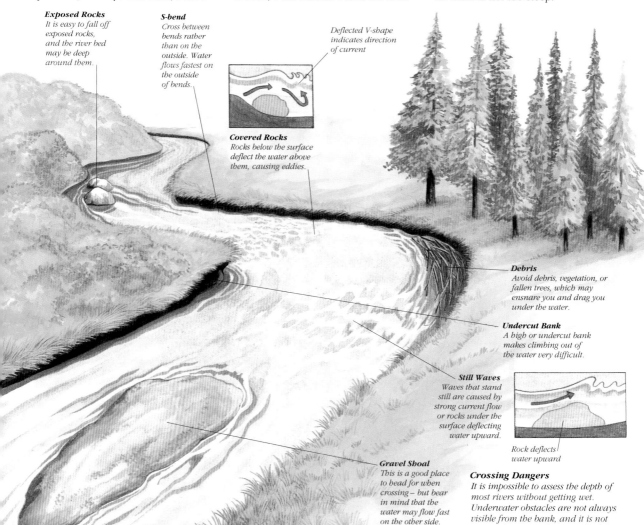

Exposed Rocks
It is easy to fall off exposed rocks, and the river bed may be deep around them.

S-bend
Cross between bends rather than on the outside. Water flows fastest on the outside of bends.

Deflected V-shape indicates direction of current

Covered Rocks
Rocks below the surface deflect the water above them, causing eddies.

Debris
Avoid debris, vegetation, or fallen trees, which may ensnare you and drag you under the water.

Undercut Bank
A high or undercut bank makes climbing out of the water very difficult.

Still Waves
Waves that stand still are caused by strong current flow or rocks under the surface deflecting water upward.

Rock deflects water upward

Gravel Shoal
This is a good place to head for when crossing – but bear in mind that the water may flow fast on the other side.

Crossing Dangers
It is impossible to assess the depth of most rivers without getting wet. Underwater obstacles are not always visible from the bank, and it is not easy to determine the strength of the current and the force of the water.

WADING

Wear some kind of footwear to protect your feet and to give yourself firm footing. Be ready for deep mud, vegetation, or sudden changes in river depth. Study the water before you enter it, watching to see what the waves do, and whether there are signs of any underwater obstructions *(see opposite)*. Always cross very slowly.

Loosen the straps of your backpack so that if you fall it can easily be discarded

Use a stout, strong pole for support

Direction of Journey

Direction of Flow

Crossing in a Huddle
Three people can form a tripod shape to cross a river. Link arms closely, and lean in toward the center, bending forward slightly at the waist. The strongest person should be upstream, and he should make the first moves. The others should support him in case he falls. This is a stable formation, and is very effective in shallow, fast water.

Direction of Flow

Direction of Journey

Direction of Flow

Direction of Journey

Crossing Alone
Use a pole as your probe, then, in the water, as a third leg, maintaining an extended "T" shape – like a tripod. Place the pole upstream of you and lean on it as you lift your leading foot, moving your foot sideways across the current and replacing it firmly on the riverbed. Take short, shuffling paces, to ensure that the current does not force your leg backward and cause you to fall over.

Crossing in a Line
Several people can cross in a line, with the strongest person upstream, and the others providing stability, supporting anyone who might fall. The leader will decide where to cross, and should take the first steps. Everyone should link arms, with the weakest and lightest person in the middle. Cross slowly and carefully. Keep well balanced, putting each foot down deliberately.

SWIMMING

If the water is too deep to wade, you may have to swim. Make a float to help you get across. Before entering the water, look for a suitable landing place on the opposite bank.

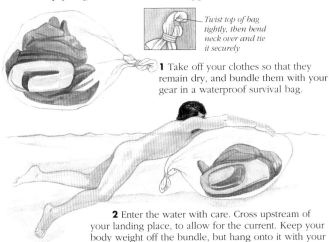

Twist top of bag tightly, then bend neck over and tie it securely

1 Take off your clothes so that they remain dry, and bundle them with your gear in a waterproof survival bag.

2 Enter the water with care. Cross upstream of your landing place, to allow for the current. Keep your body weight off the bundle, but hang onto it with your arms. Kick your legs to propel you along.

HYPOTHERMIA

Strip off (except for footwear) before entering the water. Consider wearing waterproof or windproof clothes to give some protection. The cold makes you feel lethargic. Immediately after crossing, dry off and dress in warm, dry clothing, if possible making a hot, sugary drink. Help anybody who dithers. Work in pairs. The leader should check the group carefully for the symptoms of hypothermia, and be prepared to give treatment. If sufferers are not warmed immediately, they may become so chilled that they will die *(see page 163)*. Wrap them in dry insulation, followed by a plastic or foil blanket. Feed them foods and hot drinks that are high in sugar, because this energy is absorbed quickly. The signs of approaching hypothermia usually appear in the following order:

■ Shivering, goose pimples, and pale, numb skin.
■ Apathy, confusion, irrational behaviour, amnesia, incoherence, and belligerence.
■ Lethargy, then bursts of sometimes frenetic energy.
■ Lapses of consciousness, along with slow and shallow breathing and an erratic heartbeat.
■ A slow and weakening pulse. This can eventually lead to cardiac arrest *(see page 176)*.

DANGEROUS WATER

ALL WATER CROSSINGS should be considered dangerous. Fluctuations in rainfall can radically change the safety of any crossing point. The only way to ascertain depth and current is to send one person across first, attached to a lifeline secured to the bank and controlled by a member of the team. If forced to swim, always use a reliable float, and particularly in rapids, rocks, or fast-moving waters, wear a brightly colored safety helmet. (Lightweight climbing or cycling helmets are perfect.)

USING ROPES TO STAY SAFE

If crossing dangerous rivers on your own, a safety rope can only be used by looping the rope around a rock or tree, tied with quick-release knots. With two or more people, controlled safety ropes can be used, very greatly lessening the danger. Always use safety ropes, but ensure that the slack rope does not entangle those in the water.

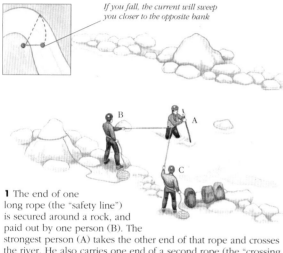

If you fall, the current will sweep you closer to the opposite bank

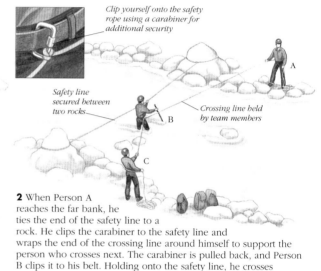

Clip yourself onto the safety rope using a carabiner for additional security

Safety line secured between two rocks

Crossing line held by team members

1 The end of one long rope (the "safety line") is secured around a rock, and paid out by one person (B). The strongest person (A) takes the other end of that rope and crosses the river. He also carries one end of a second rope (the "crossing line"), whose other end is held by another person (C). This rope has a carabiner knotted in its center *(see page 147)*. Person A wears a helmet and boots and uses a pole to probe the way.

2 When Person A reaches the far bank, he ties the end of the safety line to a rock. He clips the carabiner to the safety line and wraps the end of the crossing line around himself to support the person who crosses next. The carabiner is pulled back, and Person B clips it to his belt. Holding onto the safety line, he crosses slowly on the upstream side of it, using a pole. Person C pays out the crossing line, while Person A pulls in the other end.

3 As each person reaches the far bank, he unclips the carabiner from his belt and attaches it to the safety line. It is then pulled back to the near bank. The backpacks can be hauled across in the same way, their strong carrying straps clipped securely to the carabiner. The safety line may need tightening to keep the backpacks out of the water.

4 The last person across the river (C) unties the safety line from the rock. He loops the end of the safety line around himself and crosses the river, probing his path with a pole. The other team members pull in the slack in the crossing line, ready to support him if he falls.

BUILDING A BRIDGE

Guide first log with ropes so that it falls straight

Slide second log along first to opposite bank

1 To build a bridge, first lower a long log across the river with ropes. The end of the log that remains on the first bank should be braced against a short log, which is held in place with pegs.

2 With the first log in place, slide a second log along it until the end reaches the opposite bank. Roll the second log off the first one onto the bank. Try to keep the logs close together.

3 Shinny along the logs to the other bank and put a short log under their ends to prevent them from sinking into the ground. Peg the logs in place so that they do not spread apart.

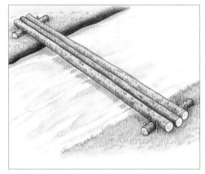

4 Slide a third log along the other two. Place a short log under their ends on the first bank and peg them together, as in Step 3. You can make the bridge as wide as you like, but three logs are usually enough.

CROSSING WATERLOGGED GROUND

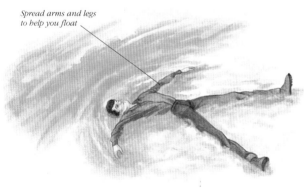

Spread arms and legs to help you float

Lean on backpack to help spread your weight

By Yourself

Quicksand and bog are merely waterlogged ground, so if you fall in, you should be able to float or swim across, providing you can spread your weight over as large an area as possible to avoid sinking. First try running across, stepping on tussocks of grass. If you begin to sink, discard your backpack and fall onto your back. Spread out your arms and legs and swim slowly to the bank on your back by sculling (see page 162). Do not panic or struggle .

With Help

If you are not alone when you begin sinking in quicksand or boggy ground, another person can lie at the edge of the quicksand, pass you the end of a long branch, and pull you out. Again, it is important not to struggle or panic, since quick movements will stir up the surface and cause you to sink faster than if you just float or move slowly. You may find that, if you lean on your backpack, it will help spread your weight and prevent you from sinking further.

BUILDING A RAFT

IF YOU HAVE a lot of supplies and equipment to transport across a river, or if you want to travel downstream but do not have a boat, a raft is the simplest form of craft to build. The traditional materials used in raft building are logs, but you can also use bamboo or oil drums, if they are available. The basic principle of construction is to make as few cuts as possible in the logs of the raft so that it will remain buoyant, and so that the raft will be as stable as possible when floating. A raft should not be used on a river where there are likely to be rapids, since it may break up and you may be injured. If you use logs to build your raft, it is best to cut leaning trees, since you can accurately gauge where they will fall. If possible, test your raft in shallow water before launching it on a deep river.

1 To form the deck, cut 12 to 14 thick, sturdy logs to the same length. Cut six more logs, each about 1 ft (30 cm) longer than the intended width of your raft. They will act as retainers, holding the raft together. Before fixing the deck logs together, lay two long logs across two of the shorter poles to act as a launching bed *(see page 156)*.

2 Using a large knife, cut a notch along the whole length of each of the retaining logs, leaving 1 ft (30 cm) at each end. The notches should be about half the depth of each log. Take care not to cut too deeply and weaken the retaining logs.

3 Make sure that each notch is of the same length and reasonably level. The long logs that will make up the deck will need to lie flat on these retaining logs, to make the deck as level as possible.

4 Lay two notched logs, carved face upward, at opposite ends of the launching bed. These will form the base supports. Begin laying long logs between these two supports to form the deck of the raft.

5 Lay each end of the long poles in the notches of the support logs, working from the outside toward the middle of the raft. Alternate the thickness of the logs so that their weight is even from one end of the raft to the other, turning them so that they fit neatly into one another.

6 The last log should be a nice, tight fit, bracing all the other logs against each other to keep the raft together. Even in the water, however, you may have to take steps to keep the logs in position, adding extra lashings as necessary. You should expect some water to seep between the logs.

7 Place the last two notched logs, carved face down, across the raft, on top of all the deck logs. These will act as the cross retainers. Remember that, in the water, the logs will be floating up into these retainers, which serve to hold all the pieces of the raft together.

8 The two retaining logs on each end, above and below the deck, must be firmly bound together, tensioned as tightly as possible. Keep the knots uppermost, so that once the raft is in the water they can easily be checked and tightened if necessary.

9 Lash the retaining logs on both sides of the deck, using square knots *(see page 35)*.

10 Make sure that the lashings are secure, and knotted well. If you have time, you can also lash between each lengthways log.

11 Lash two pieces of wood together to form a cross. It should be strong enough to carry the weight of the rudder.

Lash crosspiece of rudder securely

12 Wedge the crosspiece into the rear of the raft, between two deck logs, to make sure that it will fit. Adjust the lashing if necessary. Do not lash it in place at this stage.

13 Make a paddle *(see page 157)*. This will act as a rudder, and enable you to steer the raft. If you want to stand up while you are steering, you may have to extend the tiller (the paddle handle) by lashing a long branch to it.

RAFTS AND RAFTING

■ Instead of logs, you could use thick stems of bamboo for the deck of your raft. Lash two layers of bamboo together, since a single layer would probably not support your weight. Instead of lashing retainers above and below the raft, you can cut holes in the sides of the stems and thread thin branches or rope through them to link the bamboo stems together to make a deck. Lash between each of the stems for added security.

■ You will not know how your raft floats until it is launched. With certain types of wood, a loaded raft may float slightly below the water's surface, although this is not a serious problem.

■ A raft will turn relatively slowly, so take this into account when steering.

■ Try to avoid collisions with the bank or large objects, since they are likely to distort the raft and break lashings.

14 Make sure that the rudder will fit on the crosspiece, and then lash it securely. In order to prevent the crosspiece and rudder from breaking when the raft is launched, take them off the raft. Secure them in place once the raft is in the water. The raft should be big enough to carry you and your gear safely across or down the river. Try to make sure the raft will float before loading it up.

USING RAFTS AND BOATS

IN MANY WILDERNESS areas, dense vegetation and tough terrain make river, lake, or coastal travel the best option. However, you should bear in mind that venturing onto water is dangerous, especially when using improvised boats. You must therefore ensure that your boat is suitable for the particular water you intend to cross, whether it is improvised or not. Water conditions can change very rapidly, turning a relatively safe journey into a hazardous one. For this reason, you should not venture onto water unless you are experienced or have no other option. Always wear some form of lifejacket.

LAUNCHING A RAFT

A raft must only be used on slow-flowing waters. Build it close to the water, since it may be too heavy to carry to the bank. Before putting the raft in the water, tie it to an immovable object, leaving enough slack in the rope to enable the raft to be launched.

Using Levers
Launch the raft by levering up one side with poles, so that it slides into the water.

Floating
Once you are satisfied that the raft will not fall apart in the water, you can lash the rudder onto it, and begin loading your equipment in the center.

SAILING A RAFT

For long journeys down a straight river, rig up a mast and sail to take advantage of the wind – as long as the wind is blowing in the direction you want to go. Without a keel, the rudder will only control direction in a light wind, but it will enable you to keep the raft straight. If the bow digs into the water, reduce the area of sail. You will only be able to move downstream with the current.

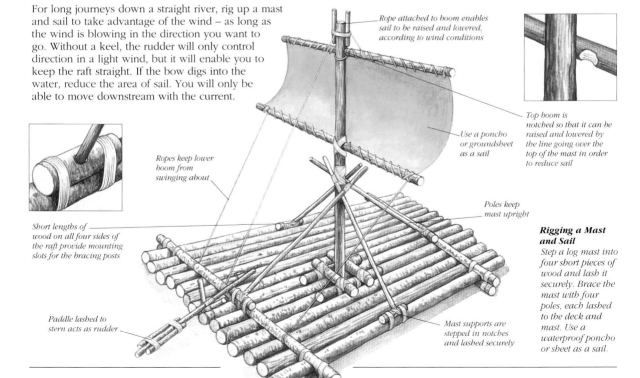

Rope attached to boom enables sail to be raised and lowered, according to wind conditions

Top boom is notched so that it can be raised and lowered by the line going over the top of the mast in order to reduce sail

Use a poncho or groundsheet as a sail

Ropes keep lower boom from swinging about

Poles keep mast upright

Short lengths of wood on all four sides of the raft provide mounting slots for the bracing posts

Paddle lashed to stern acts as rudder

Mast supports are stepped in notches and lashed securely

Rigging a Mast and Sail
Step a log mast into four short pieces of wood and lash it securely. Brace the mast with four poles, each lashed to the deck and mast. Use a waterproof poncho or sheet as a sail.

CHOOSING A BOAT

Every small boat has its strengths and weaknesses, and must never be used for the wrong purpose, in conditions beyond its capabilities. Some designs, such as the coracle, are only suited to mild, fairly slow waters, while others, for example the modern inflatable, can be used in conditions in which other boats would be totally unsuitable.

Inflatable
An inflatable can be used in relatively adverse sea conditions, and is a favorite craft among scientists and explorers. It can still be steered even when swamped by heavy seas. However, surface ice and other obstacles can puncture the floating compartments. When using an inflatable, you should keep the weight forward to prevent the boat from being lifted from the surface and blown backward.

Outboard Motor
A flat-bottomed boat with an outboard motor is best for use in wide, steadily flowing rivers. It is capable of covering long distances. An outboard motor weighs down the stern of a narrow boat, particularly when the propeller digs in, and must be counter-balanced by weight in the bow. The length of its propeller shaft will reduce the draft of the boat to a certain extent.

Coracle
A coracle requires skill in construction and use. It consists of a framework of pliable branches lashed into a half-sphere shape, and covered with an animal hide or tarpaulin shell. A coracle is suitable only for the most sheltered and slow-flowing waters.

Kayak
The traditional Inuit kayak is the basic design for the toughest modern kayaks capable of negotiating rough waters. Craft with skin or fabric shells are not as robust as fiberglass versions, but they are lightweight, and can easily be carried around rapids too difficult to negotiate by boat. Skill is required when paddling a kayak, particularly when it is loaded with equipment, or when it is being used in rough water. With no keel, kayaks capsize easily.

BOATING TIPS

- Always wear a lifejacket, or improvise with empty water bottles in your pocket.
- Secure every item of equipment by rope to your vessel.
- Do not overload the craft.
- Research the river you intend to use before launching your vessel.
- If you are using an outboard motor, accelerate to get the boat planing, then throttle back to keep it on the plane.

MAKING A PADDLE

1 To make a paddle, strip a strong, green branch of stems using a knife. Cut a smooth wedge shape at one end.

2 Bind two shorter, straight pieces of wood at the end on the sides of the wedge to act as the blade of your paddle.

3 Lash a third piece of wood to the center, forcing it into the gap, and against the wedge shape at the end of the handle.

Finished Paddle
The finished paddle may require relashing when it gets wet, since the string may stretch.

USING VEHICLES

THE BASIC REQUIREMENTS for off-road vehicle travel are well-distributed weight, the correct tires inflated to the right pressures, and good driving. Four-wheel drive, a high power-to-weight ratio, and other modifications help, but they increase fuel consumption and tire wear. Never take less than two vehicles on an expedition; if possible, take three so that one can be towed by the other two without either of them straining. A large-wheeled truck with high axle clearance can carry your heavy equipment, with two four-wheel-drive, short-wheel-base vehicles to carry passengers and give tows. You should complete a vehicle maintenance course before driving into wild areas.

CHOOSING AN EXPEDITION VEHICLE

The most powerful four-wheel-drive vehicles available can go almost anywhere, but use up too much fuel to be viable for an expedition. Gasoline engines are lighter and cheaper than diesel engines, and provide more power. However, large diesel engines can provide a lot of power in very low gear, for steady movement over rough terrain. In addition, diesel fuel is often a quarter of the price of gasoline – and diesel engines use less fuel. A long wheel base provides a lot of internal space, but makes it difficult for the vehicle to negotiate very rough ground without getting bogged down or stuck on obstructions.

Roofrack
A roofrack should have high, strong sides, and be able to carry bulky equipment that will not fit inside the vehicle. Ideally, the roofrack should be designed so that the gear can be lashed on with ropes. Carry only solid items such as crates on the roofrack.

Ideal Vehicle
There are a great many different kinds of sturdy vehicle that can be used for expeditions. The vehicle that you choose should ideally have most of the features shown below.

Access Ladder
Having a ladder leading up to the roof allows easy daily loading and unloading, plus access for using the roof of your vehicle – for observation, filming, and safety, as well as a cool spot for resting off the ground.

Engine
Engines that use gasoline are lighter, more powerful, and generally cheaper than those that run on diesel fuel. However, diesel engines can run powerfully at very low speeds, and tend to last longer than gasoline engines. In addition, diesel is usually much cheaper than gasoline in many countries.

Tires
Radial tires are best for off-road driving, but you should take care not to damage their sidewalls on rocks. Deflate tires slightly before crossing soft sand, then increase their pressure once you are back on a solid road.

High Axle
Good ground clearance is necessary for crossing rough ground. If your vehicle does not have a high axle, you are more likely to get bogged down in soft ground, and may even damage the chassis by getting stuck on a rock.

Four-wheel Drive
Four-wheel drive is essential on rough or boggy tracks and in sand. If you cannot get a four-wheel-drive vehicle, you should at least have a front-wheel-drive one, so that you can get out of soft ground if you get stuck (see opposite).

Spare Tire
Several spare tires must be carried, but think carefully about where on the vehicle you keep them. Although easily accessible if bolted on to rear doors, hoods, and roofracks, they are likely to get damaged or stolen.

DRIVING IN EXTREME CONDITIONS

Always drive slowly and carefully, particularly in extreme conditions. Stop the vehicle and scout ahead on foot if you are in any doubt about the state of the road. Then proceed at walking pace, if necessary. Always use the right tires for the conditions – for example, snow tires on icy, snow-packed tracks. Tire pressure can be reduced on soft ground, but must be increased when you return to the road. Check your vehicle before starting out on a drive.

Muddy Tracks
Go slowly along muddy tracks, taking care not to slide, spin the wheels, ground the chassis on rocks, or bog down the vehicle. Stay in the center of the track. Use four-wheel drive unless on firm roads, when you can save fuel and tire wear in two-wheel drive.

Crossing Water
Drive slowly and steadily through water, having inserted the wading bungs, and stopped up the axle breathers. Cover the engine's electric parts with canvas, leaving air intakes clear.

Crossing Sand
Sandy ground can vary from a firm, flat surface to deep, soft dunes. There may be boulders that could smash the engine sump. When driving on sandy ground, be alert and do not be tempted to travel too fast for the conditions.

DAILY CHECKS

Before setting off each morning, you should always make the following checks to your vehicle:
- Check the fuel, oil, and water, and the brake and hydraulic fluids, as well as the axle oil levels.
- Start the engine and allow it to warm up.
- Walk around the vehicle and check the tire treads and sidewalls, wheel nuts, steering arms, lights, and all external fixings.
- Check the brakes. Inspect the engine for oil or water leaks, and also for any exhaust problems.

RECOVERY FROM SOFT GROUND

1 If your vehicle gets stuck in mud, sand, or snow, and you cannot get out even using four-wheel drive, try backing out, "rocking" between reverse and first gears. If this fails, a passenger should try pushing the vehicle while you continue to drive forward. Admit defeat early, before you get in too deep.

2 If pushing fails, or you have no one to help you, dig down in front of the wheels to free them, and build a gradual upward slope in front of the holes. Try to drive gently forward and out. Do not rev the engine, since this may cause the wheels to spin and dig in even deeper.

Wood in front of wheels provides a solid surface on which to drive

3 If you cannot drive out even after digging out the wheels, lay pieces of wood or sand ladders, if you have them, in front of the wheels. Even a blanket may help to give the tires more grip. Drive out carefully. You may have to keep replacing the wood as you drive over it, until you reach solid ground.

WINCHING

If you have a winch, you can use it to get out of soft ground. Attach the cable to a tree or other strong point. Run the cable over a log to keep it clear of the ground. Gently drive and winch at the same time.

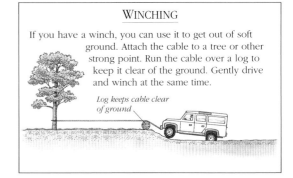

Log keeps cable clear of ground

OTHER TRANSPORTATION

IN AN URBAN environment, we regard traveling by bicycle, horse, or motorcycle as enjoyable forms of recreation. In the wilderness, however, they can provide a practical means of moving ourselves and our equipment from one place to another. Animals and vehicles must not be overloaded or driven too hard, but should be used well within their maximum capabilities. This may mean that you have to travel more slowly than you might on foot. Your choice of pack animal, bicycle, or motorcycle will depend upon the terrain you will cross, the duration of your journey, and the luggage you need to carry.

USING ANIMALS

Camels
Camels can each carry about 600 lb (272 kg) at a steady rate over rough terrain. They can be used in various terrains and conditions, from snow to soft sand. However, they can be willful and difficult to control.

Elephants
Elephants are enormously strong, but they walk quite slowly and are not the first choice for carrying equipment. They have specialized needs and work only with one handler, sometimes taking several months to gain trust in a new owner. They need a large amount of food, which must be carried.

Dogs
A seven-dog sled team can pull 600 lb (272 kg) about 20 miles (32 km) per day. Very hardy, Huskies can live out in the snow and enjoy pulling sleds. However, they need a lot of fresh meat, which must be added to the load.

Horses
Pack horses must be fed, watered, and rested daily, and need regular rest days, but they can cover 50 miles (80 km) per day for a few days at a time, carrying 200 lb (90 kg) at 4 mph (6 km/h). Mountain-bred horses are best for wilderness treks.

LOOKING AFTER ANIMALS

Animals must be looked after very carefully. Although it is important not to treat them as pets, their needs must be met. Establish a daily routine for watering and feeding them, and always stick to this routine. Treat any injuries immediately. Look after your animals before you look after yourself. Pack animals should be groomed before being saddled or loaded, to ensure that no grit rubs their backs under their loads. Elephants need daily bathing to prevent their skin from becoming sore, as well as dust baths to keep fly bites to a minimum. Hooved animals, such as horses and mules, must have their hooves cleaned every day with a hoof pick. If they will be walking on roads, they will need shoes. Other animals that are sometimes used for carrying luggage include llamas, oxen, yaks, donkeys, and even sheep.

Brush animal's coat before loading or saddling up

Grooming
Groom animals regularly, checking for injury, sores, and ticks at the same time. Pay particular attention to legs and hooves, watching how each animal walks. Any stiffness or tenderness must be treated immediately.

USING MOTORCYCLES

Heavy-duty motorcycles can be used to cross almost any terrain, but they must be properly looked after. It is essential to load a motorcycle correctly, taking into account both weight and balance. Spare parts and tools will add appreciably to the load you have to pack, but daily servicing must become a routine.

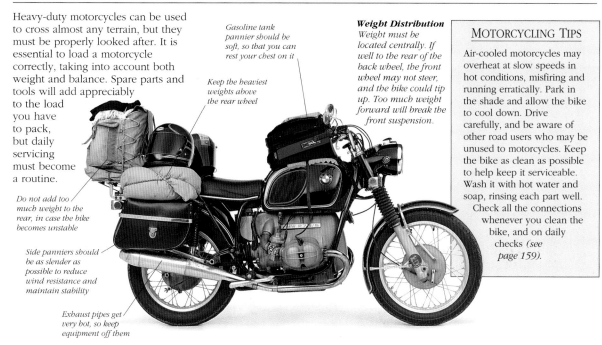

Gasoline tank pannier should be soft, so that you can rest your chest on it

Keep the heaviest weights above the rear wheel

Do not add too much weight to the rear, in case the bike becomes unstable

Side panniers should be as slender as possible to reduce wind resistance and maintain stability

Exhaust pipes get very hot, so keep equipment off them

Weight Distribution
Weight must be located centrally. If well to the rear of the back wheel, the front wheel may not steer, and the bike could tip up. Too much weight forward will break the front suspension.

MOTORCYCLING TIPS

Air-cooled motorcycles may overheat at slow speeds in hot conditions, misfiring and running erratically. Park in the shade and allow the bike to cool down. Drive carefully, and be aware of other road users who may be unused to motorcycles. Keep the bike as clean as possible to help keep it serviceable. Wash it with hot water and soap, rinsing each part well. Check all the connections whenever you clean the bike, and on daily checks *(see page 159).*

USING BICYCLES

Mountain bikes can be regarded as an aid to walking. On rough ground, consider wearing a backpack rather than loading the bike with panniers, which make the bike too heavy to carry. Keep well separated from other bikes – and any other users of the track or road. When wearing a backpack, keep your speed down, particularly when descending steep hills.

All-terrain Transport
Mountain bikes can be used in almost all terrains and conditions. You should be prepared, however, to get off and carry or push the bike up steep hills or across streams or mud.

Wear a windproof jacket, and keep a pullover handy for when you stop

Wheels can be easily buckled, particularly when the bike is carrying heavy gear

Gaiters keep pant legs out of the chain, and can prevent pants from being ripped by vegetation

Cycling Gear
You can wear almost anything for cycling, but pants should be held in at the ankle by gaiters so that they do not catch in the chain. Always wear a helmet and goggles.

Handlebars must be able to support your upper body and the weight of your loaded backpack

Footwear can be light hiking boots or special cycling boots that fit into pedal cages

IMPROVISED REPAIRS

There is a limit to the number of spare parts that you can carry, so do not risk breaking anything on your bicycle. If you do need to make repairs, you should ride very gently afterward until you can get the part fixed permanently. Wire is useful for replacing rivets on broken chains, rejoining snapped cables, and attaching brake levers. Duct tape will temporarily seal punctured inner tubes. If you lose your pump, you can stuff a flat tire with grass and leaves until you can get it pumped up again.

APPENDIX A

ABANDONING SHIP

LEAVING THE SAFETY of a ship at sea is a very serious and dangerous action. Even if it is very badly damaged, a ship can offer you warmth, shelter, water, and food. It will also contain radios, flares, and other lifesaving equipment. You should only leave at the last moment, for no other reason than that it is too dangerous to remain. The signal to abandon ship is always given by the captain, the person best qualified to judge when that moment has arrived. Before leaving a vessel, take with you every piece of equipment that might be useful to you, as well as all the food and freshwater you can carry.

Liferaft
Most commercial seagoing vessels are equipped with liferafts or lifeboats. These can range from a basic inflatable boat to one that has a canopy and emergency tools and provisions.

EVACUATION

Ideally, you should never jump into the water. Instead, climb down a ladder into a liferaft. Getting wet seriously reduces your chances of survival *(see opposite)*. However, you may have no other option but to jump. First ensure that your lifejacket is securely tied around you but not inflated, in case it gets caught on something as you jump. Check for debris in the water, then jump from the lowest part of the vessel.

1 Cover your mouth and pinch your nose to prevent seawater from entering. Your free arm should grasp your other shoulder to keep that arm in position, your elbow keeping your lifejacket flat.

2 Keep your head up and your spine straight. Jump into clear water. Keep straight in the air. Then, just before entry, cross your legs and ankles and lock them.

3 Pull the cord on your lifejacket to inflate it, or blow in the mouthpiece. Keep clear of the sinking vessel. Swim slowly backward, using your legs.

RULES TO REMEMBER

- Do not abandon your vessel unless it is absolutely certain that it will sink.
- Before you jump into the water, make sure that your lifejacket is securely tied around you, and that you have on adequate clothing to help keep you warm.
- Never inflate a lifejacket before entering the water.
- If you need to attract attention, use the whistle on your lifejacket, or splash or wave with one arm.
- Swim well under any burning fuel, or use breaststroke and splash a breathing hole for your head.
- Even if you are in sight of land, never swim against the tide.

FLOATING WITH A LIFEJACKET

HELP
The Heat-Escape-Lessening Posture (HELP) is designed to reduce the amount of heat escaping from your body's core. Draw up your knees and fold your arms to conserve heat in your abdomen.

Huddle
If you are in a group, place children in the center and form a huddle, keeping everyone as close together as possible, ideally with chests touching. Do not allow anyone to fall asleep.

DROWNPROOFING

In salty water, humans are very buoyant. This applies even to non-swimmers wearing clothes – so relax and do not panic. If you cannot float on your back and keep your head above water without getting swamped by waves, the following method will enable you to float quietly and come up for air at regular intervals.

1 If you relax, you will float naturally just below the surface of the water. Let your face lie in the water, and tread water with your legs as you come up to the surface to breathe.

2 Exhale in the water, and scull (scoop water) with your hands to raise your head just clear of the surface. Make sure your lungs are completely empty, and then take a deep breath.

3 Put your face back in the water, mouth closed, and bring your arms forward to rest at surface level. Allow your legs to float out behind, until you need to take another breath.

FLOTATION AIDS

Gather all the debris you can find to help you float. You may find driftwood or garbage discarded by ships.

Using Debris
Debris can be used to help keep you afloat.

SURVIVING IN COLD WATER

You will lose more valuable body heat (and die quicker) if you swim than if you remain still, so it is best to hang quietly in your lifejacket in the HELP position, or use debris to improvise a float. Keep on your clothes, including your shoes – they retain water, which your body warms, like a wetsuit. Keep your head and shoulders out of water, to conserve heat in your body's core.

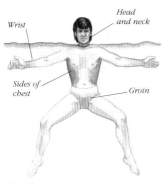

Wrist

Head and neck

Sides of chest

Groin

Heat-loss Areas
Large volumes of blood circulate close to the surface of the skin above these critical areas. The HELP position keeps them covered (see opposite).

MAKING A BUOYANCY AID

Even if you can swim, a buoyancy aid is vital for helping to keep your head above water so that you can breathe, and so that you do not lose body heat from your head. You can improvise a buoyancy aid from a pair of pants.

1 Tie pant legs together close to the cuffs, tightening the knot with your teeth while treading water with your legs.

Catch air by throwing open pants over your head

2 Holding the belt or fly, throw the pants forward over your head, catching as much air as possible. Repeat if necessary.

3 Place your head between the pant legs. Hold the waist shut below the water. Reinflate the pants as required.

Inflated pants will help keep your head above water

WARNING

Even if you are floating in the water and rescue seems out of the question, keep calm and do not panic. You must think clearly to survive. Exposure to the cold will make you feel sleepy – you must fight this. Boredom is equally destructive, so start counting the time to keep your brain occupied.

SURVIVING AT SEA

IF YOU HAVE to abandon your vessel at sea, all available liferafts must be used, loaded to safe capacity with survivors. Put children, the infirm, and any injured people in the center. In warm waters, if there are too many people to fit into the liferaft, some people can hang on to the sides. They should change over regularly with those in the raft. Put all the food and equipment in plastic bags or containers and attach them to the vessel with cord. Tie everybody on with a lifeline. Check food supplies, estimate the number of days you could remain afloat, and begin rationing immediately.

Shark
There are hundreds of species of sharks around the world, some of which may threaten humans. Sharks are attracted to the sounds of distress and the smell of blood. Take care not to attract them.

ADAPTING A LIFERAFT

Although you can obtain liferafts complete with emergency equipment and supplies, many liferafts are very basic, designed more for easy storage on the mother ship than for extended use. In a basic liferaft, you must immediately improvise a shelter from rain, wind, or spray, and devise the means of putting up a sail.

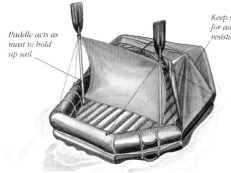

Paddle acts as mast to hold up sail

Keep shelter up for added wind resistance

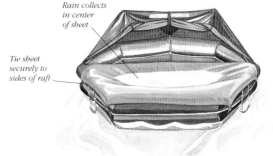

Rain collects in center of sheet

Tie sheet securely to sides of raft

Improvising a Sail
A large poncho or sheet strung between two upright paddles will propel the liferaft before the wind, although the craft will be difficult to steer unless you can improvise a rudder. Tie the paddles securely to the sides of the liferaft.

Collecting Rainwater
Obtaining freshwater can be very difficult at sea. Stretch a plastic sheet across the liferaft during rain to collect the rainwater. Scoop it immediately into containers to prevent it from becoming contaminated with salt spray.

Making a Sea Anchor
A bucket streaming along behind the liferaft on a line will keep you facing into the weather so the raft does not capsize. If distress signals were sent before you abandoned your vessel, you should try to stay in the same place so that rescuers can find you. A sea anchor will also limit drift caused by the wind.

DEALING WITH SHARKS

Sharks may approach a liferaft out of curiosity. If they get too close to the liferaft and you think they may damage it, you can discourage them by making loud noises and deliberate movements. They will often depart if jabbed firmly on the nose with something hard, such as a paddle. The danger increases if a shark is hungry, and has smelled blood or excreta, or sensed weak and uncertain movements; all of which indicate an easy meal. Shark-repellent chemicals should be reserved until a shark circles in toward the liferaft, making sudden movements that indicate imminent attack. To discourage sharks from rubbing along the bottom of the liferaft, float a cloth or blanket behind it.

LIVING IN A LIFERAFT

Protection from the sun, rain, and waves is vital. You should try to catch fish with the hook and line in your survival kit *(see page 28)*, or with a net *(see below)*. However, if you do not have any fresh water, you should not eat, since the body uses up precious water for digestion. Keep as still as possible to avoid losing even more water through perspiration. One person must be on watch at all times, collecting water and looking for land.

Catching Food
Tie a shirt or other garment to a paddle attached to the side of the liferaft. This will form a trawl net for surface-swimming fish. Take great care not to fall in, or lose the paddle. You may also be able to find shore creatures, such as crabs, clinging to driftwood and debris.

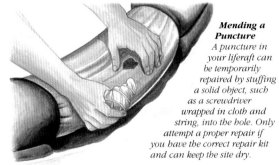

Mending a Puncture
A puncture in your liferaft can be temporarily repaired by stuffing a solid object, such as a screwdriver wrapped in cloth and string, into the hole. Only attempt a proper repair if you have the correct repair kit and can keep the site dry.

SIGNALING FROM A LIFERAFT

Getting noticed in a liferaft can be difficult, but flares can be used for signaling to ships or aircraft. Some flares are meant to be used only at night, offshore, or in fog, while others are best seen in daylight. Some can be held in the hand, while rockets must be fired into the air with a special gun.

BY DAY

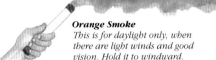

Orange Smoke
This is for daylight only, when there are light winds and good vision. Hold it to windward.

Signaling with the Arms
If you can see a ship or plane, stand up in the liferaft and lift your arms up and down.

BY NIGHT

Red Parachute Flare
This bursts at 300 ft (91 m) and is visible for about 7 miles (11 km). It stays visible for longer than other types of flare.

Red Handheld Flare
Hold this flare as high as possible, in your hand or tied to the end of a paddle. It will be visible for up to 3 miles (5 km). Use it in poor visibility, darkness, or high winds.

Anticollision White Flare
This is carried on craft to indicate presence and reduce collision risk. Use this flare once other flares have run out. It is most visible at night, or at close range.

SIGNS OF LAND

As you grow used to the view from your liferaft, you will soon notice anything unusual that might indicate that land may be nearby. For example, cumulus clouds *(see page 132)* in a clear sky generally form over land. They often have a greenish "lagoon glare" caused by sunlight reflecting from shallow water. Although single seabirds may be a long way from land, flocks of birds are usually never more than 62 miles (100 km) from the shore. They often return to land in the late afternoon to roost on beaches and cliffs and in fields.

Seal
Seals in the water are a sure sign that land is nearby, since they never venture very far from the shore.

HEALTH PROBLEMS

Sunburn, windburn, and saltwater boils are the most common health problems at sea. Keep covered and out of the sun. Keep saltwater off your skin, and ensure that the liferaft is as dry as possible. Wash in freshwater if you can, and use oil or barrier cream to prevent boils. A raw fish diet creates little waste, so bowel movements are few, and constipation may make them painful. The only solution is to eat less than you normally would, especially if you are short of fresh water.

DANGEROUS CREATURES

UNLESS PROVOKED, INJURED, hungry, or disturbed, most animals will avoid humans. You can, however, provoke them by mistake, particularly when they have young, which even nonaggressive herbivores will protect fiercely. You are a visitor to their world, which you must respect. Some dangerous species are either lethally poisonous or behave naturally in ways that make them dangerous to us.

Grizzly Bear (Ursus)
The grizzly bear is not, by nature, aggressive, and is more likely to run away than attack a hiker who encounters it. However, the dangerous exception to this rule is a female with cubs, which should be avoided at all costs.

NORTH AMERICA

Much of North America is still wilderness. The continent is largely temperate, although it includes mountains, arid plains, and hot deserts. In remote forests, large predators such as the grizzly bear and the North American timber wolf *(Canis)* survive, while small, venomous creatures such as the diamondback rattlesnake *(Crotalus)* and the brown recluse spider *(Loxoscees)* inhabit warmer regions. In temperate regions, most creatures dangerous to humans become torpid or hibernate during the winter.

Coral Snake (Micrurus)
There are many species of coral snake in North America, all of which have red, black, and yellow stripes. Other species live in southeast Asia and South America. The snakes can be up to 3 ft (1 m) long. Although they are venomous, they have short fangs, so most bites are to the hands and feet.

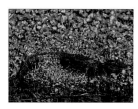

American Alligator (Alligator)
This lives in swamps in the southeastern United States. It lies in wait for its prey, remaining immobile for hours at a time, but it can move extremely fast.

SOUTH AMERICA

Much of South America is tropical rainforest *(see page 145)*. Thousands of species of animal live here, many of which are venomous. Insects and snakes are the most abundant creatures, thriving in the lush, tropical vegetation. There are also larger animals such as wild pigs and jaguars, and amphibians that can be dangerous to humans. On the southernmost tip of the continent, the bull elephant seal *(Mirounga)* can be very aggressive during its rutting season.

Piranha (Serrasalmus)
This feared South American fish has razor-sharp teeth, and schools of them will attack a wounded animal, stripping the bones clean.

Poison Arrow Tree Frog (Sminthillus)
The skin of this South American frog secretes one of the most toxic substances known to man. Only a minute amount on skin can kill.

Sea Snake (Laticauda)
Some Indo-Pacific sea snakes are very venomous, but they are not aggressive.

Scorpionfish
(Scorpaenidae)
Scorpionfish live in the Atlantic, Pacific, and Indian oceans, and the Mediterranean Sea. Their long spines are venomous and can cause extremely painful stings if stepped on (see page 180).

EUROPE

Europe's once extensive forests are now towns and suburbs, the odd wild boar surviving only in remote areas. However, the hornet *(Vespa)* and the adder *(Vipera)* can kill, their small amount of poison stimulating anaphylactic shock *(see page 180).*

Black Widow Spider
(Lactrodectus)
Found in hot, dry regions around the Mediterranean, as well as in North America, the black widow is one of the most feared spiders in the world. Its bite is not always fatal, but panic can accelerate the spread of the poison throughout the body, contributing to heart and respiratory failure.

AFRICA

Many African animals can be dangerous to humans if provoked, the large predators requiring particular respect. There are also deadly snakes, such as the black mamba *(Dendroaspis)* and the boomslang *(Dispholidus).* The biggest threat, however, is the malaria-carrying mosquito *(Anopheles).*

Puff Adder (Bitis)
Found near water in semi-arid areas of Africa, as well as the Arabian Peninsula, the puff adder is thickset, with a large, flattened head and short tail. It is usually straw-colored, with dark brown markings. The puff adder is a long-fanged viper, which means that its fangs can penetrate clothing. Its bite can be deadly.

Hippopotamus
(Hippopotamus)
This is said to be one of the most dangerous animals in Africa. It lives in rivers, and although it is usually harmless, it will attack if its escape route is blocked or its young are threatened.

ASIA

Most of southeast Asia is tropical forest, uninhabited by humans except for a few primitive tribes. Creatures here that can be dangerous to humans include the estuarine crocodile *(Crocodylus),* the Indian krait snake *(Bungarus),* and the red-back spider *(Lactrodectus).*

Tiger (Panthera)
The tiger lives in southeast Asia, and is generally reclusive, avoiding humans. Nevertheless, a tiger can be a formidable predator if provoked, especially if it is a female defending her cubs.

Funnel-web Spider (Atrax)
Funnel-web spiders are found in Australia, and their bite can be fatal. They are named for the type of web they produce, and are most active at night, especially in relatively cool, damp areas.

AUSTRALIA

Some of the world's most venomous and aggressive creatures live in Australia. They include the deadly poisonous fierce snake *(Parademansia);* the aggressive great white shark; and the lethal stonefish (Synanceidae) and death puffer fish *(Arothron).*

Great White Shark
(Carcharodon)
This inhabits both temperate and tropical waters. Some sharks can be very aggressive (see page 164).

DEALING WITH DANGEROUS ANIMALS

It is better to avoid danger than have to deal with it. Make as much noise as possible when walking through brush. Most animals will run away. Avoid females with young. If you do encounter a predator, freeze, then back away slowly. Do not run – you could trigger the animal's instinctive chasing response. If you do incite a charge, run in a zigzag pattern, or rush at the predator, waving your arms and shouting. Learn the habits of the animals in your area so that you can avoid them. If you are bitten, do not panic *(see page 180).* Use a mosquito net at night to avoid dangerous insects. Shake out your clothes and boots before putting them on in the morning, in case scorpions and spiders have taken refuge in them during the night.

NATURAL HAZARDS

W E SEE DISASTERS regularly on television, becoming to an extent inured to them. We do not think that disaster could ever happen to us. It is, however, important to understand that certain kinds of disaster are common in many parts of the world – in these areas precautions should be taken. You must always take serious heed of warnings given by locals, particularly local radio.

FOREST FIRE

Causes of Fire
Forest and brush fires can easily start when ground vegetation is dry. A campfire may spread, or the sun may ignite dry vegetation through a piece of glass. If a fire begins close to you, try to smother it immediately with a sleeping bag, or beat it out with a coat, before it gets out of hand. The importance of supervising and keeping campfires under control cannot be overstated.

SIGNS AND PRECAUTIONS

You will smell the fire first, and may notice animals becoming nervous. If the wind is blowing toward the fire, move into the wind. If the wind is behind the fire, the flames will move very fast. Seek a road, a natural break in the trees, or a river, and stay there until the fire has passed. Do not travel uphill. If there is no possibility of escape, it may be best to run through the flames, taking refuge in the area beyond.

AVALANCHE

Snowslide
Avalanches are hazards in all snow-covered mountain areas. Always seek local advice before venturing into any such area. Common sense can minimize the risk, which increases throughout the day as snow is warmed by sunshine on steep, south-facing slopes (north-facing in the southern hemisphere). An avalanche may be caused by an earthquake, by loud noises, such as shouting, or by skiers.

PRECAUTIONS

If an avalanche starts above you, ski or run downhill away from it as fast as you can. Duck into any solid rock overhangs or shelter. If caught, drop your backpack and other gear. Cover your mouth and nose with your arms, and lie flat, trying to keep your head above the rising snow. When the avalanche has stopped, clear a space around your head so that you can breathe. Shout loudly when you hear rescuers.

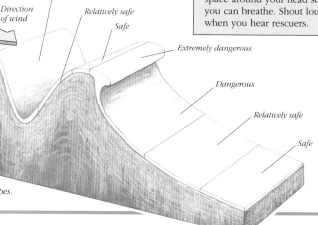

Direction of wind

Dangerous

Relatively safe

Safe

Extremely dangerous

Dangerous

Relatively safe

Safe

Danger Zones
Snow naturally creeps downhill because of gravity, so the snow at the bottom of a hill is denser and more stable than that at the top. Avalanches thus occur easily toward the top of a hill, particularly on convex slopes.

THE VOLATILE EARTH

Earthquakes and volcanic activity follow the edges of the plates of the Earth's lithosphere. These plates move against each other, causing tension to build up. Earthquakes occur when these tensions are released, usually along fault lines, as a sudden movement. The movement may only be a few inches, or several yards. Volcanoes also occur in areas of geological weakness, when molten material from the Earth's upper mantle forces its way to the surface.

Ring of Fire
Most earthquakes and volcanoes encircle the Pacific Ocean plate – the "Ring of Fire."

▲ VOLCANOES   EARTHQUAKE ZONES

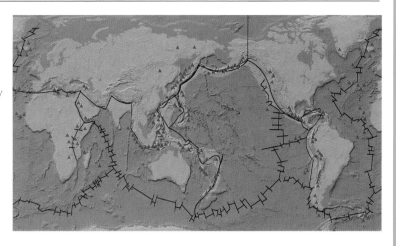

EARTHQUAKE

Feared Disaster
The most feared natural disaster, earthquake damage is so bizarre as to be completely unpredictable. Get to the top of a hill or a beach (away from cliffs). Keep out of buildings, lying flat on the ground in open areas. Stop your car, but remain inside. In a well-built cellar or ground floor, keep close to the walls, preferably under a strong table.

AFTER AN EARTHQUAKE

Even though an earthquake appears to have finished, there may still be further tremors. Keep clear of all damaged structures, which may topple over and fall on you. Watch out for live electric cables. Ruptured sewage and water pipes make disease the biggest hazard of earthquakes, so boil and filter all your drinking water *(see page 74).* Tune in to local radio stations and obey all public service instructions.

TSUNAMI

An earthquake under the sea can cause waves up to 100 ft (30 m) high, which may swamp coastal areas. There is little you can do in the face of such a wall of water.

GIANT WAVE

VOLCANOES

Eruptions
Live volcanoes are part of the tectonic activity of earthquake areas. They produce lava, ash, hot gases, mud flows, and flying debris ("volcanic bombs"). Lava flows are rarely fast enough to catch people, but hot gas clouds, ash (actually pulverized rock), and volcanic bombs are lethal. Strong sulfur dioxide affects lungs and skin. You must avoid places where lava might flow, such as stream beds. Leave the area immediately.

PRECAUTIONS

If you notice increased volcanic activity, leave the area. Once an eruption has started, ash and mud flows will make roads slippery and dangerous, as well as destroying buildings and cutting off escape routes. Keep dust masks (or wet cloths) ready in case the air becomes contaminated. Wash any debris from your skin as soon as possible.

EXTREME WEATHER

WEATHER CHANGES ARE the product of differences in atmospheric temperature and pressure. Extreme weather results when these differences become larger than usual, and can be deduced from the study of proper weather maps, called synoptic charts. Using data gathered at certain times daily from all over a region, these charts can help in the detection or prediction of serious storms. Warnings can then be issued, and steps taken to minimize danger and prevent loss of life. Extreme weather is often seasonal, and may be confined to certain regions.

WORLD WEATHER

The forecasting of extreme weather is based upon predicting how various enormous masses of air are likely to interact with each other. Large land masses create stable high-pressure systems, which are upset by low-pressure systems, or depressions. Below is an idealized synoptic chart, showing extreme weather conditions.

Weather Forecast
A map on which weather is marked is called a synoptic chart. Once all the available information has been gathered from weather stations and satellites and marked on the chart, likely weather conditions can be forecast for up to a week.

Good weather with high pressure, trapping pollution to create smog

Squall line along which tornadoes are likely to run

Spiked lines show where fronts of heavy, cold air are pushing under lighter warm air

Blizzards

Atlantic gales

An occluded front is indicated by spikes and bumps together, where cold fronts catch up with warm ones and keep them off the ground

Low-pressure systems, or cyclones, bring cloudy weather

High-pressure systems, called anticyclones, are stable, with good weather, clear skies, and cumulus clouds

Isobars join areas of equal air pressure

Symbol shows direction and strength of wind

A hurricane is indicated by an isolated isobar of warm, low-pressure air surrounded by rotating, high-speed winds

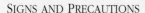

WINDSTORMS

Severe windstorms can affect any part of the world, at any time of year, and there is nothing that anybody can do to prevent or prepare for them. Extreme storms, such as hurricanes and tornadoes, uproot trees, destroy buildings, and block railroads and streets. At sea these storms can cause waves large enough to capsize ships.

Tornado
A tornado develops when warm, low-pressure air rises to meet high winds descending through storm clouds. This creates a swirling vortex of wind that may reach 400 mph (644 km/h).

SIGNS AND PRECAUTIONS

You can see and hear a tornado coming – get out of its way fast. Outdoors, take shelter in a cave, or lie in a ditch with your arms over your head. Indoors, close doors and windows facing the tornado, and open those facing away from it. Get out of vehicles and mobile homes.

Hurricane
A hurricane is a tropical storm caused by hot air rising from the sea, creating low pressure and drawing high, spinning winds and thunderstorms together.

SIGNS AND PRECAUTIONS

Abnormal rises in barometric pressure, followed by a sudden drop, may indicate a hurricane. Evacuate the area when a hurricane has been spotted. If outdoors, avoid coasts and rivers, and shelter in a cave or deep gully. If indoors, clear up loose objects that might cause damage when blown around. Board up windows. Shelter under strong furniture in a cellar.

RAINSTORMS

Sudden, very heavy rain can saturate the surface of the land, preventing the usual percolation of water through the soil and underlying rock. Instead, most of the water flows over the surface, and may wash away soil, vegetation, and buildings. It may also overwhelm drainage systems and short out power lines.

Flood
Floods can be caused by rivers and reservoirs breaking their banks, and by sudden, heavy rainfall. They are usually worst in very dry areas, where the surface of the ground is saturated immediately, and the topsoil is washed away. It is fairly easy to predict which low-lying areas are likely to flood during heavy rain, so you should avoid them if you think a flood is imminent.

PRECAUTIONS

If you can predict a flood, save as much drinking water as possible. Collect food, matches, and bedding, and move to high ground, or to the upper floors of a building. Unless there is any danger to the building in which you are taking refuge, stay put until the flood waters drop, or until you are rescued. Walking or driving through a flood can be extremely dangerous.

PRECAUTIONS

Wear rubber-soled shoes and sit on something completely dry that will not conduct electricity. Keep off the ground, offering as low and small a profile as possible. Keep away from anything tall or metal. Lightning strikes create huge flashes, a shockwave, and much heat, which can injure people even though they might not be hit.

Electrical Storm
When rising warm air meets colder air, static electricity is created as water droplets are violently agitated. This static electricity has enormously high voltage, flashing between water particles, striking the first object it encounters as it runs to earth by the easiest route. Even if you are struck by lightning, you may still survive.

SIGNALING

I T IS VITAL, before leaving on any expedition, that people know your plans, route, and expected arrival times. If overdue, somebody will thus know you are lost, and roughly where. Indicating your position and the problem is simple. The basic international distress signals are "SOS" (Save Our Souls), transmitted by Morse Code using a mirror, flashlight, or smoke signals, or by Semaphore; and the radio call "May Day," from the French "M'aidée," ("Help Me").

SEMAPHORE

Sender and receiver must have a clear view of each other. Use binoculars to ensure accurate reading. When sending, count slowly from "one thousand and one" to "one thousand and six," moving deliberately to each new letter. When receiving, draw the arm positions, then determine the letters when the message is complete.

GROUND-TO-AIR SIGNALS

Waiting to be rescued, you must be able to attract the attention of aircrew, then indicate exactly what you need.

If there is no need to be rescued but you need supplies, you must make this clear *(see below)*. Pilots willingly

risk airplane and crew to attempt a landing in a dangerous place. Their dedication must not be abused.

USING MARKERS

Ground Markers
These signals are international. "FILL" is the mnemonic for remembering them. Pilots will take great risks if they see "I" for "serious injury." Make the signs as large as possible, from sticks or stones, or by drawing in the dirt.

 NEED FOOD AND WATER

 INDICATE DIRECTION TO PROCEED

 BELIEVED SAFE TO LAND HERE

A YES (OR Y FOR YES)

I SERIOUS INJURY/NEED DOCTOR

□ NEED COMPASS AND MAP

↑ AM TRAVELING THIS WAY

N NEGATIVE

JL DO NOT UNDERSTAND

LL ALL IS WELL

USING THE BODY

Marshaling Aircraft
These signals can be used to marshal a helicopter safely in to land, or to communicate with aircrew. You must stand straight and exaggerate all movements. Brace yourself when a helicopter lands – its downdraft may bowl you over.

FLY TOWARD ME/ PICK ME UP

HOVER/ NEED MECHANICAL HELP

DESCEND

(WAVING RIGHT ARM) MOVE TO MY LEFT

(WAVING LEFT ARM) MOVE TO MY RIGHT

FLY TOWARD ME

INDICATING DIRECTION OF SAFE EXIT

USING THE SUN

Using a piece of reflective material with a hole punched in the center, look through the hole in the direction of the sun. Tilt the reflector downward until a bright flash of sunlight is reflected onto the ground. Move the flash up into the sky and onto an aircraft. Tilt the reflector slightly to attract the pilot's attention, but avoid blinding him.

Heliograph
A heliograph can reflect the sun to attract attention.

MORSE CODE

Morse Code can be sent by radio, whistle blasts, heliograph, or smoke clouds. It is easier to transmit Morse than to receive it, so send very slowly. Pause after each word. AAAAAA means I have a message; TTTT means I am receiving you; and R (roger) means message received. Send slowly.

A	• —	N	— •	1	• — — — —
B	— • • •	O	— — —	2	• • — — —
C	— • — •	P	• — — •	3	• • • — —
D	— • •	Q	— — • —	4	• • • • —
E	•	R	• — •	5	• • • • •
F	• • — •	S	• • •	6	— • • • •
G	— — •	T	—	7	— — • • •
H	• • • •	U	• • —	8	— — — • •
I	• •	V	• • • —	9	— — — — •
J	• — — —	W	• — —	0	— — — — —
K	— • —	X	— • • —		
L	• — • •	Y	— • — —		
M	— —	Z	— — • •	SOS	• • • — — — • • •

APPENDIX B

FIRST AID

IN ORDER FOR injured people to come through a survival situation alive, the correct first aid must be given immediately. Consequently, every person in your party must know what to do, and be confident enough to take action immediately. Without the professional backup of ambulances and hospitals, the continued care of seriously injured people is a major problem, but you can treat minor injuries and keep serious casualties stable until further help is available. Although there are innumerable injuries and ailments that could affect you or a member of your party, as long as you learn the basic principles of first aid, you can apply them to almost any situation.

BASIC FIRST-AID KIT

Your first-aid kit should contain specially selected items to enable you to deal with most medical emergencies, helping you to stabilize a casualty's condition until you can get him to a doctor. There are a lot of kits available, but it is best if you assemble your own basic kit, including the items shown below.

LIMB ADHESIVE BANDAGE · DIGIT ADHESIVE BANDAGE · SPOT ADHESIVE BANDAGE

Adhesive Bandages
Use these to keep small cuts from going septic, and for covering blisters.

GAUZE DRESSING · GAUZE BANDAGE · CREPE BANDAGE

Bandages
Bandages are useful for a variety of purposes, from keeping dressings in place and binding wounds closed, to tying up broken limbs to prevent further damage.

Safety Pins
Safety pins are useful for securing bandages, and as temporary sutures.

Painkillers
Save painkillers for when you really need them, for instance when you are making an emergency move.

Gauze Padding
Pads of gauze absorb blood and keep wounds clean until they can heal.

Scissors
A pair of scissors is perhaps the most valuable first-aid tool. You should buy the best-quality, blunt-nosed kind that you can find.

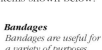
ANTISEPTIC WIPE · ANTISEPTIC CREAM

Antiseptic
Use antiseptic wipes to clean wounds. Antiseptic cream can be put on minor wounds to help them heal properly without becoming infected.

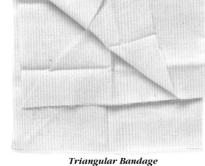
Triangular Bandage
This can be used to make a sling for supporting a broken arm, or as a large bandage, for example around a foot. It can also serve as a scarf (see page 142).

Foot Felt and Corn Pads
Blisters and other foot problems are common when you have a lot of walking to do, so foot felt and corn pads are helpful for preventing small wounds from becoming large ones. Cut the felt to fit over the sore spot. Hold in place with an adhesive bandage.

CORN PADS · FOOT FELT

ASSESSING VICTIMS

When approaching the scene of an accident, take time to stand back and assess the scene. Turn off vehicle ignitions to prevent fire, and sort out any other hazards that could cause further injury. Look quickly at all the victims, ensuring that nobody remains trapped or hidden from view. Then assess each of the injured, deciding who is so badly injured that he will die anyway; who requires immediate life-saving treatment; and who can wait. Do not panic. Act with assurance and efficiency – people may die if you do not.

WARNING

Do not try to move victims until you have discovered what is wrong with them (unless there is a greater danger in leaving them where they are). You could paralyze those with spinal injuries (see page 178).

THE ABC OF RESUSCITATION

1 To check an unconscious victim, place two fingers under her chin and a hand on her forehead. Tilt her head back to open her **airway**. Remove any obstructions from her mouth.

2 Listen and feel for the victim's **breathing.** If she is breathing, place her in the recovery position *(see below)* If she is not breathing, start rescue breathing *(see below).*

3 Check the victim's **circulation** by feeling for a pulse at the side of her windpipe (carotid artery). If there is no pulse, begin cardiopulmonary resuscitation immediately *(see page 176).*

RECOVERY POSITION

1 If a victim is unconscious but breathing, bend her near arm up at a right angle to her body. Hold the back of her far hand to her near cheek. With the near leg straight, pull the far knee toward you.

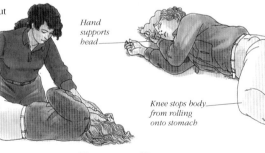

Hand supports head

Knee stops body from rolling onto stomach

2 With the victim on her side, place her uppermost leg at right angles to her body. Her head will be supported by the hand of the uppermost arm. Tilt her head back so that she will not choke if she vomits.

RESCUE BREATHING

1 To ensure an open airway, first clear the victim's mouth of obstructions. Then place one hand under his chin and one on his forehead, and tilt his head back.

2 Pinching the victim's nose shut, clamp your mouth over his mouth, and blow steadily for about two seconds until his chest rises. Remove your mouth and let his chest fall, then repeat.

3 Listen for the victim's breathing and check his pulse. If he still has a pulse, give 10 breaths per minute until help arrives or the victim is breathing by himself. If the pulse has stopped, combine rescue breathing with chest compressions *(see CPR, page 176).*

CARDIOPULMONARY RESUSCITATION

If a person's heart has stopped, give cardiopulmonary resuscitation (CPR). This consists of chest compressions to maintain the circulation of blood to the brain, combined with rescue breathing *(see page 175)* to oxygenate the blood. Give chest compressions at a rate of 80 per minute, counting "one-and-two-and...".

Find end of breastbone with two fingers, then slide other hand down to touch index finger

1 Place the heel of your hand two finger-widths up from the end of the breastbone, and your other hand on top of the first. Press down firmly, then release.

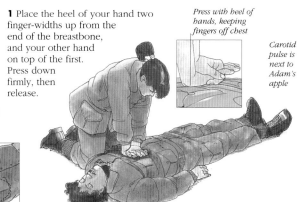

Press with heel of hands, keeping fingers off chest

Carotid pulse is next to Adam's apple

2 Check for a pulse. After 15 chest compressions, give the victim two breaths of rescue breathing *(see page 175)*. Repeat until the pulse restarts, medical help arrives, or you are too exhausted to continue.

CHOKING

Slapping the Back
To dislodge an obstruction from a person's airway, sit her down with her head lower than her chest. Slap her firmly between the shoulder blades five times.

Abdominal Thrusts
If back slaps do not work, stand behind the victim, interlock your hands beneath her ribcage, and pull sharply upward. The sudden pressure of her exhaled air should clear the throat obstruction.

WARNING
Lie an unconscious victim down and alternate five back slaps with five abdominal thrusts. Follow the ABC of Resuscitation *(see page 175)*.

CHOKING IN CHILDREN

Bending the child over your knee, strike it between the shoulder blades with the heel of your hand. Hold a baby over your arm. Do not use abdominal thrusts on babies.

BACK SLAPS

SHOCK

1 Lay the victim down, on a coat or sleeping bag, if possible. Raise his feet higher than his head. Loosen his clothing, reassure him, and take his pulse.

2 Cover the victim with a coat or sleeping bag. Check his breathing and pulse rates, particularly if he is unconscious. Be ready to resuscitate him if his heart stops.

Sleeping bag keeps victim warm

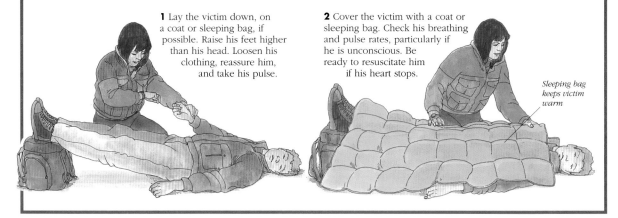

SEVERE EXTERNAL BLEEDING

1 Press the edges of the wound together. If you cannot remove a foreign body from the wound, press the skin up to the sides of the object.

2 Lie the victim down. Check for fractures, then raise his bleeding limb and apply pressure on the wound with a gauze pad until the bleeding stops.

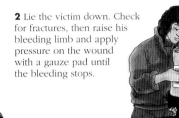

Press fingernail gently

3 Apply a sterile dressing to the wound, padding all sides of a protruding object.

4 Bandage the wound firmly, but do not impede circulation. Do not push in or pull out a protruding object.

5 Gently press a fingernail or toenail. If the color does not quickly return to it, rebandage more loosely.

NOSEBLEEDS

High altitude can sometimes cause bleeding from the nose. The victim should sit down with his head forward, and pinch the bridge of his nose where the blood vessel passes across the bone.

Treating Nosebleeds
Pinch the bridge of the nose until the bleeding stops.

KNOCKED-OUT TOOTH

Replace the tooth in its socket and keep it in place with a sterile pad. If it is dirty you can rinse it in milk, but do not touch the root with your fingers. If the tooth will not replant, the victim can store it in his cheek until he receives medical attention.

Replanting Tooth
Replacing a tooth in its socket gives it the best chance of taking root again.

BLEEDING VARICOSE VEINS

Apply pressure on wound site

1 Varicose veins in the legs can easily be damaged, losing a lot of blood. Lift the leg and press hard on the site.

2 When bleeding has slowed, bandage the leg firmly over a clean pad. Check to ensure that circulation is not impeded *(see above)*.

BROKEN LEG

1 To treat a broken leg, first dress any puncture wounds. Put padding between both legs. If you have to move the victim, apply traction by pulling the leg straight gently but firmly from the ankle, while supporting the knee. This may reduce the pain.

Bind good leg to broken leg for support

2 Immobilize the broken leg by binding the good leg to it. Tie the knots on the good leg. Wrap a figure-eight bandage around the feet and ankles to support them.

3 To move the victim, make a stretcher by pushing two strong branches through the sleeves of jackets with their zippers and buttons done up.

Sleeves should be pushed inside for strength

MOVING VICTIMS

Moving a seriously injured person over rough ground is a nightmare – both for the uninjured carrier, in terms of physical effort, and for the victim. To avoid worsening the injury during the move, the injured part must be comfortably secured and immobilized.

Broken Ankle
Support a broken ankle with clothes secured with bandages.

4 Test the stretcher to ensure that it is strong enough to hold a body. Then carefully roll the victim onto his side and push the stretcher underneath him.

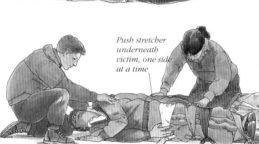

Push stretcher underneath victim, one side at a time

MOVING A CONSCIOUS VICTIM

1 Pad the injured part as firmly as you can. With the victim standing, grip one of his arms and place your other arm between his legs. This technique can also be used for an unconscious person, but you will have to lift him to his feet first.

Put your arm through victim's legs ready to grasp his knee

Bend your knees to take victim's weight

WARNING

Do not use any of these methods of moving a victim if he has a back or chest injury. In such cases, it is best to leave him where he is, rather than risk making his injury worse. An unconscious victim should ideally be strapped to a stretcher.

2 Pull the victim over your shoulder as you stand up, taking the strain with your leg muscles, not your back. He should rest comfortably across your shoulders. Once you are walking, you can grasp his knees and hand with one hand, leaving your other arm free for balance.

LIFTING AN UNCONSCIOUS PERSON

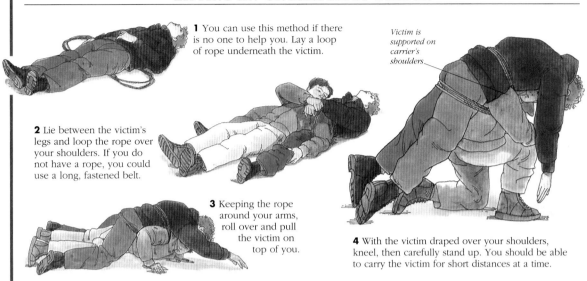

1 You can use this method if there is no one to help you. Lay a loop of rope underneath the victim.

Victim is supported on carrier's shoulders

2 Lie between the victim's legs and loop the rope over your shoulders. If you do not have a rope, you could use a long, fastened belt.

3 Keeping the rope around your arms, roll over and pull the victim on top of you.

4 With the victim draped over your shoulders, kneel, then carefully stand up. You should be able to carry the victim for short distances at a time.

BROKEN ARM

2 Gently ease a triangular bandage behind the injured arm. If the arm is broken near the elbow, it may be too painful to bend. In this case, bandage the arm to the upper body, which will act as a splint.

Place bandage beneath arm

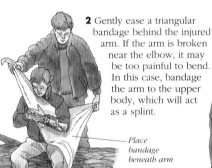

3 Bring the bandage up over the injured arm and tie its ends together so that the knot rests on the uninjured shoulder.

1 You can splint a broken arm with a piece of bark or wood to protect it from further damage.

4 Bring the bottom corner of the bandage around the elbow and pin it in place. Gently lift the arm off the chest and place padding behind it. You may also want to place padding under the sling where it goes around the victim's neck, to prevent it from chafing.

BROKEN HAND

1 Wrap the injured hand in clean gauze to protect it from further damage.

2 Support the injured hand with a triangular bandage tied around the victim's neck. This elevated sling helps to reduce swelling in the injured hand, and stops any bleeding. You can splint broken fingers with bark.

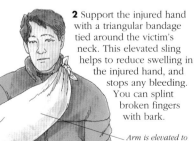

Arm is elevated to reduce swelling

ANIMAL BITES

Minor Bites
Animals carry bacteria in their mouths, and these bacteria cause a wide variety of infections, such as tetanus and rabies (see page 183). Pour water over the wound for at least five minutes, as soon as possible after you have been bitten. Cover the wound with a sterile dressing.

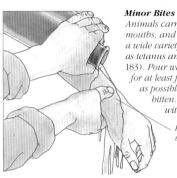

Pour cold water on wound to clean it

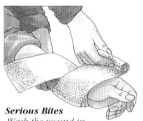

Serious Bites
Wash the wound in cold water, then apply pressure with a gauze pad to control bleeding. Raise the area above the heart. Bandage the wound and seek urgent medical help.

WARNING
In some countries, notably Australia, spiders can give poisonous bites. If bitten by a Sydney funnel-web spider, apply pressure to the bite and seek urgent help. A bite from a red-back spider, however, should be treated with an ice compress, not pressure.

SNAKE BITES

Washing the Wound
Do not panic if you are bitten by a snake. Panic increases the heartbeat, taking the venom around the body. If you can correctly identify the snake as a mildly poisonous species, wash the wound, then bandage it firmly. Do not wash the bite if you cannot identify the snake. A snake can be identified by its venom, and its bite can be treated accordingly.

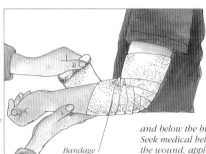

Bandage firmly

Applying Pressure
If you are bitten by a snake in a country where such a bite can be fatal, or you cannot be certain of identifying the snake correctly, immediately apply direct pressure to the bite wound. Bandage the area firmly above and below the bite to localize the venom. Seek medical help immediately. Do not cut the wound, apply a tourniquet, or try to suck out the venom.

INSECT STINGS AND TICK BITES

Bee and Wasp Stings
Carefully remove the sting with tweezers, taking care not to squeeze the poison sac, thereby injecting even more venom into the wound than it has already. Some people can have severe allergic reactions to the stings of bees and other insects (anaphylactic shock). They should be treated for shock, and may need to be resuscitated (see page 175). Seek medical help.

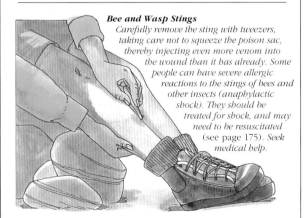

Removing Ticks
Ticks have strong jaws, which will remain embedded if the body is pulled away, causing infection. Dab an embedded tick with insect repellent or a cigarette to make it loosen its grip, then remove it carefully with tweezers.

INJURIES FROM MARINE ANIMALS

Stings
Sea anemones, jellyfish, and corals often release stinging cells when touched. These stick to a victim's skin and discharge venom. If you are stung, wash the area thoroughly with vinegar or alcohol to neutralize the stings. Pick off the stings using gloves.

Puncture Wounds
If you step on a spiny creature such as a sea urchin, its spines may break off and remain embedded in your skin, generating pain and rapid infection. Immerse the affected part in water as hot as you are able to bear in order to deactivate the venom and remove the pain. Remove the spines if you can. Seek medical help.

POISONING

Contact Poisoning
Some poisons affect the skin and must be washed off thoroughly before treatment as for burns (see page 182). Alcohol helps remove all residue. Contaminated clothing must be removed and thoroughly washed or discarded.

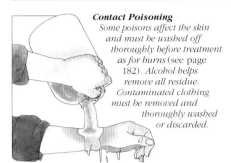

WARNING
Do not induce vomiting in the victim to prevent a poison from being absorbed into the bloodstream unless you know what has been ingested, since some caustic substances may cause damage on the way back up.

Internal Poisoning
It is important to find out what the victim has ingested, so that the correct treatment can be given. If the victim is unconscious but breathing, put her in the recovery position. Seek medical help immediately.

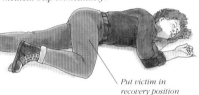

Put victim in recovery position

BLISTERS

1 Never burst a blister caused by a burn *(see page 182)*. If you must pierce a blister to continue walking, first cleanse the area with alcohol. Sterilize a needle to red heat in a flame. When the needle has cooled, slide it into the edge of the blister parallel to the surface of the skin.

2 Carefully apply pressure to the blister on the side away from the needle, squeezing out the fluid.

3 Cover the blister with a clean dressing. Take care not to rub the site of the blister.

CRAMP

Massage muscles to loosen them

In Leg
Unaccustomed walking or running, and loss of mineral salts through excessive sweating, may cause a cramp. To relieve a cramp in the knee or leg, raise the affected leg in the air and massage the muscles until they relax.

In Foot
To relieve a cramp in the foot, gently massage the ball of the foot, stretching the toes.

WARNING
Take great care to ensure that a cramp is just due to muscle strain, and does not indicate a more serious complaint. For example, a snake bite can cause muscle paralysis, while tetanus can cause lockjaw. If in doubt, always seek medical attention for a serious cramp.

DIARRHEA AND VOMITING

Diarrhea and vomiting can signify many serious conditions. In the wild, they can kill through dehydrating the sufferer *(see page 69)*. The most likely causes of diarrhea and vomiting are food poisoning or drinking contaminated water, although serious infectious diseases should not be ruled out.

Fluid Treatment
Maintain your fluid level by frequently taking one teaspoon of salt and one teaspoon of sugar in a quart of water.

BURNS

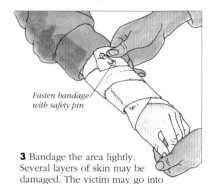

Fasten bandage with safety pin

1 Considerable tissue damage can be prevented by immediately plunging the burned area into cold water and leaving it there until the skin has cooled.

2 All burns are very susceptible to infection, and must be protected with a clean, non-fluffy dressing. Do not put any ointment on the burn.

3 Bandage the area lightly. Several layers of skin may be damaged. The victim may go into shock *(see page 176)*. Seek medical help.

THE EFFECTS OF HEAT

Dehydration

The gradual loss of water and salts from the body causes headache, dizzyness, nausea, and sweating. The victim may have pale, clammy skin, muscle cramps, and breathing problems. Move him to a cool place and give him plenty of food and electrolyte solutions.

WARNING

If a heatstroke victim is cooled too quickly, for example by immersion in cold water, his body temperature may drop too far, causing shock. Take care to cool him down slowly.

Heatstroke

Heatstroke is the result of depletion of body fluids or exposure to a significant heat source. It can cause feverishness, severe headache and vomiting, the cessation of sweating, and unconsciousness. The victim's body heat must be reduced by placing her in the shade, preferably under a sleeping-bag liner soaked in cold water. Fanning her face will help to cool her. Do not immerse her directly in cold water.

Raising the feet eases blood flow to the vital centers

Fanning helps to cool patient down

FOREIGN OBJECTS

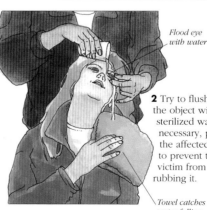

Flood eye with water

1 For a foreign object in the eye, separate the eyelids and examine the whole eye. Do not attempt to remove anything embedded in the eyeball. Seek medical attention immediately.

2 Try to flush out the object with sterilized water. If necessary, patch the affected eye to prevent the victim from rubbing it.

Towel catches water falling from eye

OBJECT IN EAR

Carefully pour tepid water into the ear until the foreign body floats out. If it does not, do not try to pull it out. Cover the ear and seek medical help.

FLUSHING OUT OBJECT

REMOVING A FISHHOOK

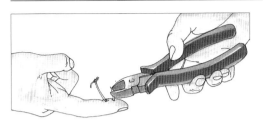

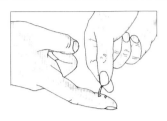

1 If the barbed end of the fishhook is visible, cut it off with wirecutters close to the skin. If the tip of the barb is buried in the skin, you may be able to press on the eye of the hook and pull on the line to remove it.

2 Gently pull the shank the way it entered the skin. Cleanse the area with antiseptic solution, and put a bandage on it to stop bleeding.

EYE INJURY

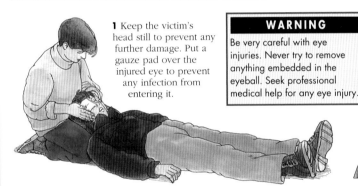

1 Keep the victim's head still to prevent any further damage. Put a gauze pad over the injured eye to prevent any infection from entering it.

2 Bandage across both eyes to keep the pad in place, and to prevent the victim from moving the injured eye.

Bandage both eyes to keep injured one still

DANGEROUS DISEASES			
Disease	**Where Found**	**How Transmitted**	**Symptoms**
HIV/AIDS	Worldwide	Via bodily fluids, such as blood	Persistent influenza, colds, sores, general ill health, fatigue
Cholera	Africa, Asia	Through insanitary conditions	Nausea, diarrhea, vomiting, cramps, dehydration, shock
Infectious hepatitis (Hepatitis A)	Worldwide	From the feces of infected people	Chills, fever, headache, bone pain, enlargement of liver and spleen
Poliomyelitis	Warm climates	From water infected with the virus	Paralysis
Typhoid	Mexico, Far East, Africa	From water contaminated with *Salmonella* bacillus	Headache, abdominal pain, delirium, fever
Yellow fever	West Africa, South America	Via a mosquito bite	Headache, fever, limb pain, vomiting blood, constipation
Tetanus	Worldwide	Through bacterial spores entering wounds	Lockjaw, fever, stiff face and back muscles, sweating, asphyxia
Rabies	Almost worldwide	Via the saliva of infected animals	Fever, appetite loss, hyperactivity, thirst, inability to drink, coma, death
Bubonic plague	Almost worldwide	Through flea bites from infected rodents	Coughing, swollen lymph glands
Pneumonic plague	Almost worldwide	From breathing in virus	Coughing, labored breathing

Worldwide Disorders
There are a great many diseases around the world that can be picked up by a traveler who is unprepared. They can be caused by viruses or bacteria, and are transmitted via food or water, or in the feces of infected people. Some are carried in animal or insect saliva and are transmitted by bites. Many of these diseases could prove fatal in a survival situation, in which proper medical attention may be unavailable. Before venturing into areas where these diseases are prevalent, therefore, you should have appropriate vaccinations. Diseases transmitted in water can be avoided by purifying all water before drinking it (see page 75).

GLOSSARY

Anticyclone Winds rotating outward from area of high barometric pressure, producing good weather.
Aerobic exercise Endurance exercises designed to increase amount of oxygen taken in by the body.
Aiming off Deliberately heading to one side of a destination point, so that you know in which direction to turn in order to complete your journey.
Anaphylactic shock Shock caused by sudden, massive allergic reaction.

Back bearing Compass bearing taken from a feature and plotted on a map in order to find one's position in relation to that feature.
Bearing Angle of travel, taken by compass, measured in degrees or mils (thousandths of an inch) from north.
Belay Pay out or pull in rope attached to someone, in order to act as support if that person falls.
Billycan General-purpose metal container for cooking.
Bivy sack Weatherproof sleeping bag cover that can be used instead of a tent.
Bow drill Fire-starting instrument consisting of a bow that turns a pointed stick (the drill) in a wooden hearth to create friction and produce sparks.
Bowline Knot that will not slip or come undone by itself. Usually used to secure a loop.
Breathable fabric Fabric with treated surface that allows body moisture to escape through pores, but prevents rain from seeping in.

Calorie A unit of heat related to the energy values of foods. The calorie is correctly termed a kilocalorie (or large calorie), which is the amount of heat needed to raise the temperature of 2.2 pounds (1 kg) of water through 1.8°F (1°C).

Carabiner Clip useful for joining ropes.
Chimneying To climb or descend a gap between rock faces by supporting oneself using the hands and feet on opposite sides of a fissure.
Cirrus clouds High, wispy clouds formed of ice crystals.
Conical projection System of projecting a globe onto a cone, then opening it out to form a map.
Contour lines Lines on a map, joining points of land that are of the same height above sea level.
Contouring To negotiate a hill by remaining at the same height as you walk around it, moving along the imaginary contour line.
Concave slope Hill whose summit can be seen from the ground.
Contact poisoning Skin rash or ailment caused by touching poisonous substance, such as a plant with irritant hairs or sap.

Convex slope Hill whose summit cannot be seen from the ground.
Cord Rope, string, or cord used for lashing.
Core Center of the body, whose temperature must be maintained to sustain life.
Core layer First layer of clothing next to skin.
Crampons Metal spikes that fit to soles of boots, providing grip on ice.
Cumulus clouds Mass of rounded clouds forming above horizontal base. Usually associated with high-pressure zones and fine weather.
Cumulonimbus clouds Tall bank of dark cumulus clouds that may contain thunderstorms.
Cyclone Winds rotating into area of low barometric pressure, causing bad weather.
Cylindrical projection Method of mapmaking in which an image of a globe is projected onto a cylinder, and then unrolled to make a flat surface.

Damper bread Unleavened bread made from flour and water. Often cooked over an open fire.
Daypack Small backpack used to carry supplies for short trips away from the main camp.
Dehydration Results when the body loses more water than it takes in. Signified by nausea, headache, and eventual collapse. Drink so that urine remains clear or only slightly yellowish.
Detouring Navigational technique of veering away from a set course to avoid an obstacle, then returning to the course once the obstacle has been passed.
Dome tent Stable tent supported by curved poles.
Double fisherman's knot A specialized knot used for joining ropes together, and for making secure connections. It is particularly used in rock climbing *(see page 149)*.

Edging Rock climbing technique of placing edge of foot in a crack instead of on a protrusion.

Fitness rating Measurement of how quickly pulse rate returns to normal after exercise. Depends upon age, gender, and health.
Flare A signal used at sea, in the form of a flame or light.
Flysheet Outer skin of tent that can be used as a shelter by itself in warm weather.
Frostbite The freezing of body tissues, causing damage and eventually death.

GPS Global Positioning System used for navigation. Radio signals are sent to and from satellites to determine a position on the ground.
Gaff Hook used for landing fish.
Gaiters Fabric or plastic worn around lower legs to protect them from dampness, rocks, or thorny vegetation.
Geodesic dome Stable dome structure made from interlocking struts. Commonly used in tent frames.
Gillnet Net usually strung across a stretch of water,

designed to catch fish by the gills as they try to swim through it.

Gradient A slope. Gradient can also mean the amount that a slope rises from the horizontal.

Grid reference Position on a map, given in relation to the lines of the direction grid.

Guyline Cord with one end attached to a tent to act as a stabilizer when the other end is pegged into the ground.

Hand drill Pointed stick rotated between the hands in a wooden "hearth" to cause friction and produce sparks to light a fire.

Handrail Navigational technique in which a linear feature in the landscape, such as a river or road, is followed until a bearing can be taken to another feature that was previously out of sight.

Hawser-laid Type of rope formed from twisted strands.

Heatstroke Condition in which body becomes overheated, sometimes resulting in collapse.

Heat exhaustion Condition of collapse, due to excessive exposure to heat, exertion, and a lack of water to replace water lost by the body.

Heliograph Reflector used for signaling with the sun.

HELP Heat-Escape-Lessening Posture, used when floating in water. Designed to keep abdomen covered to reduce loss of heat from body core (*see also* Core).

Hurricane Tropical storm characterized by whirling winds. May be hundreds of miles across.

Hypothermia Condition in which body loses heat from its core. Fatal if not treated early enough.

Igloo Dome-shaped shelter made from snow blocks.

Inner tent Basic tent that can be used in conjunction with weatherproof flysheet.

Invertebrate Animal without backbone. For example, insect and shellfish.

Isobar Line on a weather map connecting areas having the same atmospheric pressure at the same time.

Kayak Small, one-person canoe based on traditional Inuit sealskin boat.

Kernmantle Type of rope consisting of a central core of twisted strands surrounded by a woven sleeve.

Kindling Sticks of wood or other fuel used to get a small fire going from initial flames.

Kukri Large knife traditionally used by Gurkhas in Nepal. Useful for several different purposes.

Lashing Method of joining items together using ropes.

Latrine Hole in ground used as camp toilet.

Layering principle Method of insulation using thin layers of clothing.

Magnetic variation Difference between magnetic north and grid north.

Manteling Rock-climbing technique used to negotiate overhangs and bulges in a rockface.

Mercator projection Method of projecting earth onto flat surface in order to make a map.

Middle layer Layer of clothing worn on top of second layer and underneath outer layer.

Morse Code Alphabet consisting of dots and dashes, used for signaling. Can be adapted to sounds, printing, or visual signals, such as smoke or light.

Mountain bibs Pants, usually insulated, with high waistband and suspenders.

Muscarine Poisonous substance found in *Amanita muscaria muscaria* fungus. Causes convulsions, hallucinations, and sometimes death.

Occluded front Weather system in which cold air of a depression meets warm air and forces it upward.

Omnivore Creature that can live on a wide variety of foods, including both meat and vegetation.

Outer layer Layer of clothing worn on top of other items, to act as an outside barrier against the air.

Panniers Bags attached to sides of pack animal, bicycle, or motorcycle.

Pemmican Cake of dried meat or fish mixed with congealed fat, originally devised by Native Americans as a method of preserving meat.

Phillips screwdriver Screwdriver with cross-shaped tip, which fits into special screws with cross-shaped slots. Named after original manufacturer in the United States.

Pitfall trap Container set in ground and disguised, in order to trap ground-crawling animals, particularly insects.

Primary forest Forest that has never been cut.

Prussik loop Knot formed of loops of rope over a second rope. Particularly used in rock climbing.

Prussiking Descending or ascending a rockface using prussik knots attached to a fixed rope.

Pulk Sled pulled by a person.

Purse seine Large fishing net with drawstring edge.

Quicksand Waterlogged sand whose loose particles spread apart easily, to engulf anything that falls into it.

Quinze Shelter consisting of hollowed-out heap of snow.

Rappel To descend a rockface supported by a rope.

Reamer Instrument for boring or widening a hole.

Recovery position Medical position of prone body designed to enable victim to vomit without choking, and to breathe without throat being blocked by tongue.

Ridge Long, narrow hill, or the apex of two long slopes.

Ridgepole Central, horizontal support of pitched roof.
Ridge tent Basic tent with pitched roof and two pointed gables at the same height.
Ring of Fire Region around edge of Pacific Ocean where earthquakes and volcanic eruptions are common, due to the collision of plates of the Earth's lithosphere.

Saddle A ridge rising to a hill or peak at each end. Named for its resemblance to a riding saddle.
Sculling Keeping afloat by scooping water with hands toward body.
Sea anchor Device dragged from vessel in order to limit drift due to current.
Second layer Layer of clothing worn on top of underwear. Can be added to or removed to moderate body temperature.
Secondary forest Forest that has been cut down at least once, and has grown back in a more tangled form.
Semaphore Alphabet formed by position of arms, or both hands holding flags. Used for signaling.
Shear lashing Method of joining two spars by lashing them together with cord.
Shock Medical condition of total collapse of bodily systems, following an injury or accident.
Snowmobile Vehicle with motorcycle engine and tracks or skis for crossing snowy ground.
Sod house Building constructed of blocks of sod.
Solar still Device using the heat of the sun to distil contaminated water, so that it evaporates, then condenses on a surface as pure freshwater.
Step test Method of determining fitness by stepping on and off a raised block for a measured length of time, then taking one's pulse to see how long it takes to return to normal (*see* Fitness rating).
Stratocumulus clouds Combination of stratus (layered) and cumulus (rounded) clouds, forming a thick sheet.
Stratus clouds Continuous sheet of thin cloud, sometimes forming fog, or bringing drizzle.
Sunblock Cream or lotion put on skin as a barrier against ultraviolet rays from the sun.
Sundial Instrument for determining time or direction by measuring a shadow cast by the sun.
Survival bag Insulated bag that can be used as tent or sleeping bag in extreme conditions.
Synoptic chart Map showing synopsis of information on weather conditions in a particular region at a certain time, marked in symbols. Used by meteorologists to correlate information and forecast probable weather.

Taste test Step-by-step test for assessing unfamiliar plants for palatability and whether they are safe to eat.
Tepee Conical structure formed by three or more sticks leaning together.
Tick Arthropod that lives on blood from mammals. Can transmit disease.
Tickling a fish Technique of catching a fish with the hands. Accomplished by stroking the underside of a resting fish to calm it, then grabbing it and throwing it out of the water.
Tinder Small, fine, combustible material used for starting a fire.
Toilet can Container used for holding human waste when it is not practical or legal to dig a latrine.
Tornado Whirling winds and funnel-shaped cloud, caused by hot air being sucked up into thundercloud.
Travois Improvised vehicle for carrying a load, consisting of two poles joined by a platform, dragged behind a horse or man.
Trench foot Fungal condition of skin, caused by excessive dampness. Particularly prevalent in humid areas, such as jungle.
Tsunami Enormous wave caused by earthquake on the seabed. Such a wave may travel for hundreds of miles and swamp coastlines for a long way inland.

Vegetation still Device for extracting water from vegetation. Foliage is enclosed in plastic, and as the air inside the plastic heats up, the vegetation gives off water vapor. This vapor condenses as water droplets on the underside of the plastic and can be collected.
Vent To open clothing zippers and buttons to allow excess body heat to escape.
Volcanic bomb Rocks, ash, and gas exploding from erupting volcano.
Volcano Conical protrusion of land, through which molten material and gas from the Earth's mantle escapes.

Wick Ability of fabric to allow body moisture to seep away from skin, yet prevent outside moisture from reaching it.
Winch Cable with a hook on one end, used for pulling. Sometimes attached to vehicles. Can be used to pull vehicle out of soft ground.
Windchill Increased effect of cold temperatures caused by wind.
Wire saw Twisted wire attached to handles.

Yukon stove Oven constructed from hardened clay, consisting of cone-shaped chimney with fire at bottom.

CHECKLIST FOR SURVIVAL

THIS LIST IS anything but exhaustive, but it is intended to give you headings from which to create lists of your own, for whatever activity you are undertaking. Use it to trigger your thinking, to determine what might be necessary – as well as to help you remember things you may have forgotten. It may also remind you of other things you may need that are not on this list. Always keep a list of the equipment you take with you into the wilderness. The next time you go, you will know which items to leave behind, and which ones you cannot manage without.

BAGS AND PACKS
Backpack
Daypack
Moneybelt
Washkit

SHELTER
Tent with poles and pegs
Sleeping bag
Sleeping bag liner
Bivy sack
Sleeping mat
Tent repair kit
Sewing kit

TOOLS
Large knife
Pocketknife
Survival kit

COOKING, EATING, AND DRINKING EQUIPMENT
Stove
Waterproof matches
Fuel
Fuel bottles
Stove maintenance kit
Billycans
Plate
Dish
Utensils
Plastic mug
Water filter
Water purification tablets
Water bottles
Large water container
Can opener
Pan scrub
Plastic bags
Food

PERSONAL GEAR
Towel
Washcloth
Sunscreen
Insect repellent
Soap
Toothbrush
Toothpaste
Lip balm
Shampoo
Razor
Toilet paper

NAVIGATION EQUIPMENT
Compass
Binoculars
Map in plastic bag
Flashlight
Batteries

CLOTHING
General
Underwear
Socks
Boots
Light hiking boots
Pants
Shirt
Jacket
Hat
Sunglasses
Belt

Tropical Regions
Cotton underwear
Long-sleeved, cotton, ripstop shirt
Cotton ripstop pants
Windproof jacket
Hat

Mosquito face net
Mosquito bed net
Insect repellent
Ankle & wrist bands
Belt
Sunglasses
Jungle boots

Desert Regions
Cotton underwear
Cotton long-sleeved shirt
Cotton pants
Windproof jacket
Lightweight boots
Sunglasses
Hat
Scarf/bandanna

Polar Regions
Thermal underwear
Heavy shirt
Fleece jacket
Hooded parka
Insulated mountain bibs
Cotton inner socks
Wool outer socks
Inner boots
Heavy insulated boots
Inner gloves
Warm mid-layer mittens
Heavy outer mittens
Balaclava
Goggles
Glacier glasses
Snowshoes
Crampons
Cross-country skis
Ski poles
Ice ax
Ice hammer

SIGNALING EQUIPMENT
Whistle
Heliograph
Paper
Pencils and pens

MISCELLANEOUS
Rope
String or cord
Climbing helmet
First-aid kit
Candle lantern
Magnifying glass
Flint and steel
Firestarter blocks
Disposable cigarette lighter

OPTIONAL EQUIPMENT
Books
Games
Radio
Camera
Film
Lifejacket

INDEX

A

ABC of resuscitation 175
Abramis 98
Acacia 72
Acanthocybium 101
Acer 88, 93
Aconitum 84
acorns 88, 93
Acorus 86
adder 167
Aegopodium 82
Aesculus 88
Agaricus 91
aiming off 131
air pollution 13
airway, checking 175
Alaria 93
Aleuria aurantia 90
Alligator 166
Allium 82
almond 88
Amanita 91
Amaranthus 83
American alligator 166
animal bites 180
animals, caring for 160
ankle, broken 178
Anacardium 88
Anopheles 167
anticyclone 170
antibiotic tablets 29
ants 94, 98

B

back bearings 128
backpack,
    carrying 134
    improvised 135
    packing 134
baking in mud 117
Balistidae 109
bamboo
    edible 83
    pot 116
    shelter 53
    shovel 33
banana tree, getting water
    from 73
baneberry 89
Barbarea vulgaris 82
bark water container 77
barracuda 101
barrel cactus
    as water source 72
    getting water from 73
Basella 83
basket fish trap 107
bass 100
Batrachoididae 101
beachapple 85
Beaufort wind-speed scale 133
bed, improvised 31
beefsteak fungus 90
bees
    edibility 94
    collecting 96
belaying 147
Betula 83
bicycles 161
Big Dipper 125
billy tea 93
binoculars 26, 123
birch 83
bistort 82
bites, treating 180

Arachis 86
Arenga 83
arm, broken 179
Arothron 167
arrowhead 86
ascending a rockface 146
aspen 83
assessing
    companions 123
    terrain 122
    victim 175
asthma 13
Astralagus 86
Atrax 167
Atropha 89
avalanche 168

Bitis 167
bivy sack 43
blackfly 137
black locust 85
black mamba 167
black widow spider 167
bleeding, controlling 177
blinding mangrove 85
blisters, treating 181
bog arum 87
boggy ground, crossing 153
Boletus 90
boomslang 167
boots
    choosing 24
    cleaning 25
bottle fish trap 107
bow drill 63
bowl, carving 113
bream 98
breathing
    rate 12
    checking 175
bridge, building 153
brown recluse spider 166
bullhead 99
Bungarus 167
buoyancy aid, making 163
burns, treating 182
buttercup 84
butterflies 94
buttons 29

C

California laurel 85
Calla 87
calorie needs 15
Calvatia utriformis 90
camels 160
camp
    safety 56
    tips 40
campsite
    choosing 40
    cleaning up 64
cancer 13
candle 28
cannibals 13
Cape gooseberry 14
carabiner 149, 152
carbohydrate 14
Carcharodon 167
cardinal beetle 95
cardiopulmonary resuscitation
    176
carnivores 14
carob 83
carp 98
carrageen 82, 93

carrion flower 72
Carya 88
cassava 87
Castanea 88
caster bean plant 84
cauliflower fungus 90
caves 55
Ceratonia 83
Ceylon spinach 83
chemicals 13
Chicorium 93
chicory 93
chimneying 148
choking 176
Chondrus 93
chopping wood 33
chub 98
Cicuta 84, 87
cinnabar moth 95
circulation, checking 175
Cladonia rangiferina 91
clay pot, making 113
clothes
    desert 142
    fabrics 22
    jungle 144
    layers 22
    polar 138
    washing 57
cloudberry 89
clouds 132, 165
clover 93
Clupea 100
coconut palm 83
Cocos 83
coiling rope 36
Colocasia 87
compass
    making 124
    using 130
cone shell 95
Conium 84
contact poisoning 181
contouring 131
contours 127
cooking on hot rocks 117
coracle 157
coral snake 166
cord, improvised 34
Cortinarius 91
Corylus 88
cowbane 84, 87
cowhage 85
crabapple 89
crab
    cage 107
    dressing 97
Crambe 82
cramp, relieving 181
cranberry 89
Crocodylus 167

cross-country skiing 139
Crotalus 166
cyclone 170
Cyperus 86
Cyprinus 98

D

dace 98
daffodil 87
damming stream 108
damper bread 117
dandelion 82
Dasyatis 101
dates 14
daypack 134
deadly nightshade 89
death camas 84, 87
death cap 91
death puffer fish 167
dehydration 69
Dendroaspis 167
descending a rockface 146
desert, crossing 142
destroying angel 91
detouring 131
dew, collecting 70
diamondback rattlesnake 166
diarrhea 69, 181
Digitalis 84
Dioscorea 87
direction, finding 124
Dispholidus 167
distance
    estimating 131
    measuring 129
dock 82
dogsled 140
dome tent 43

double fisherman's knot 184
drying frame 118
Duchesnea 89

E

ear, foreign object in 182
earthquakes 169
earthworms, cooking 97
easing back pain 19
Echinocactus 72
edging 146
eel, skinning 111
electric eel 99
electrical storm 171
Electrophorus 99
elephant seal 166
elephant 160
environment
    affecting health 13
    protecting 65
Esox 99
estuarine crocodile 167
eucalyptus 93
Euthynnus 100
Excoecaria 85
exercise, benefits of 19
eye
    foreign object in 182
    injury 183
    protection 142

F

fat 14
feet
    features of 12
    keeping clean 24
Ferrocactus 72
fiber 14
fierce snake 167
fire
    carrying 61
    cleaning up 65
    lighting methods 62
    types 61
fireplace, building 54
first-aid kit 174
fish
    drying 118
    filleting 110
    skewering 111
    skinning 110
    where to find 105
fishhook
    in finger 183
    making 102
    using 104
fishing
    bait 103
    floats 102
    harpoons, making 103
    ice 104
    landing, 105

line 28
    lures, making 102
    net, making 106
    netting 108
    spearing 104
    trap, making 107, 109
Fistulina hepatica 90
fitness rating 18
flares 165
flashlight 26, 96
flint blade 33
floating
    aids 163
    HELP position 162
    survival 163
    with lifejacket 162
    without lifejacket 163
flood 171
flour, making 92
fly agaric 91
flysheet 42
food safe 57
fool's mushroom 91
footholds for climbing 146
forest fire 168
foxglove 84
Fragaria 89
frostbite 140
fruit 89
fuel
    for fire 59
    for stove 114
fungus 14
funnel-web spider 167

G

gaff 105
gaiters 25
galingale 86
geodesic dome tent 43
gillnet, using 108
glass knife 33
Glechoma 93
Global Positioning System 128
Gluta 85
goutweed 82
gradients 127
grasshopper 94
great white shark 167
grid references 127
Grifola frondosa 90
grizzly bear 166
ground ivy 93
ground-to-air signals 173
grubs, collecting 96
guyline 42

H

hand drill, using 63
handholds for climbing 146
handrail, using 131
hay fever 13

hazel 88
hearing, sense of 12
heart 12
heat-loss areas 163
heatstroke 182
Helianthus 86
heliograph 28, 173
hemlock 84
hen-of-the-woods fungus 90
herring 100
Hippomane 85
hippopotamus 167
honey ants 97
honey, collecting 96
hornet 137, 167
horse chestnut 57, 88
horses 160
Hudson Bay pack 137
human body, features of 12
hurricane 171
huskies 160
Hydrophis 166
hygiene 57
hyperactivity 13
hypothermia 151

I

Ictalurus 99
igloo 50
Indian krait snake 167
industrial solvents 13
inflatable boat 157
insect
    eating 96
    identifying 94
    stings 180
    trapping 96
isobars 170

J

Jatropha
    glandulosa 85
    integerrima 85
    podagrica 85
jellyfish 95, 180
Jerusalem
artichoke 86
joints 12

Juglans 88
jungle
  equipment 25, 144
  types 145
juniper 89
Juniperus 89

K

kayak 157
kelp 93
kindling 59
kiwi fruit 14
knife
  glass 33
  sharpening 32
  using 33
knots 35
kukri 32

L

Laburnum 85
Lactrodectus 167
land, signs of 165
Laportea 85
latrine 56, 64
laver 82, 93
lip balm 27
leeches, removing 145
Leuciscus 98
liferafts 164
log cabin 54
Lupinus 84
Lycopersicon 87

M

mackerel 101
magnetic variation 129
magnifying glass 29, 62

Makaira 101
Malus 89
Manihot 87
manioc 87
manteling 148
map 26
  contour 126
  making 129
  projections 127
maple 83, 93
matches, waterproof 27, 28, 62
Megalops 100
Mercator projection 127
Metroxylon 83
Micrurus 166
migration 130
minerals 14
Mirounga 166
monkshood 84
Morchella 90
morel 90
Morone 100
Morse Code 173
mosquito 145
moths 94, 96
motorcycles 161
mountain bikes 161
Mucuna 85
mud oven 115
multipitch ascents 147
muscarine poisoning 91
mussels, cooking 97

N

Narcissus 87
navigation 130
needle as compass 124
Neoregalia 72
Nepenthes 72
nettle 93
nettle tree 85
night vision, retaining 137
nosebleed, treating 177
nuts 14, 88
Nymphaea 86

O

occluded front 170
omnivores 14
Onchorhynchus 98
Opuntia 72
orange peel fungus 90
Ornithogalum 87
outboard motor 157
ovens 115

P

pack frame, making 135
paddle, making 157
Pagellus 98

palm 83
panniers 161
panther cap 91
Panthera 167
papaya 14
Parademansia 167
Parthenocissus 89
Passiflora 89
passionfruit 89
peanut 14, 86
pemmican 119
Perca 99
perch 99
persimmon 14
periwinkles, cooking 97
pesticides 13
Physalia 95
Picea 83
pickerel 99
pike 99
pilewort 87
pine
  drinks from 93
  eating 83
Pinus 83
piranha 99, 166
Pistacia 88
pitcher plant 72
pitfall trap 96
pocketknife 32
poison arrow tree frog 166
poison
  ivy 84
  oak 84
  sumac 84
poisoning 181
polar equipment 138
pollution 13
Polygonum 82
Populus 83
Portuguese man o' war 95
Porphyria 82, 93
Portulaca 82
potassium permanganate 29
potato 87
predators, dealing with 167
preservatives 118
prickly pear 72
prismatic compass 124
protein 14
protractor compass 124
Prunus 88
prussik loop 149
prussiking 149
Pseudosasa 83
puff adder 167
puffball fungus 90
pulk 140
purse seining 108

Q

quinze 51
Quercus 88
quicksand 153

R

rabies 183
rafts 154, 156
rain, collecting
  on land 70
  on liferaft 164
rainstorms 171
Raja 100
ramps 82
rappeling 147
Ranunculus 84, 87
razor blade compass 124
razor clams 97
recovery position 175
red-back spider 167
reflecting the sun 173
reflector 28
reindeer moss 91
rescue breathing 175
rhengas tree 85
Ricinus 84
roach 98
Robinia 85
rock tripe 91
roots
  digging for 92
  preparing 92
rope
  coiling 36
  damaged 36
  improvised 34
  joining 37
  type 34

Rubus 89
rudd 98
Rumex 82
Rutilus 98

S

Saccharum 83
saddle 126
Sagittaria 86
sago palm 83
sail
    on liferaft 164
    on raft 156
Salmo 100
salmon 100
salsify 86
saltwater
    boils 165
    distilling 75
sandstorm 143
Sapium insigne 85
scalpel 29
Scardinus 98
Scomberomorus 101
Scophthalmus 100
Scorpaenidae 101, 166
scorpionfish 101, 166
sea anchor, making 164
sea anemone 95
sea kale 82
sea lettuce 93
sea snake 166
sea urchin 94
seawater, condensing 71
seaweed, using 93
Sedum 82
seeds, collecting 92
semaphore 172
Serrasalmus 99, 166
sharks, dealing with 109, 164
sharpening knife 32
shear lashing 37
shellfish 95, 97
shelter
    A-frame 52
    bamboo 53
    jungle 53
    lean-to 48
    natural 55
    snow 50
shock, treating 176
sight 12
Silva compass 29, 124
skate 100
skin 12
skinning
    eel 111
    fish 110
slugs, gathering 97
smell, sense of 12
Sminthillus 166
smoker, building 119
snails 94, 97
snake bites 180

snow equipment 138
snowmobile 140
snowshoes, making 139
soap, improvised 57
socks 24
sod house 55
Solanum 87
solar still 71
Sorbus 89
SOS 172
Southern Cross 125
space blanket 31
Sparassis crispa 90
spearfishing 104
Sphyraena 101
spider bites 180
splinting 178
spoon, carving 113
spruce 83
stagnant water 75
Stapelia 72
starfish 94
starflower 87
stars, navigation by 125
steam cooking pit 115
step test 18
stingray 101
stings 180
Stizostedion 99
stonefish 109, 167
stoves 114
strawberry 57, 89
stress 13
stretcher, making 178
stretching 19
Strychnos 89
sugar palm 83
sugarcane 83
summer purslane 82
sunblock 27
sun
    navigation by 125
    signaling with 173
sundial, making 125
sweet chestnut 88
sweet flag 86
sweet vetch 86
swimming 151
Swiss Army knife 26
Synanceia 101
Synanceidae 167
synoptic chart 170

T

Tamarindus 83
tandan 99
Tandanus 99
Taraxacum 82
taro 87
tarpon 100
taste
    sense of 12
    test 83
Taxus 85

tepee
    fire 60
    smoker 119
teeth
    cleaning 57
    features of human 12
tench 98
tent, repairing 47
termites
    collecting 96
    nests 125
terrain, assessing 122
Tetrapturus 101
thread 29
Thunnus 100
tickling a fish 104
ticks, removing 180
tiger 167
Tinca 98
tinder 58
toadfish 101
toilet can 56
tomato 87
tools, improvised 33
tooth, replacing 177
tornado 171
Toxicodendron 84
Trachinidae 109
Tragopogon 86
travois, making 135
Triakis 101
Trifolium 93
triggerfish 101
trout 98
tsunami 169
tuna 100
turbot 100

U

Ulva 93
Umbellularia 85
Umbillicaria 91
Unconscious person 175
Urolophus 101
Ursus 166
Urtica 93
utensils 27, 115

V

varicose veins 177
vegetarian diet 14
vegetation still 73
venting 22
Vespa 137, 167

victim
    assessing 175
    moving 178, 183
Vincetoxicum 87
vine, getting water from 73
Vipera 167
Virginia creeper 89
vitamins 14
Vitis 89
volcanoes 169
vomiting 181

W

wahoo 101
wall pepper 82
walleye 99
washing
    clothes 57
    dishes 41
wash kit 27, 57
wasps 95
water chestnut 86
water lily 86
water
    bad 75
    containers 26,76
    digging for 70
    from dew 70
    from ice and snow 73
    from plants 71, 72, 73
    from soil 71
    needs 69
    signs of 69
    sterilizing tablets 29
    where to cross 150
waterborne diseases 75
weaverbirds 125
weever fish 101
winching 159
windchill 141
wind-speed 132
windstorms 171
wintercress 82

Y

yam 87
yellow-staining mushroom 91
yew 85
Yukon stove 115

Z

Zigadenus 84, 87

ACKNOWLEDGMENTS

AUTHOR'S ACKNOWLEDGMENTS

This book is the sum total of the work of a great many people, from the very top of Dorling Kindersley downward. It involved a tremendous amount of coordination – of artwork, photography, equipment, and materials, as well as editorial and design work. The creative team of editor Lynn Parr and designer Lee Griffiths made it all happen, and the work was made enjoyable thanks to the superb professionalism and good humor of the photographers Tim Ridley, Andy Crawford, and Steve Gorton. The upper echelons of the DK hierarchy were very closely involved throughout the whole project. Inception required a good many most convivial meetings with Publisher Christopher Davis, Editorial Director David Lamb, Managing Editor Krystyna Mayer, and Managing Art Editor Derek Coombes. As we got under way, Krystyna Mayer kept a necessarily tight rein (while offering support and guidance), and Derek Coombes personally supervised one of the location shoots. And throughout, I was gingered up by personal comments from Peter Kindersley. I would also like to thank Commando Forces and the Royal Marines for giving me both the training and the opportunity to learn and develop the techniques and ideas shown in this book.

PUBLISHER'S ACKNOWLEDGMENTS

For equipment and materials:
Airborne Industries Ltd.; Armory Fitness Centre; Cotswold: The Outdoor People (Free 192-page catalogue, 0285 860612); Cruisermart Discount Marine; Dr. T.J. Dean, Institute of Hydrology, National Environmental Research Council; Ellis Brigham Mountain Sports; Europa Sport; Sally Gilbert; Goodlife Foods Ltd.; Sheila Metcalf; Paul Goodyear, Nomad Pharmacy Ltd.; Olympus; Plastimo Manufacturing UK Ltd.; Jim Sharp, Aberdeen Weather Centre; Roger Daynes and Richard Olivier, Snowsled; Survival Group Ltd.; The Colt Car Company Ltd.; Zamberlan; Zodiak UK Ltd.

For research and advice
Shane Winser, Expedition Advisory Centre; Tom Sheppard, Royal Geographical Society; Deborah McManners, M.D.; Ray Rogers.

For picture research
Catherine O'Rourke, Anna Lord, and Joanna Thomas

For page make-up and computer assistance
Jonathan Harris and Chris Clark

Illustrations
Key: t top, b bottom c center, l left, r right
Coral Mula: 25b, 30b, 34b, 42t, 50, 51t, 51 c, 53, 54, 55t, 55c, 56t, 56bl, 57b, 64, 65, 70, 71, 73t, 77, 91bl, 92, 93, 96, 97, 104, 105, 106, 108, 109, 110, 111, 115, 117, 118tl, 123t, 126, 127tr, 128, 129, 131, 134t, 136, 143bl, 145, 146, 147, 148, 149, 150, 151, 152, 153, 156, 159, 160, 162, 163, 164, 165, 168, 173
John Woodcock: 33, 51b, 55b, 56br, 57cr, 61cr, 71br, 73br, 75tr, 77tr, 97bl, 107br, 111, 113br, 115br, 116br, 118cr, 123tr, 128br, 143br,
Jim Robins: 175–183
Colin Newman: 198-101

Maps
James Anderson and **James Mills-Hicks** of **Dorling Kindersley Cartography:** 16-17, 166-167, 169, 170

Models
Peter Griffiths: 40-41, 68-69, 100-101, 122-123
David Donkin: 132

Photography
All photography by **Steve Gorton**, **Tim Ridley**, and **Andy Crawford** with assistance by **Nicholas Goodall**, **Sarah Ashun** and **Gary Ombler** except:

Charles Badby: 157tr
Bruce Coleman Ltd.: David Austen 139cl; Jen & Des Bartlett 125br; Erwin & Peggy Bauer 16cl, 43cl; N. G. Blake 91tl; Bob & Clara Calhoun 84c; John Cancalosi 88c; Alain Compost 167cr; Raimund Cramm GDT 137c; Gerald Cubitt 17cr, 169bc; Adrian Davies 90tc, 90bc; A. J. Deane 132cl; Jack Dermid 84cr; Nicholas Devore III 143cl; Hans & Joachim Flugel 69cl; Michael & Patricia Fogden 130tc, 133cl, 145c; Jeff Foott 13tr, 95c, 133c; Christer Fredriksson 20-21, 160tr; Michael Freeman 103br, 167c; C. B. & D. W. Frith 166br; R. Glover 120-121; Keith Gunnar 2, 38-39, 126cr, 139bc, 139br, 160cr, 168bl; Pekka Helo 89tl; Carol Hughes 69tr, 75c, 143tr; Johnny Johnson 166tc; Steven C. Kaufman 43bl; Stephen J. Krasemann 91bc, 145tr; Harald Lange 17br; Olivier Langrand 69tl; Wayne Lankinen 166c; Luiz Claudio Marigo 168tl; George McCarthy 90cr; 91c; 165bc; Fredy Mercay 126br; John Murray 15cl; S. Nielsen 132bl; Charlie Ott 89cr, 143cr; Robert Perron 15tc; Dieter & Mary Plage 17tl, 66-67, 122tc, 169bl, 171c; Dr. Sandro Prato 17bl; Andy Purcell 13cl, 90tr, 91tc, 132cr; Hans Reinhard 13br, 75cr, 89tr, 91tr, 125bc, 133tl, 166cb, 171tr; Gary Retherford 145tl; Norbert Rosing 140br; Leonard Lee Rue III 160cl; Frieder Sauer 91br; John Shaw 90tl, 143tc; Kim Taylor 13tl, 69cr; 90br; R. Wanscheidt 132cb; Peter Ward 145bc; Bill Wood 95tc Joe van Wormer 13tc
Cotswold Camping: 24tl, 24br
Peter Crump: 137tc
Michael & Patricia Fogden: Endpapers
Hutchison Library: Christina Dodwell 157bl; John Egan 171bc; Brian Moser 169cl; Dr. Nigel Smith 15tl; J. Wright 16bc
Images Colour Library Ltd./Horizon International: Andris Apse 78–79
Land Rover UK Ltd.: 158bc, 159tl, 159tr, 159c
Hugh McManners: Jacket, 160tl
Mountain Camera: John Cleare 126bl
Lynn Parr: 84tc, 140tc
Phoenix Mountaineering Ltd.: J. Timper 43c
Planet Earth: Jack Jackson 164tc; Marty Snyderman 167bl
Plastimo Manufacturing UK Ltd.: 162tc
The Royal Geographical Society: Martha Holmes 157tl; Nigel Winser 157c
The Harry Smith Collection: 85tl, 85tc, 85cl, 85c, 85bl, 87tl, 87cl, 87bc, 87cr, 88tl, 88bl, 88tr, 88tc, 88bc, 89bl, 89br
Stockfile: F. Witmer 161bl;
Tony Stone Images: 132tc,171tc
Vango Scotland Ltd.: Tim Greening 43tr
David Ward Jacket
Tony West: 10–11
Wild Country: 41tr, 43tc
Zefa: 126cl

Additional Photography
Beth Chatto 82tr, 82cr, 84 tl, 86cr, 87tr, 87tc; Eric Crichton 82tl, 84cl, 89bc; Andrew de Lory, 82bl, 83cr, 85cr, 89ct; Andrew Lawson 86 ct; Edrom Nurseries, Berwickshire 84 br; Royal Botanic Gardens, Kew 87br; Jerry Young 166br, 166tl, 166bl, 167t, 167br, 167tr